NEW
TREASURES
OF THE PAST

• Sculpted head found in the sepulchre of a Maya king at Palenque, Mexico

NEW TREASURES OF THE PAST

FRESH FINDS THAT DEEPEN
OUR UNDERSTANDING OF
THE ARCHAEOLOGY OF MAN

BRIAN FAGAN

Grange BOOKS

A QUARTO BOOK

Published by Grange Books
An imprint of Books & Toys Limited
The Grange
Grange Yard
London SE1 3AG

ISBN 1 85627 220 6

Reprinted 1992

This book was designed and produced by
Quarto Publishing plc
The Old Brewery, 6 Blundell Street
London N7 9BH

Senior Editors Maria Pal and Sandy Shepherd
Editor Lydia Darbyshire
Art Editor Iona McGlashan
Designer Ted McCausland
Picture Researcher Carina Dvorak
Art Director Moira Clinch
Editorial Director Carolyn King

Typeset by Comproom Ltd, London
Manufactured in Hong Kong by Regent Publishing Services Ltd
Printed by Star Standard Industries (PTE) Ltd

CONTENTS

INTRODUCTION
FROM A TREASURE HUNT
∾ TO A SCIENCE ∾

Right *Austen Henry Layard 1817-1894*

Left *Heinrich Schliemann 1822-1890*

Glittering gold, buried pharaohs, lost civilizations and unsolved mysteries – these are the romantic ingredients that conjure up an image of archaeology even today. The cartoonist's depiction of eccentric, pith-helmeted professors unearthing inscriptions in the shadow of mighty pyramids has been around for generations. It dates from the nineteenth century, when you could find a lost civilization in a few weeks. Those were the heroic days of archaeology, the days when archaeologists were adventurers rather than scholars, brilliant writers instead of academics.

There was Sir Austen Henry Layard, law student turned traveller, who became so fascinated by ancient Mesopotamia in the 1840s that he unearthed the Assyrians of the second book of Kings from the ancient cities of Nimrud and Nineveh. He actually found two Assyrian palaces in a month.

On the other side of the world, John Lloyd Stephens and his architect friend Frederick Catherwood travelled to the central American rain forests, in 1839 in search of mysterious temples buried in clinging undergrowth. They returned to describe the Maya civilization, an indigenous American society which was quite unlike anything on the banks of the Nile or Tigris. Small wonder that archaeology became a romantic pastime associated with mystery and fabulous treasure.

Today, archaeology is still a fascinating, even sometimes romantic subject, but the study of the past has come a long way since the days of Layard. If anyone symbolizes the change in archaeology, it is Heinrich Schliemann, German businessman turned archaeologist, who found Homeric Troy at Hissarlik, in Turkey, in 1871. When he excavated the Hissarlik mounds, he employed engineers who had managed the building of the Suez Canal to supervise his vast

The heroic days of archaeology. In the 1840s British archaeologist and adventurer Austen Henry Layard, **far left**, excavated ancient city mounds in what is now Iraq and discovered several Assyrian royal palaces at Nimrud and Nineveh. Like an alien chieftain he commanded large teams of local workers, relying on their prodigious efforts to unearth and haul winged bulls, **below**, and other spectacular antiquities to the banks of the Tigris and onto rafts. They were then shipped by steamer to England and taken to the British Museum. Layard's Assyrian finds documented vividly the existence of a shadowy ancient civilization mentioned in the Old Testament.

On Stone by W.L. Walton.
Frontispiece Vol I.

Printed by Hullmandel & Walton

LOWERING THE GREAT WINGED BULL.

John Murray, Albemarle Street, 1848

trenches. This was archaeological discovery on a large scale, excavation designed to yield the maximum number of spectacular discoveries in the shortest possible time.

As Schliemann toiled, a team of German scholars in Greece was dissecting the ruins of ancient Olympia, the site of the first Olympic games, but in a very different way. Architects, excavators, draughtsmen, photographers and epigraphers all worked together not only to dig, but to reconstruct and preserve Olympia. The results of their work were published in lavish style, the finds housed in a special museum at Olympia itself. Archaeology was on its way from being a glorified treasure hunt – it was starting to become a science.

John Lloyd Stephens or Heinrich Schliemann would not recognize archaeology today. They would find some of their successors working at the same spectacular sites as they did over a century ago – Hissarlik, Nimrud, Chichén Itzá, Copán – but the trenches are much smaller, the analyses and interpretations more minute than those of yesteryear.

Stephens would marvel at the intricate photographic apparatus that now records the inscriptions at Copán that his friend Frederick Catherwood took weeks to sketch, ankle-deep in mud. Schliemann would be astounded to see students on their knees collecting tiny soil samples from the walls of trenches at Hissarlik. He probably moved more earth in a week than modern archaeologists would excavate in years. A prime example of modern archaeology is the discovery in 1982 of the Coppergate helmet. The basement foundation of York's Coppergate development was receiving a last-minute scraping before a modern building was to rise where an ancient Viking town and a Victorian factory once stood. A huge mechanical digger (JCB) extended its bucket into the deep hole. An expert 'ganger' stood in front of the machine, guiding the driver as he carefully scraped the bottom of the basement level for the last time. Suddenly the bucket hit an obstruction. The ganger called a halt, thinking they had snagged the base of the massive brick chimney that had once stood there. To his astonishment, the obstruction was not brick but metal.

He removed the damp soil from it and fingered the rusty brown object. It had yellow strips that looked like gold, some of it inscribed with unfamiliar letters. The surprised ganger called over an archaeologist who was watching the construction project. The archaeologist knelt to examine the find. He realized at once that it was a metal helmet, only the third ever found in Britain.

Everyone working on the Coppergate development knew that they were probing deep into York's ancient history every time they demolished an old building. York was founded as a Roman military base in AD71. It prospered under the Romans and was an important Anglo-Saxon archbishopric and international trading centre between the seventh and early ninth centuries. The Vikings captured the town in 866 and made it the capital of their only lasting kingdom in England. By 1068, York was the second largest and the richest city in England.

This great medieval city continued to prosper and remained a great social centre right up to the Industrial Revolution. Surprisingly, this revolution passed York by. It therefore survived into the twentieth century with an extraordinary legacy of ancient buildings – and rich, undisturbed archaeological treasures. Today, archaeologists of the York Archaeological Trust watch every major construction project in the city centre. So the ganger on the Coppergate development did not

Above *The Coppergate helmet restored. Found in 1982, this is a superb example of the type of helmet worn by royal or noble Anglo Saxons in Northumbria at about the time of the first Viking attacks in the late eighth century AD. The iron helmet has brass bindings, two cheek pieces attached by iron hinges, and a chain mail neck guard, mostly of iron. The* brass eyebrows end in fanged animal heads, with a third one above the junction of the eyebrows. The Latin inscription on the narrow brass strips between neck and nose and from the top down to the ears can be roughly translated as reading, 'In the name of our Lord Jesus Christ, the Holy Spirit, God the Father and all we pray. Amen. Oshere of Christ.'

have to look far for an expert.

Within minutes of the discovery, a team of skilled diggers was trowelling away the soil from the vicinity of the magnificent find. They soon found that the helmet was lying inside a wooden shaft filled with sticky clay which had helped to preserve the metal and the original shape of the helmet in an airtight seal.

With infinite care, the excavation team photographed and drew plans of the find. They carefully excavated the rest of the shaft, and exposed the long noseguard of the helmet, which was adorned with a stylized animal head and pronounced eyebrows, in brass. As darkness fell, the helmet was eased from the shaft and handed over to conservators.

To study the helmet further they turned to modern medical technology. A body scanner produced computerized X-rays which revealed that a chain-mail neck guard and a cheek piece lay still buried within the helmet. With painstaking care, the technicians cleaned the curtain of two thousand individual metal links that had protected the wearer's neck. The decoration on the brass noseguard was so well preserved that the technicians could reveal the layout lines made by the helmet's designer when he carved the original master mould for the animal motif.

The helmet was an Anglo-Saxon masterpiece, owned by a man named Oshere about AD750. He probably wore a woollen cap to protect his head from chafing, because the iron helmet had no lining. Even Oshere's inscription was preserved, invoking the protection of his Maker: 'In the name of our Lord Jesus Christ, the Holy Spirit, God the Father and all we pray . . .'. Of Oshere we know little, but his helmet has become one of Britain's great archaeological treasures.

The Coppergate helmet is eloquent testimony that archaeologists still make spectacular discoveries. But many of archaeology's most dramatic discoveries today would have been impossible even a generation ago. The X-ray technology used to probe the York helmet was unthinkable when Leonard Woolley excavated the Royal Tombs of Ur of the Chaldees in the 1920s. He used such crude artifices as plaster of Paris to recover the perished wooden parts of ceremonial lyres and royal standards. Today's archaeologist uses fibreglass, nuclear physics, lasers, even space satellites to discover, recover and interpret the past.

THE THREADS OF HISTORY

If the nineteenth century was the era of romantic spectacular discovery, the twentieth century is that of scientific technology and the small object. Many of the sites described in this book are unspectacular in themselves, but are remarkable in the information they have yielded about the past.

Late in 1618, 220 settlers were shipped from England to settle the 8,000 ha (20,000 acre) tract of land called Martin's Hundred, facing the James River in Virginia. The settlers built what proved to be a short-lived community that included a small palisaded fort and a fledgling township named Wolstenholme Towne. This was little more than a hamlet of timbered and thatched houses.

At first the local Indians were friendly, but in March 1622 they attacked the James River settlements without warning. The town and fort were set on fire and nearly 350 people perished in the raid. Half the Martin's Hundred population was massacred or taken hostage. The survivors eked out a precarious existence for a few more years, but virtual starvation and contagious diseases eventually wiped them out. Martin's Hundred was almost forgotten for 350 years.

Left and above *Between 1976 and 1981 the York Archaeological Trust's excavations in Coppergate, in the heart of the ancient city of York, revealed what life was like from about AD400 when the Romans departed and AD1068, when the Normans arrived. The waterlogged soil preserved intricate details of tenth-century daily life: items such as leather shoes, textiles, and wooden utensils, as well as seeds, pollen grains and animal and insect remains. Most of the goods found were of local manufacture, but the inhabitants also enjoyed wines from Germany's Rhineland, imported lava grindstones from the continent, whetstones from Norway, amber from Denmark and silk from the Byzantine Empire. A silk cap from a nearby excavation provided an incredible detail of ancient trade. The silk has an identical weaving fault to a fragment found in excavations in the city of Lincoln to the south. Perhaps lengths from the same bale of silk were sold in both cities!*

In 1970 Ivor Noël Hume, the resident archaeologist at Colonial Williamsburg, was directing an excavation on the James River as part of a project to restore a colonial plantation named Carter's Grove. In his search for vanished outbuildings he came across seventeenth-century postholes, pits and graves. Fortunately, Noël Hume and his wife Audrey had spent their earlier archaeological careers working in the foundations of London, so they were well prepared for the complex excavations that followed.

The excavations explored an area of 0.81 ha (2 acres). On one site Noël Hume found a complex of pits and postholes that included a large pit 9m (30ft) in diameter. He dissected this with infinite care. The pit turned out to be an abandoned cellar, reached by a flight of clay steps. At first there were no clues to the construction of the house, until six large postholes were found extending below the clay floor.

What sort of house had stood over the cellar? After weeks of searching historical records, the Noël Humes came across a memorandum penned in 1650 by the Secretary of the Dutch colony of New Amsterdam, now New York. He described how impecunious farmers would start by living in a cellar-like underground house. They would line the walls with timber and bark, floor the excavation with planks and then erect a roof and eaves above ground – the missing structure in the Martin's Hundred house. 'They can live dry and warm in these houses with their entire families for two, three, and four years . . .' wrote the worthy secretary.

If this was the design of the Martin's Hundred house, who then had dwelt in it? There were no written records such as title deeds, just the artifacts found in the cellar. These included a cannon ball and three short strands of gold and silver wire, each as thick as a sewing thread. One short length of woven gold thread had been twisted and glued to a point. Noël Hume knew enough about seventeenth-century costume to identify these fragments as the remains of once elegant clothing.

Clothing was an accurate barometer of social status in the seventeenth century. Prominent officials and officers setting off for Virginia would have been resplendent in their golden thread and dangling points, so much so that in July 1621 the governor and his council passed a resolution that suppressed drunkenness and gaming and 'excess in cloaths [and] not to permit any but ye Council & heads of hundreds to wear gold in their cloaths'. One of the council members who supported the resolution was the head of Martin's Hundred. His name was William Harwood, the only man there who would have been legally permitted to wear gold adornment on his clothing.

But Noël Hume knew that a garter does not a governor make. He argued, for example, that people might have worn gold before the law was passed, or even old hand-me-downs, especially in a society where life expectancy was short. Fortunately, William Harwood's identity hangs on more than thread. A 1623 census listed Harwood as the only person at Martin's Hundred owning a 'peece of Ordnance, 1 wth all things thereto belonging'. This would account for the 3kg (6lb 9oz) cannon ball found in the house.

The Martin's Hundred excavations are a superb example of the complex, detective-like nature of modern archaeology. Gone are the days when an archaeologist spent months on end excavating a city mound in the Near East with several hundred workers and a handful of trained helpers. Today's finely tuned excavation methods and analytical techniques may move more slowly than the lost-civilization-in-a-week excavations of the past, but they yield a much more fine-grained picture of the past. Above all, modern techniques enable us not only to describe ancient life but to interpret it as well.

*A telltale skull, **left**, probably from a victim of the Indian attack that devastated Wolstenholme Towne, shows that his forehead was split with a spade or cleaver; a cut on the left brow indicates that he was scalped. In 1970, archaeologists digging near the eighteenth-century mansion at Carter's Grove, Virginia, uncovered evidence of Martin's Hundred, a Virginia Company settlement **left**. The large hole in the background was dug for a cellar, and the middle ground post hole patterns show the layout of the dwelling and others around it. Several rubbish pits from that time can be seen to the left.*

*Colonial Williamsburg archaeologist Ivor Noël Hume, **above**, excavated Martin's Hundred and is reconstructing its tragic history from a complex jigsaw puzzle of archaeological and historical clues. Today, the visitor can tour the plantation and the Wolstenholme Towne fort, **left**, a partial reconstruction based on skilful archaeological excavation. Nothing remained of the original fort except postholes in the subsoil, which marked the positions of the palisades and interior structures, and four large posts which marked the site of the most prominent structure, a watchtower. The Wolstenholme Fort covered 929m² (10,000ft²) and was large enough to accommodate most of the settlers. It is the oldest British timber defence work ever excavated in its entirety.*

A FEAT OF ENGINEERING

No monuments of antiquity have inspired so much speculation as the pyramids of Giza across the Nile from modern Cairo. We know they were built by the ancient Egyptian pharaohs of the Fourth Dynasty, in a massive spurt of energy between about 2700 and 2500BC. We know that enormous teams of artisans and unskilled labourers moved more than 8.4 million m^3 (11 million yd^3) of stone and fashioned them into pyramids, temples and causeways. Astonishing though it may seem, they did so without wheeled transport or any beasts of burden at all. What surveying and alignment methods did the Egyptians use to erect these stupendous monuments? How did they quarry and transport the stone used in their construction? These questions have puzzled archaeologists for more than a century and spawned a massive project to reveal the grand design behind the constructions.

Mark Lehner is a young Egyptologist working with the American Research Center in Egypt. He heads the Giza Plateau Mapping Project, a long-term research plan that began in 1984. He is using the high technology of modern surveying to produce the first complete, and highly detailed map of every feature on the Giza plateau, where the pyramids stand. Lehner believes that his project will fill many gaps in our knowledge of one of the world's great construction projects. Using electronic distance measurers and photogrammetry, he is searching for the humble dwellings used by the pyramid labourers, for long-forgotten building ramps, even ancient surveying marks.

The first archaeologist to prepare an accurate survey of the pyramids was the great British Egyptologist Sir Flinders Petrie (who scandalized Victorian ladies in the 1880s by working in his red underwear). He argued that the Egyptians had quarried the stone for the pyramids elsewhere and brought it to the construction site by barge. His successors wrote of thousands of barge-loads of stone arriving from far away with the Nile floods every year. But Lehner's survey locates the main quarry for the Great Pyramid directly to the south of the towering artificial mountain. The local limestone was ideal for building pyramids and is stratified in such a way that stone masons could easily have cut it into blocks with the simplest of tools.

But how did the Egyptians move blocks weighing between 2.5 and 15 tonnes 137m (450ft) up the rising

(preceding page) For more than a century archaeologists have speculated on how the Pyramids of Giza, some of the greatest monuments of antiquity, were constructed. Today, using sophisticated mapping and surveying equipment, they believe they are nearer the answer than ever before.

The Great Sphinx, **right**, carved from a rocky outcrop, has a lion's body and a 4m wide (13ft) human face, thought to be that of the pharaoh Khafre. The archaeologist Mark Lehner and expert geologists and surveyors are tracing the intricate history of building and reconstruction. With the aid of highly accurate mapping and measuring systems the Egyptians are restoring the Sphinx in this the most comprehensive of its many restorations.

pyramid? For generations, scholars have believed that the architects built mud-brick ramps that sloped right up the pyramid. Lehner, with his much more complete information, disagrees. No debris from mud-brick ramps has been found, and a straight ramp would have had to be more than a kilometre (at least a mile) long! His survey located traces of subsidiary ramps and embankments that had been built of limestone chips, gypsum and a local clay. Tonnes of this debris now fill the quarry for the Great Pyramid. Lehner pointed out that the remains of the ramp from the quarry to the pyramid must survive somewhere in the landscape. Logic suggested that these remains would have been dumped into the empty quarries – where Lehner duly located them.

What is different about this research is that it has replaced the speculation of generations with logic based on systematic field research. Lehner's highly accurate maps allow him to theorize far more convincingly than his predecessors did. He hypothesizes that a broad ramp led to the base of the pyramid, then wrapped around the rising structure and grew along with it. Teams of workmen dragged the massive stones up the ramps, building extensions for the 'construction highway' as they went along. Lehner's comprehensive bird's-eye view of the Giza plateau convinces him that there would have been no space for any other form of ramp. Too much construction was going on nearby, and the ground falls away sharply on the north side of the pyramid.

The Giza Plateau Mapping Project solved several other mysteries as well. Generations of scholars have tried to explain how the ancient Egyptian architects measured the pyramid bases so accurately and levelled the structures as they built them. One ingenious theory argued that they dug a grid of water-filled canals and that the water line provided a baseline for excavating the foundation trenches to a uniform depth. Lehner disagrees. He points out that the builders had already piled up massive heaps of rubble to form the core of the pyramid. Using high technology he has combed every inch of the plateau and has located a series of regularly spaced holes around the perimeter of the Great Pyramid, connected by depressions let into the rock floor. Lehner believes that

the surveyors fixed stakes in the holes, then poured water into the depressions. Next they measured and cut the stakes to the true level, and then stretched string along the tops of the stakes that served as a reference line for aligning the pyramid structure.

As famous as the pyramids is Pharaoh Khafre's human-headed, lion-bodied Sphinx. It has been excavated and restored by everyone from the Romans to Napoleon's soldiers, but no one had ever studied the details of the Sphinx before Lehner did. He assembled a team of experts – not only archaeologists and surveyors, but geologists as well. They spent two years cleaning, measuring and mapping the recumbent figure, colour coding each element of the Sphinx to show when it was assembled or restored.

Today, the Sphinx's head stands 23.7m (78ft) above the plateau. It was excavated out of solid rock by cutting away the surrounding stone in blocks. Lehner believes that these blocks were then used to build the pharaoh's mortuary temple nearby or were hauled off for use in the pyramid itself. So precise is Lehner's

NEW DEVELOPMENTS

Until World War II, most archaeology was confined to Europe, the Near East, the United States and Mexico. These were the areas where most archaeologists lived and worked, the regions where universities and wealthy private individuals supported field research. Only a handful of archaeologists worked in more remote parts of the world, like sub-Saharan Africa, Australia and Peru. Many of them were amateur excavators who were colonial administrators, missionaries or businessmen. As late as the 1950s, there were few archaeologists in Africa south of the Sahara, and fewer than half a dozen of them were professional scholars, mainly directors of local museums. The number of archaeologists working in Peru was tiny until the explosion of archaeological fieldwork throughout the world in the 1960s.

research that he believes that he may be able to trace individual blocks by studying their fossil content.

But what was the purpose of the Sphinx? Some Egyptologists believe that the pharaoh erected it and a nearby solar temple to guard the 'city of the dead' at Giza. The new research team argues that the Sphinx represents the pharaoh under the protection of the falcon-headed god Horus, the god of kingship, presenting offerings to the sun-god Ra. It marks a crucial moment in Egyptian history when Ra became all-important instead of the hawk-like Horus.

The Giza project has brought to life a bustling, crowded ancient landscape. For instance, excavations and core drillings about 46m (150ft) beyond the temples in front of the Sphinx revealed a ledge in the sand-covered bedrock at least 15m (50ft) deep. Egyptian archaeologist Zawi Hawass believes that this was once the rock-cut port at which the barges brought by canal from the Nile berthed. The survey team has also located the workmen's village in a sand-filled depression south of the Great Pyramid.

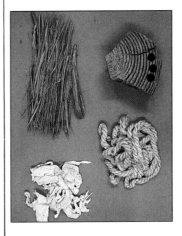

Radiocarbon dating has replaced the guesswork of the archaeology of old, allowing much more accurate chronologies to be reached. Typical samples suitable for dating include wood, rope, reed, and linen, left. Scientists at the Oxford Radiocarbon Accelerator, above, are now pioneering the use of an accelerator and mass spectrometer which will make it possible for them to date sites 75,000 years old or more. This new technique allows the use of samples 1/1000th the size of previous ones.

Three developments led to this rapid expansion and the discovery of the remarkable archaeological finds described in these pages. The first was the invention of radiocarbon dating by University of Chicago and Nobel Prize-winning chemist Willard Libby around 1946. This unique time-measuring device was based on the fact that radiocarbon elements in organic substances, such as wood and charcoal, decay at known rates. Radiocarbon dating provided the first global way of dating the past based on something more than objects of known age or intelligent guesswork. For the first time an archaeologist working in, say, Syria, could compare the date of an early farming village with an equivalent settlement thousands of kilometres away in Mexico. So instead of studying purely local sites, archaeologists could think for the first time of a 'world prehistory' for all of humankind.

This revolutionary invention – it was nothing less – coincided with a second development, a great stirring of nationalism and ethnic pride in many Third World countries and among minorities such as the North American Indians. Archaeology began to move to centre stage as a way of providing cultural and intel-

lectual roots for new nations and ethnic minorities. In Africa, for example, although written history began on the coasts with Arab traders in the late first millennium, in some parts of the interior it began as late as the advent of European colonial rule in the 1890s. The only other sources for African history were some short-term oral histories. But now there is the archaeologist's spade. Archaeology has become a powerful force in fostering nationalism and a sense of national pride.

The Mexican government has long believed that national pride can be enhanced by melding prehistoric Indian, early Spanish and other Mexican cultural traditions into a single sense of 'Mexican-ness', and archaeology plays a key role in this type of nationalism. Take the great city of Teotihuacán for example, which lies 56km (35 miles) northwest of Mexico City. Between about 200BC and AD750 Teotihuacán was the centre of a vast empire which traded as far as the Gulf of Mexico and the Pacific. Even the mighty Aztecs revered it as an intensely sacred place. Once a complex of crowded neighbourhoods and teeming *barrios*, the scale of Teotihuacán,

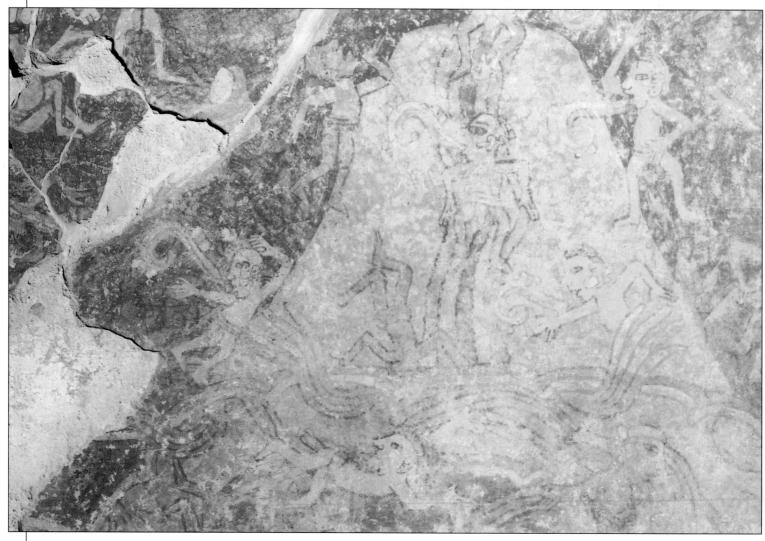

with its vast pyramids and imposing ceremonial plazas, still overwhelms the visitor. This is precisely what the architects intended – a symphony of structures and open spaces that made the individual seem insignificant in the presence of the gods.

A century ago Teotihuacán was a crumbling mass of decayed pyramids and overgrown ruins. At intervals, Mexican archaeologists carried out large-scale excavations and reconstruction work there that continue to this day. Americans have assisted too, using the latest computer technology to map every segment of the city. The preliminary map was completed in the 1960s, but a team of pottery and computer experts continue to labour over the collections of pottery from thousands of compounds and houses. So precise is this research that the archaeologists have even been able to identify an enclave occupied by foreign merchants from the prosperous Valley of Oaxaca, more than 320km (200 miles) to the southeast.

Today, tens of thousands of tourists visit Teotihuacán every year. It is one of the great archaeological sites of the world, as much a symbol of Mexican nationalism as it is a cultural treasure of humanity's past.

The forces of nationalism coincided with a third development, an explosion of knowledge in archaeology itself, as the popular imagination was fired by the past. In the 1950s a handful of universities offered training for professional archaeologists. Now there are hundreds, not only in Europe and North America, but in every part of the world. The past 20 years, the era of the ecological movement and anti-nuclear protest, have seen a new awareness of the past and the final acceptance of archaeology, not as an eccentric form of treasure hunting but as a meticulous, scientific enterprise. The pith-helmeted professor is gone forever, replaced by teams of fieldworkers who probe the past with scientific techniques that were unimagined in Austen Henry Layard's day. The treasures of the past they reveal are not rich gold and dramatic civilizations, but a multitude of fascinating details about our ancestors. In the chapters that follow, we will explore some of the achievements of archaeologists as familiar with two-million-year-old humans as they are with the almost-forgotten factories that once signalled the beginnings of the Industrial Revolution.

A partially reconstructed wall painting from a building at Tepantitla, Teotihuacán, **left.** *The painting is thought to depict the Rain God Tláloc, an important figure in the Mexican pantheon. Many wall paintings have been found in Teotihuacán's larger buildings, most of them of religious scenes. Teotihuacán occupied an important place in Mexican religious life and was revered even in Aztec times, long after the pyramids were abandoned. Aztec legend considered the ancient city the place where the gods created the world of the Fifth Sun, the world in which their civilization flourished. But this was a finite world, destined to end in their destruction. To many Aztecs, Cortez's arrival was a sign that the world was ending.*

In its heyday, the great Mexican city Teotihuacán, **above,** *housed more than 120,000 people and covered 20.7m^2 (8 square miles). Today archaeologists are still uncovering parts of this imposing city which have lain buried for more than a thousand years. Among the many religious and public buildings they have found is the great Pyramid of the Sun which dominates the city – a vast adobe and rubble structure 64m (210ft) high and 198m^2 (650ft^2) in area.*

PART ONE
THE DAWN OF CIVILIZATION

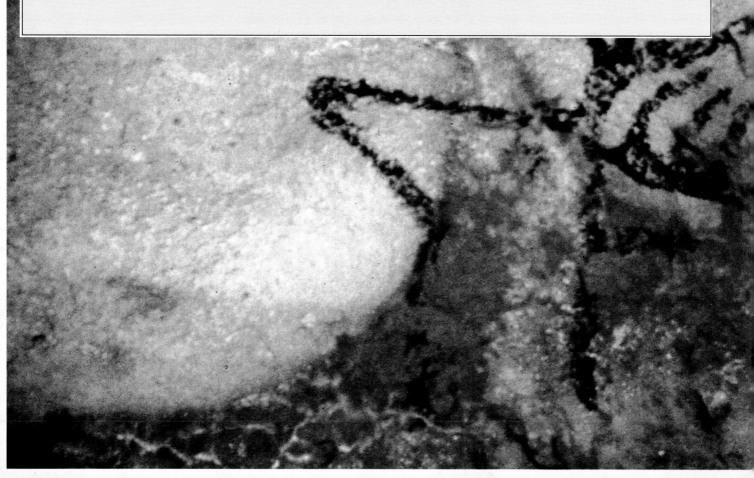

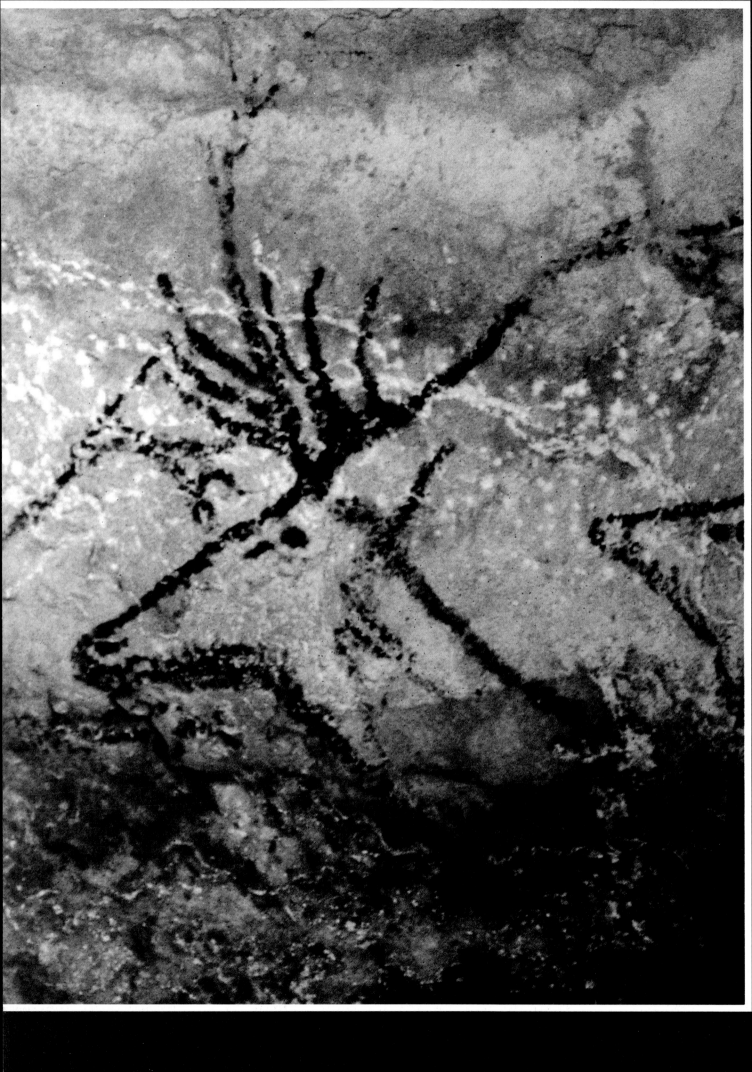

THE FIRST HUMANS

● *The fossil-rich area of Omo, in southern Ethiopia*

● *San hunter-gatherer digging for edible roots*

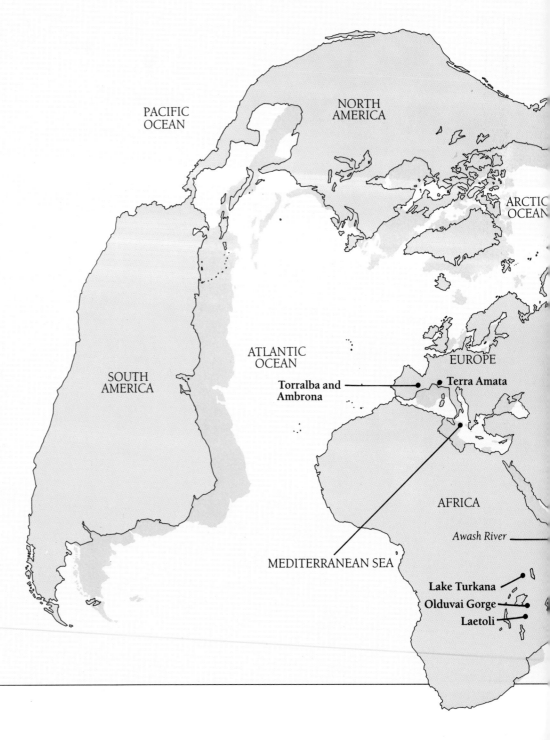

Today's archaeologists are probing deep into prehistory, into the very remotest millennia. Slowly and inexorably, paleoanthropologists have been closing in on the answer to The Question of Questions – the origins of humanity and the nature of the biological relationship between human beings and their nearest non-human relatives.

The question itself was posed by the great Victorian biologist Thomas Huxley as long ago as 1862. Even today, people speak of this search as if it were a quest for a 'missing link', an apelike human ancestor that ties us in with our primate forebears.

In fact, the story of early human evolution is much more complex and still little understood. Even the definition of a human being is in dispute. Everyone agrees that human beings walked upright and used tools made with their own hands to adapt to their natural environment. But they cannot agree on when hominids first appeared with these unique qualities, or when humans first emerged who were capable of fluent speech and rational thought.

The scientific controversies revolve around the most unspectacular of archaeological finds – fossilized skulls and occasional scatters of crude stone tools and bones. But important discoveries during the past 25 years have revolutionized our knowledge of early human evolution in East Africa more than two million years ago.

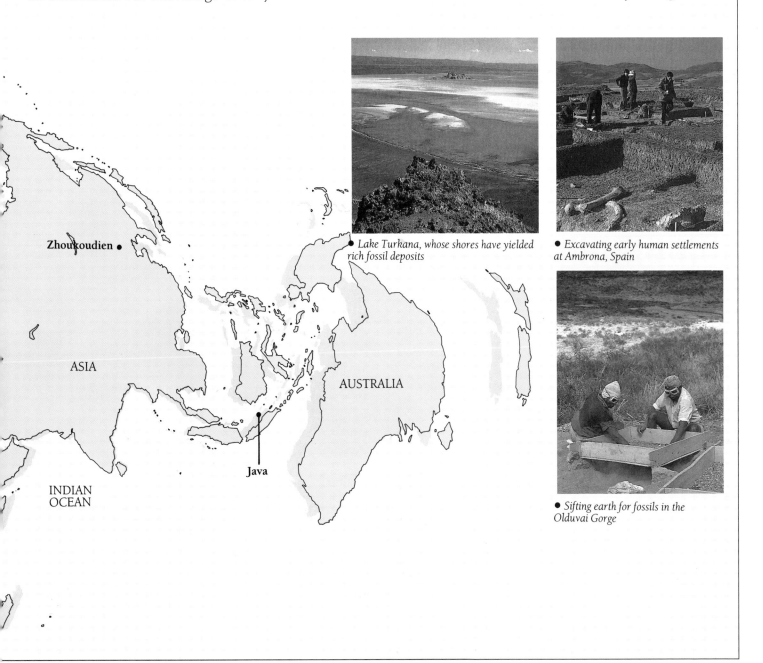

● *Lake Turkana, whose shores have yielded rich fossil deposits*

● *Excavating early human settlements at Ambrona, Spain*

● *Sifting earth for fossils in the Olduvai Gorge*

Zhoukoudien ●

ASIA

AUSTRALIA

Java

INDIAN
OCEAN

LUCY

The date was November 30, 1974. The temperature was at least 43°C (110°F) in the shade. For more than two hours paleoanthropologist Don Johanson and graduate student Tom Gray had been searching for fossils in the baking hot desert, near the Awash River in the Hadar area of northeast Ethiopia. They had found a few horse teeth and part of a monkey jaw, but little else.

The two men decided to walk back to their Land Rover through a small gully which had been combed unsuccessfully for fossils at least twice before. But as they walked through it Johanson noticed an arm fragment lying on the far slope. Immediately he recognized it as the arm of a hominid, a human-like creature. 'Too small,' said Gray. He changed his mind when Johanson pointed out the back of a hominid skull close to his hand. Then they spotted other pieces of bone on the slope – backbone fragments that were part of a pelvis. Almost immediately, Johanson realized he had made the discovery of a lifetime – the remains of one of the earliest hominids in the world.

Later that day, the entire expedition was back at the gully, laying out a measuring grid over the place where the hominid was found. It took three, long, hot weeks to screen every fragment of gravel on the slope. When the work was finished, Johanson had recovered about 40 per cent of a female hominid. The evening of the discovery, the celebrating scientists stayed up all night. Again and again, a tape recorder played the Beatles' song 'Lucy in the Sky with Diamonds'. The Awash hominid was named 'Lucy' from that day on.

Don Johanson's Lucy came from deposits that have now been dated to between 3 million and 3.75 million years ago. Johanson and physical anthropologist Tim White spent months assembling the fragmentary skeleton. They found that Lucy stood at about a metre high (just less than 3½ft tall), and was between 19 and 21 years old.

Nearby, Johanson and White found the remains of at least 13 more hominids of the same geological age – males, females and children. Johanson could not resist calling them the 'first family'. They were all from the same species of hominid, but displayed great variation in stature and weight. Some stood 1.5m high (almost 5ft) and weighed as much as 68kg (150lb), a far cry from the slender, gracile Lucy. But even she was a powerful, well-muscled creature. Lucy had a brain about the size of a chimpanzee, an ape-sized head and a forward-thrusting jaw. Despite intensive search, Johanson

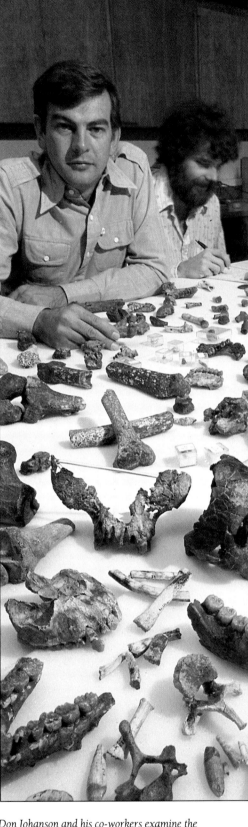

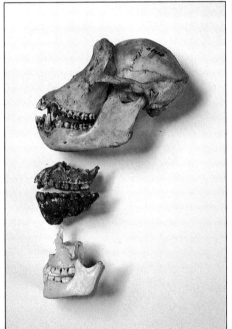

Above *At a glance a 3 million-year-old Afar hominid (middle) may resemble the chimpanzee (top) more closely than a modern human (bottom). But by taking hundreds of small measurements of skeletal anatomy and comparing them, some paleoanthropologists believe they have proved that the Afar hominids are closer to modern humans.*

Fossil hand bones of an Afar hominid, **above,** *laid out alongside a modern human hand,* **top.** *Detailed studies of the fossil hand bones hint that they were as dextrous as we are.*

Don Johanson and his co-workers examine the entire Afar fossil hominid collection, **above.** *The process of studying very early hominid fossils is painstakingly slow. The bones are first cleaned and preserved, then measured and fitted together where possible. Months of careful measurement and*

comparison follow, both to provide a detailed description of the new fossils, and to make detailed comparisons with other finds. Intense controversy surrounds the Afar fossils, which Johanson believes to represent a new form of Australopithecus, an early stage in human evolution.

found no signs that Lucy or her contemporaries ever made stone tools.

What were the Hadar hominids? Were they direct ancestors of humankind or not? A flood of controversy has engulfed Lucy and her contemporaries ever since the announcement of their discovery. Johanson and White believe that she and the other Hadar individuals are very early and direct ancestors of modern human beings, so much so that they gave them the label *Australopithecus afarensis,* meaning 'southern ape-man of the Afar' (an area of Ethiopia). But many scientists, particularly Mary and Richard Leakey, who have done most of the studies in East Africa, disagree because they consider Lucy to be off the main line of human evolution.

LAETOLI

Most of the locations where early East African fossils have been found have changed dramatically since Lucy's time. Once they were lush lake regions which swarmed with game, had plentiful wild vegetables and supported dense stands of trees which provided shade. Now they are near-desert, except for Laetoli, which is about 48km (30 miles) south of Olduvai Gorge. Several small lakes flourish near the site, and it still has trees and abundant grass. Even more important for hunters and scavengers, the great annual wildebeest migration often passes through the area.

About 3.75 million years ago, nearby Sadiman volcano was still active. One eruption spewed 1.3cm (½in) of ash-like sand over Laetoli. Soon after this uncomfortable shower it rained. Dozens of

Above *These tracks were made by two hominids at Laetoli, with a hint that a third might have walked in the footsteps of the larger one. An extinct form of horse made the trail running from lower right to upper left. The unique footprints offer an unusual perspective on early human evolution, showing that hominids were walking upright at least 3.75 million years ago. Discoveries like this amplify conventional archaeological finds – broken animal bones and concentrations of stone tools. They also provide a more complete picture of hominid anatomy than can ever be obtained from bones alone. They reveal that bipedal, upright, posture developed long before toolmaking began, perhaps thereby freeing the forelimbs for other tasks.*

Discoveries of footprints are rare in prehistory. The only other such Stone Age finds have come from deep inside prehistoric caves in France, Italy, and other parts of Europe, but these are no more than 50,000 to 15,000 years old.

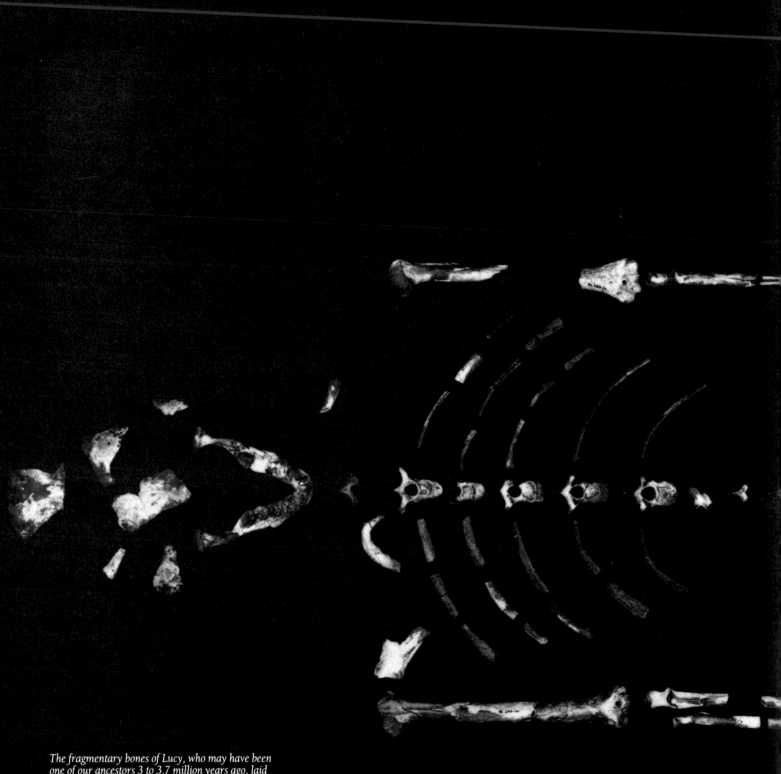

The fragmentary bones of Lucy, who may have been one of our ancestors 3 to 3.7 million years ago, laid out in a laboratory at the Cleveland Museum of Natural History. The man who discovered this controversial skeleton, Don Johanson, estimates that she was 1-1.2m (3½-4ft) tall and 19 to 21 years of age.

animals left their footprints on the wet ash, which dried quickly in the hot sun. Sadiman erupted again at least a dozen times in the month that followed, covering the footprints with successive layers of ash.

Paleontologists had known about Laetoli for years, but it was not until 1974 that they subjected it to intense scrutiny.

Then, one day in 1976, paleontologist Andrew Hill spotted some footprints in the hardened ash, exposed in a dry stream bed. The following year, a number of large elephant tracks came to light, associated with what looked very like hominid footprints. At first no one in camp believed that they were actual foot marks from so long ago, but Tim White patiently traced the original prints in a northerly direction under some sections of turf which had not been eroded by the modern stream. There was a dense tangle of roots overlying the hardened ash, so he had to work extremely slowly. One by one, White brushed the precious footprints clean and then poured preservative chemicals in them to preserve the imprints.

Slowly but steadily he and his helpers cleared more than 50 prints, covering more than 23.5m (77ft). The tracks were those of two hominids, one large, one small, and both walking in the same direction. The foot marks offer no clues as to the sex or precise age of these hominids, but they prove beyond reasonable doubt that our ancestors were walking upright 3.75 million years ago, long before they became toolmakers.

Above *The ancient dust at Laetoli tells the tale of the animals that lived there at the same time as early humans. Preserved for 3.75 million years, these footprints of a baby elephant show that the animal walked towards the edge of the stream bed, changed its mind and walked back into the stream.*

THE TOOLMAKERS

The discovery of Lucy was the culmination of generations of dedicated research, in Africa and farther afield, notably in the hands of the Leakey family – Louis and Mary, and their son Richard. After 25 years of searching in the Olduvai Gorge in East Africa, Louis and Mary Leakey unearthed well-preserved fragments of at least two early hominids. The first came to light in 1959, a robust primate that was capable of walking on two feet instead of the normal ape-like four. The bones lay among a scatter of stone tools and broken animal bones on what the Leakeys claimed was one of the earliest camp sites in the world. A year later, they found another hominid in the same ancient lake bed at Olduvai. This was a slender, anatomically more advanced hominid, also associated with stone tools and fragmentary animal bones.

Louis Leakey was an imaginative and impulsive scientist if ever there was one. He named his new and highly fragmentary find *Homo habilis,* which means 'handy man'. The label commemorated the new fossil's perceived abilities at toolmaking and its identity as a true human being as opposed to the more ape-like, robust Olduvai fossil with its heavy, crested skull.

Fragmentary finds of the same creature began to fill the gaps in our knowledge of this very early human. Its highly flexible and muscular fingers were those of a primate that spent most of its days walking upright on the ground. It had the grip and opposable thumb that enabled it to make tools, but its hands were powerful enough for it to grip branches and climb trees like

Above *In the vast emptiness of the Rift Valley, at Olduvai, the solitary figure of Dr Mary Leakey gently prises evidence of early human toolmaking from the soil. She, her late husband Louis, and her son Richard have proved in the last 25 years that human ancestors were making tools at least 2.3 million years ago.* **Below** *A sample of the Olduwan stone tools, with a hammer to give them scale.*

chimpanzees and other apes. *Homo habilis* was undoubtedly a toolmaker, probably the earliest on earth. In this and many other respects, it was light years ahead of Johanson's Lucy.

The Leakeys finds came at a time when most scientists assumed that humanity was a mere 500,000 years old. But a team of nuclear physicists at the University of California, Berkeley, dated the volcanic rocks found on the Olduvai floors to 1.75 million years ago, more than tripling the chronology of human evolution at one dramatic stroke.

LAKE TURKANA

An enormous gulf of prehistoric time separates the Laetoli and Hadar finds from the Leakeys' dramatic discoveries at Olduvai Gorge. What happened to human evolution between 3 million and 2 million years ago? Some tantalizing answers have come from one of the harshest desert environments on earth, a lava-strewn landscape in northern Kenya that is still difficult to reach and baffling for geologists to study – Lake Turkana.

There, Richard Leakey has taken up the paleoanthropological standard from his late father and heads an international team of scientists working on both shores of the lake. He first spotted the fossil deposits on the eastern shore of the lake when he was flying to Ethiopia in 1967. A quick ground reconnaissance yielded both stone tools and fossil animal bones. At the age of 23, he persuaded the National Geographic Society to underwrite a preliminary expedition to the new area. It was a gamble on the Society's part, but one that paid off with rich scientific dividends.

From the very first days of exploration plentiful, well-preserved animal fossils turned up. But the search was arduous. The terrain was so rough that most exploration was carried out on foot. Not only that, there were marauders in the area, so Leakey arranged for an armed escort to accompany the fossil hunters everywhere.

By the end of the first season, Leakey knew he had come to the right place. It was a fossiliferous area covering about 1500km^2 (more than 570 miles^2) dating to at least 2 million years ago, a period earlier than the very bottom layers of Olduvai Gorge. Leakey had also found three small hominid fragments, evidence that he was on the right track.

In 1969 Leakey concentrated his efforts on the eastern lake shore, near a sandy peninsula known as Koobi Fora. Nearby there were volcanic deposits with fossil-bearing beds sandwiched between them, places where stone tools and hominid fossils might well be found. Koobi Fora was a far larger area than the mere 9km^2 (3.5 miles^2) of Olduvai Gorge. Richard Leakey was wise enough to realize that he would have to assemble a team of scientists to study not only its hominid fossils but the local geology, ecology, site dating and archaeology as well. Leakey had no lack of volunteers, among them geologist Kay Behrensmeyer and archaeologist Glynn Isaac of the University of California, an expert on very early human artifacts.

Below *Almost 2 million years ago our remote ancestors were camping on the banks of this magnificent lake, scavenging freshly killed animals and butchering them with sharp stone choppers and stone hammers. Lake Turkana, in East Africa, has produced an enormously rich amount of highly important evidence of early human activities.*

Within a few days, Behrensmeyer found some stone tools in an eroding volcanic ash deposit. After much controversy, the ash was dated to about 1.89 million years ago, the earliest date for humanly manufactured stone artifacts found anywhere in the world.

Isaac excavated several localities near the site where the stone tools had been found, among them a dry stream bed where a group of hominids had found the carcass of a hippopotamus. They had gathered round and butchered the animal with small stone knives, crude flaked choppers and pebble hammers. The deposits in which the tools were found were so fine that there were no natural stones in them larger than a pea. So Isaac was able to show that rock lumps had been carried to the stream bed by the hominids to make tools next to the carcass. Our ancestors at that time were clearly hunters who thought hard about the best tools to cut up their food.

Another site excavated by Isaac, known as FxJj50, lies in an ancient watercourse, a place where the hominids could find shelter from the blazing sun. FxJj50 was close to water and to stone for toolmaking. Isaac and his colleagues found a cluster of stone artifacts, including choppers, crude scrapers, battered cobbles and sharp-edged

*Richard Leakey, **above**, is at present heading an international team of scientists from many academic disciplines at Koobi Fora. Here he is discussing finds with Kimoya Kimeu, an expert at finding and conserving early fossils.*

Left *From 1969 excavations at Koobi Fora, on the eastern shore of Lake Turkana in northern Kenya, have yielded tools nearly 2 million years old and have revolutionized our knowledge of early human evolution. These are slow-moving, meticulous excavations, designed to establish the associations between broken animal bones, hominid fossils and artifacts. Human settlements of this age are little more than transitory scatters of bones and broken stones; many are located near watercourses or small lakes.* **Below** *Scientists study the fossil-bearing beds at Koobi Fora.*

Right *Kimoya Kimeu, a friend of Richard Leakey's since childhood, has recently found several important hominid fossils.*

Far right *The late Glynn Isaac, who specialized in early stone tools, excavated a site near Koobi Fora, known as FxJj50. From his finds, he developed the now widely held theory that opportunism played a major role in early human behaviour, and that these sites are places where bands of hominids paused to butcher and eat game which they scavenged from kills.*

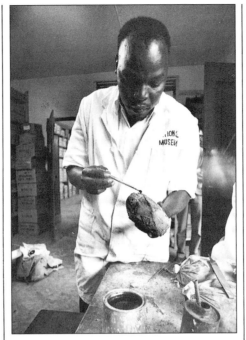

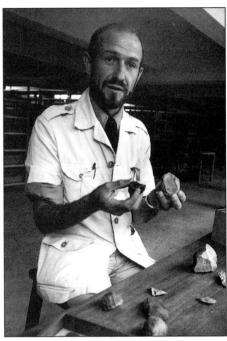

Above *!Kung San hunter-gatherers in Botswana's Kalahari Desert. Studies of these and other living peoples can throw light on very early human behaviour.*

flakes, which lay close to more than 2,000 bones from at least 20 animals, mainly antelope. Steadily, the archaeologists uncovered each stone and bone fragment, plotting their exact position before removing them for examination.

Back from the field, the archaeologists pored over the bone fragments. Surprisingly, many of them bore carnivore teeth marks and few bone joints were found, something that is characteristic of carnivore kills because the predators chew bones into small fragments. But at the same time, there were clear signs that the bones had been smashed and cut by hominids: reconstructed fragments showed signs of hammer blows and fine linear grooves that could result only from cutting bone with sharpened stones.

Opportunism is a hallmark of humankind, argued Glynn Isaac. Stone weapons and tools enabled the earliest hominids to scavenge and butcher larger and larger animals when they could find them. At the same time, they lived off predictable supplies of wild vegetable foods that tided them over short-term food shortages. Perhaps, Isaac argued, foraging for such foods provided stability in early hominid life and led to a division of labour between males and females. The site FxJj50 proved that the African savannah was an ideal ecological niche for hominids who lived by hunting, scavenging and foraging.

This theory was applied to the bones found at Olduvai. Bone by bone, Henry Bunn, Pat Shipman and other young scholars have identified cut and scratch marks made not only by carnivore teeth, but also by stone flakes, hammers and choppers. They found that the Olduvai accumulations of bones and stone tools are indeed the result of human activity, but it is very different activity from that found at camp sites.

When Bunn came to examine the bone fragments under the microscope, he found abundant evidence of deliberate butchering and meat stripping. In some cases, cut marks made by hominid tools lay *under* carnivore tooth marks. Bunn and others believed that the Olduvai 'living floors' were not, in fact, camp sites at all, but places where the hominids habitually came to butcher tasty portions of mammalian carcasses large and small.

So Olduvai was a location where our remote ancestors gathered to process meat in highly efficient, standardized ways. And

when they left, the disarticulated bones remained behind for predators such as hyenas to enjoy. Two million years ago, humans were perhaps marginal hunters, but they were certainly highly efficient scavengers, who consumed large quantities of meat when they could obtain it. In so doing, *Homo habilis* set humanity on a behavioural course that persisted for hundreds of thousands of years.

HOMO ERECTUS

Isaac and others have argued that the earliest human beings in Africa were skilled scavengers and brilliant opportunists whose way of life persisted until about 1.5 million years ago, when new, anatomically more advanced humans evolved south of the Sahara. These were the people who took advantage of a common natural phenomenon – the bush fire. They tamed fire perhaps as early as a million years ago.

It is easy to imagine how this happened. Some hunters might have come across a tree trunk burning after a sudden lightning strike. They picked up some burning brands and, enjoying the warmth when night fell, deliberately kept some logs alight, carrying fire with them wherever they roamed. From there it was a relatively small matter to learn how to create fire with friction and

to savour the enticing taste of freshly cooked meat. But of all human innovations, perhaps the taming of fire was the most revolutionary, because it allowed human beings to move outside their natural tropical range into temperate latitudes, to areas where snow fell in winter and where people would huddle by warm fires for months on end.

Who were these new, more advanced human beings? They were first identified in Java in the 1890s and 30 years later in the great Zhoukoudien cave near Beijing, where they dated to as early as 460,000 years ago. These beetle-browed people from Indonesia and China looked primitive but had modern limbs. The physical anthropologists called them *Homo erectus*.

Site FxJj50, near Koobi Fora, Kenya, during excavations in 1979, **top left**, *shows the sophisticated horizontal excavation technique used for recording every detail of the tool-bearing layers. Four skulls,* **right**, *illustrate Richard Leakey's view that three hominid lineages existed at Lake Turkana. They are* Homo erectus *(left), the gracile form of* Australopithecus *(second left), and the robust* Australopithecus, *shown in male (far right) and female forms.*

But in 1984, Kamoya Kimeu, a member of Leakey's fossil-hunting team for many years, was wandering near the base camp on the west shore of Lake Turkana when he spotted a human skull fragment. After three weeks of blisteringly hot sifting and excavation in the dry stream bed, the team revealed the remarkably complete skeleton of a 12-year-old boy who had lived about 1.6 million years ago. The sturdily built youth would have reached a height of about 1.8m (6ft) had he lived to adulthood. Like the Beijing finds, the fossil had massive eyebrow ridges, a high forehead and a larger brain capacity than *Homo habilis*. The earliest toolmaker of all had evolved into a more advanced human within half a million years. After these discoveries, few people doubt that the modern human line descended from *Homo habilis* in Africa.

THE SPREAD TO EUROPE

For all the anatomical advances chronicled by Richard Leakey's team, human life remained much the same – a constant round of hunting, scavenging and foraging. The new humans were still fundamentally tropical animals, evolving in a warm savanna environment with abundant big game and plentiful wild vegetable foods to sustain them. They seem to have wandered in small family bands over large hunting territories. These perennial movements took them out of Africa, into tropical Asia and also into what is now temperate Europe and China.

Some 300,000 years ago, a small band of these people camped by the shores of the Mediterranean near the modern city of Nice. When, in 1966, French archaeologist Henry de Lumley uncovered their small oval huts, he found that they had been erected over shallow hollows in the ground up to 15m (50ft) long. With infinite care, he cleared the hollows, exposing the bases of posts about 7.5cm (3in) in diameter that had formed the hut walls. The roof had been supported by centre posts. Perhaps skins were thrown over the saplings to make the huts waterproof. Some of them had hearths in the centre.

Fortunately for de Lumley, the Terra Amata people were bad housekeepers, who never swept out their huts. They lived among decaying, butchered elephant, wild ox and stag bones, discarded stone tools and even their own faeces. All these finds were just as rich a treasure trove as the huts themselves.

Once again the archaeologist's microscope came into play, probing ancient faeces to answer questions about pre-

Above *The Ambrona/Torralba sites in central Spain are among the most important archaeological locations in Europe, because they document some of the earliest human occupation of temperate latitudes in human history. The original excavations were conducted in the 1960s, but Clark Howell of the University of California, Berkeley, returned to the sites in 1980/81. The Ambrona North site is in the foreground of this view of the 1981 excavations, as we look south over the latest digs. Like early hominid sites, Ambrona and Torralba required meticulous horizontal excavation, to establish associations between human artifacts, butchered elephant bones, and geological stratigraphy. Such careful digging also allowed scientists to recover valuable environmental data.*

An overall view of the 1963 excavations at
Torralba, **top**, shows the 3-metre square grid used
to record the position of bones and artifacts.
Archaeologists are careful not to dislodge even small
objects until their exact distribution is documented.
Uncovering delicate elephant bones in Ambrona,
above, is a time-consuming task, often involving the
use of preservative chemicals to harden soft bone
while it is still in the ground.

Below *A stone biface tool lies beside a prehistoric elephant tusk at Ambrona, exactly where it was dropped by its user. Associations like this provide insights into prehistoric butchery practices.*

A jumble of bones from a butchered elephant carcass at Ambrona, excavated in 1963, **right**. *Originally, the archaeologist Clark Howell believed he had found a kill site in what was once a swamp, to which the hunters had driven their prey and then killed the elephants with spears. Later the band would have butchered the carcass at their leisure. However, many archaeologists now believe that big-game hunting started much later in prehistory. Thus, the Ambrona carcasses may be from animals which died of natural causes and were later scavenged by humans.*

historic diet. Nuts and seeds that flourished in late spring and early summer were plentiful under the powerful lenses. The studies also revealed that Terra Amata was a place where the hunters came year after year in search not only of wild vegetable foods, but also of shellfish, found by the hundred near the huts.

Few early archaeological sites offer such fine preservation as Terra Amata. Even fewer freeze a moment in prehistoric time in perpetuity. At approximately the same time as the Terra Amata huts were in use, another small band of hunters frequented a shallow, marshy valley northeast of Madrid. We can imagine them watching the valley floor, where great elephants would pass on regular seasonal migrations. Sometimes the lumbering beasts would wander by accident into the swamps, where they would wallow helplessly and eventually die. Sometimes, too, the watchful hunters might be able to drive them into the marsh, where they could attack the defenceless animals.

University of California paleontologist Clark Howell has spent many seasons uncovering these eventful moments in early prehistory at two major locations. At Torralba, Howell uncovered most of the left side of an elephant that had been cut up into small pieces. The butchering site was littered with crude hand axes, cleavers, scrapers and cutting tools used to dismem-ber the huge animal. The elephant was so large and heavy that the butchers could dismember only the upper side. Indeed, modern experiments with a deceased circus elephant have shown that you need a pick-up truck and a chain as well as a team of willing helpers to turn over a dead elephant!

At nearby Ambrona, Howell unearthed the remains of 30 to 35 dismembered elephants that were probably butchered individually or in small groups over long periods of time. In one place, the butchers had laid out a line of elephant bones, perhaps as stepping stones through the treacherous marsh.

Did the Torralba and Ambrona people

actually kill their huge quarry, or did they merely take advantage of animals accidentally caught in the mud? Were they and their relatives in the tropics and in China the world's first big-game hunters? The question is still hotly debated by the experts who peer at the living habits of our ancestors through microscopes. But the dramatic discoveries of the past 20 years show us that it took more than a million years for human beings to spread from their tropical African homeland into other parts of the Old World. And it was not until about 10,000 years ago that their descendants learned to master extremes of arctic cold and to survive successfully in every part of the globe.

Above *After the main features of the site were recorded the baulks, or walls, separating the different trenches were removed to recover finds which lay under them. This work was important at Ambrona, to complete site plans.*

HUNTERS
AND FORAGERS

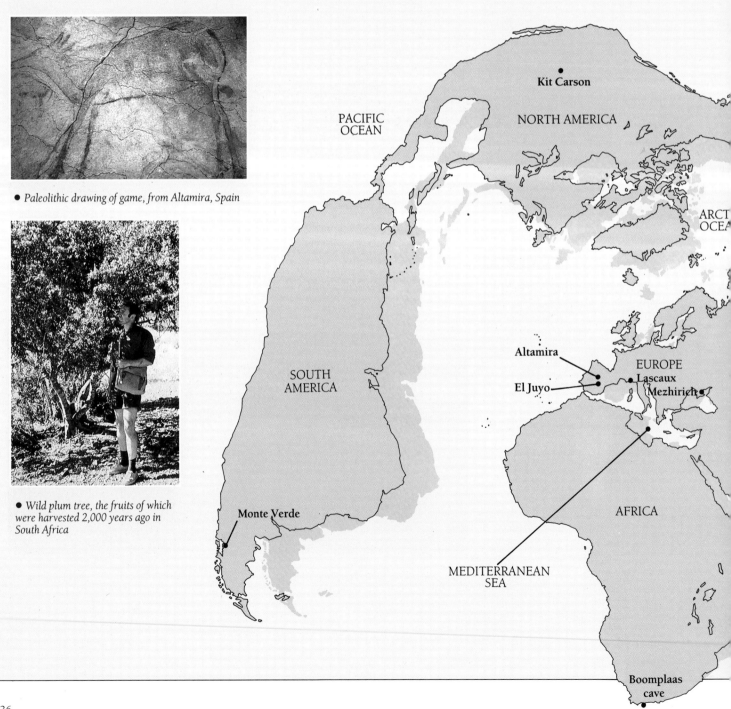

● Paleolithic drawing of game, from Altamira, Spain

● Wild plum tree, the fruits of which were harvested 2,000 years ago in South Africa

Kit Carson

PACIFIC
OCEAN

NORTH AMERICA

ARCT
OCEA

Altamira

EUROPE

El Juyo

Lascaux

Mezhirich

SOUTH
AMERICA

AFRICA

Monte Verde

MEDITERRANEAN
SEA

Boomplaas
cave

No one knows exactly when the first truly modern humans emerged, or where they did so. All we know is that anatomically modern people appeared in many parts of the Old World after 40,000 years ago. Their Neanderthal predecessors soon vanished as populations of *Homo sapiens sapiens* expanded rapidly, not only in numbers, but into hitherto uninhabited parts of the world. They did so at a time when Europe and Asia were in the grip of the last major cold snap of the Great Ice Age. Western Europe then would be unrecognizable now. Vast ice sheets covered what are now the Low Countries, great glaciers flowed down from the Alps and the land between them shivered through harsh, nine-month winters. So the human inhabitants congregated in sheltered river valleys, near game migration routes and rivers where salmon ran in spring, summer and autumn.

As early as 35,000 years ago, when the first modern human beings appeared in Europe, Africa and Asia, big-game hunting played a vital role not only in human life but also in the peopling of the globe. Many scientists believe that big-game hunting brought prehistoric peoples to the Americas more than 12,000 years ago. Bison hunting began on the North American plains at least 11,500 years ago and continued into the nineteenth century, when the Victorian repeating rifle nearly drove the lumbering, gregarious animals into extinction.

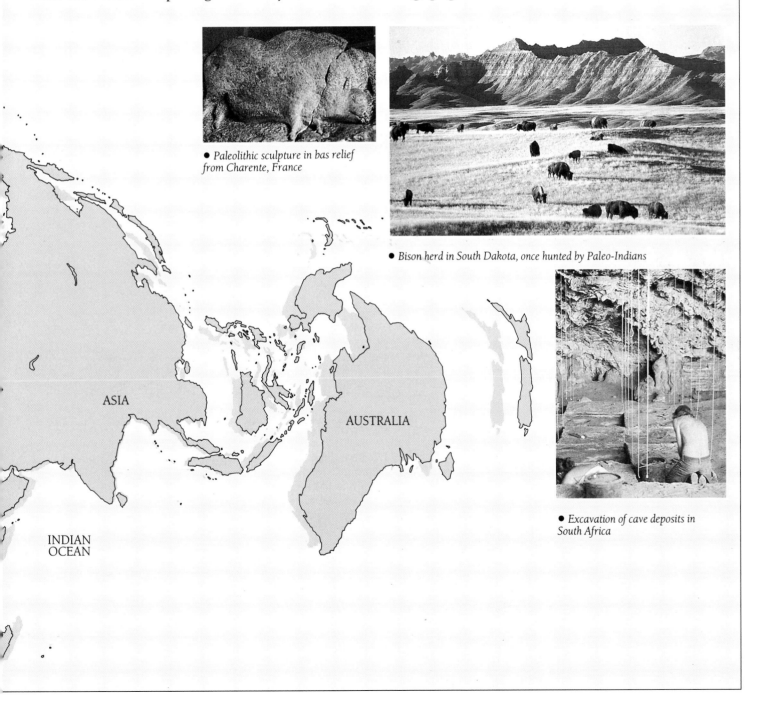

● *Paleolithic sculpture in bas relief from Charente, France*

● *Bison herd in South Dakota, once hunted by Paleo-Indians*

ASIA

AUSTRALIA

INDIAN
OCEAN

● *Excavation of cave deposits in South Africa*

THE COLORADO BISON KILL

On the Colorado grasslands the wind was blowing gently from the south on that early June day, 8,000 years ago. For days the hunters had been waiting, stalking the unsuspecting grazing bison, moving them ever so slowly upwind towards the edge of a deep, narrow gully, or *arroyo*. As dawn broke, several bands of the Paleo-Indian hunters assembled quietly and hid on either bank of the *arroyo*. The women and children waited safely out of the way.

Suddenly, the quiet of the summer morning gave way to the drumming of hundreds of hooves. A cloud of dust rose high over the horizon. Soon the stampeding bison were in sight, blindly following their leaders towards the gully. The waiting hunters heard the yells of their companions downwind of the herd and gripped their spears. Moments later, the leading bison fell headlong into the narrow gully. Bellowing, they tried to get to their feet, but to no avail. The stampeding animals at their heels stumbled on top of them, choking them to death in a crushing frantic struggle. The spearmen yelled and shouted, as more than 200 bison stumbled into the *arroyo*. They thrusted and jabbed, killing dozens of beasts on the top of the heap, while the others suffocated under the sheer weight of their companions. Minutes later, the hunt was over. A few stragglers escaped over the horizon.

The hunters watched the heaving pile of dying animals, occasionally spearing a bison that managed to get to its feet, until gradually the movement ceased. Days of careful stalking had paid off – there would be ample meat for weeks to come.

Now the real work began. The Indians worked fast and efficiently. Just like the nineteenth-century buffalo hunters after them, they probably worked in teams, processing several animals at once with sharp-edged stone knives and large hammers. First they moved the heavy carcasses out of the gully into a position where they could cut them up. The butchers laid out the legs so that they could roll each beast onto its belly. Then they cut the skin down the back and pulled it down both flanks, so that it acted as a mat for the fresh meat to lie on. Skilfully, they removed the blanket of flesh on the back, which enabled them to detach the forelegs and shoulder blades, exposing the prized meat from the hump, rib cage and body cavity.

Directly the limbs were removed, the butchers stripped the meat off them and threw the bones into the gully. If they were anything like modern hunters, they would probably have eaten some of the entrails raw as they worked. Next, they attacked the ribs and backbone, stripping off the flesh and keeping some of it to pound up and dry to make pemmican – the pounded, sun-dried paste of meat and fat that could sustain them for months. Within a few minutes, the remains of the carcass were scattered in and around the gully.

While the women stacked the meat and laid some of it out to dry in the sun, the butchers moved to yet another beast. Eventually, they could lift no more animals up the steep sides of the gully. Undeterred, they moved into the narrow defile and butchered what they could among the dense clouds of flies. Some of the dead animals were too tightly wedged into the gully to be moved, so the butchers removed just a few choice body parts and left the rest to rot. Some of the bison at the bottom of the heap lay exactly where they fell – completely untouched.

This 8,000-year-old hunt survives so vividly that it is almost as if we were beside the waiting hunters as they stalked their prey. Almost everything we know about this

incident comes from the meticulous excavation of the bison bone bed which lies near what is now Kit Carson, in south-eastern Colorado. When Plains archae-ologist Joe Ben Wheat uncovered the densely packed bones in 1955, they lay in a 52m (170ft) long concentration, together with some of the finely flaked stone projectile heads that had killed them. More than 173 bison of all ages lay in the bed, but only 13 of the skeletons were complete.

After an exhaustive analysis of the bones, Wheat believes that the kill yielded a fantastic amount – more than 25,696kg (56,600lb) of meat, to say nothing of some 1,816kg (4,000lb) of edible organs and 2,451kg (5,400lb) of fat. He used historical records of Plains bison kills to estimate that, with this amount of meat, a band of 150 people would have had enough fresh meat for a month. If they dried and preserved a third of the flesh, they would have had food supplies for several months more.

The butchered remains of more than 150 bison filled the bottom of a narrow arroyo, and lay there until Joe Ben Wheat excavated them 8,000 years later, **left**. *At the Olsen-Chubbuck site in Colorado, Wheat was able to reconstruct the most minute details of the hunt and the orgy of butchery which followed. The hunters used simple knives and hammerstones to dismember the bison, processing enough meat in a few hours to sustain a sizable band of people for more than a month. Much of the meat was dried and pounded into a lean powder known as pemmican, a vital food for highly mobile Plains Indians. The Olsen-Chubbuck site is an unusually spectacular reconstruction of a single hunt at one location. Other sites, such as the famous Head-Smashed-In jump in Alberta, Canada, were used again and again over thousands of years, right into historic times. Even so, kills like this were probably rare, with most men witnessing only one or two large-scale hunts in their lifetimes.*

BIG GAME AND THE BIRTH OF ART

Spanish nobleman Don Marcelino Sanz de Sautuola was by no stretch of the imagination an archaeologist. But he had heard of beautiful bone tools and stone artifacts that had come to light in prehistoric caves in neighbouring France. It happened that there was a deep cavern named Altamira on his property and in 1879 he started digging there. One day his young daughter came along for fun. She soon tired of the slow work and wandered off with a lantern to explore. Suddenly her father heard her exclaim 'Toros! Toros!' ('Bulls! Bulls!') Grabbing another lantern, he crawled after

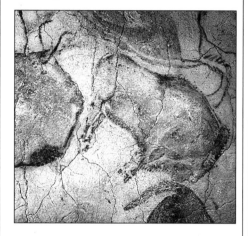

her into a low-ceilinged side chamber. Vivid brown, red and black bison danced across the ceiling, some of them cunningly painted over humps in the rock, which made them look alive.

Sautuola had seen some of the engraved antler artifacts that had come from French caves and firmly believed that he had discovered Stone Age paintings. The experts scoffed and forgot about his discovery until the early years of this century, when more paintings came to light in southwestern France and the Pyrenees. What paintings they were – life-like depictions of long extinct mammoth, long-haired 'woolly' rhinoceroses, bison, wild oxen, reindeer, horses and many other big-game animals! Northern Spain and southwestern France proved to be the seat of the world's first art tradition, which flourished more than 15,000 years ago.

Perhaps the most spectacular art discovery came in 1940, when four boys explored a hole in the woods near Montignac in southwestern France. They were astounded when their lanterns illuminated brilliantly coloured bulls, horses and stags painted on the white limestone walls and ceiling. Now known as the Lascaux caves, the remarkable paintings

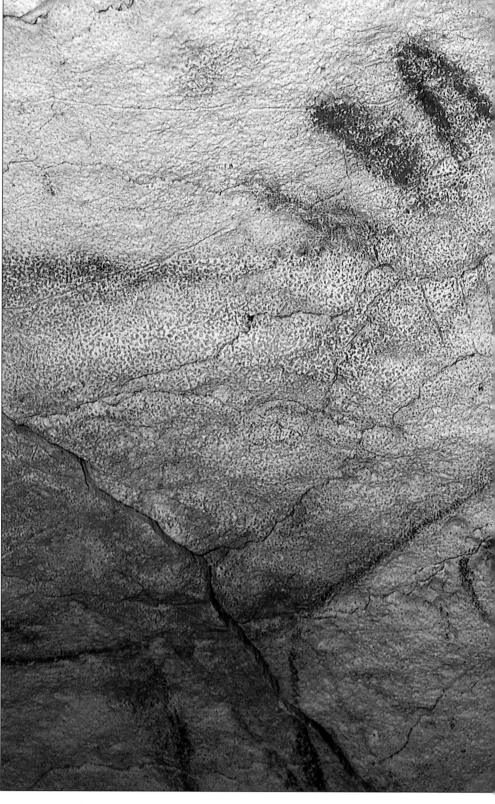

Above left *In the light of a flickering candle the Marquis de Sautuola's daughter Maria first saw the Altamira bison. The artists who painted these polychrome beasts used the natural bulges in the rock ceiling to add an additional touch of naturalism to the animals. Some experts believe the artists painted from dead animals, whereas others argue that they could paint astonishing likenesses from memory.*

Above *A polychrome hind and an outline bison from the 'Sistine Chapel' of Upper Paleolithic art – Altamira Cave. These paintings were executed perhaps as late as 12,000 years ago.*

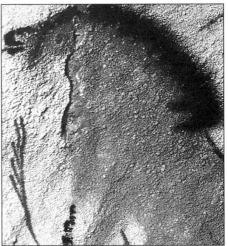

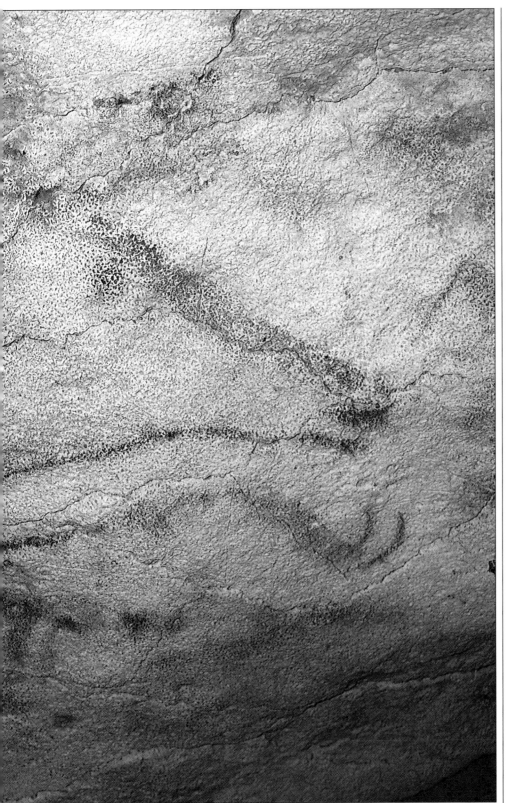

and engravings in them proved to be more than 15,000 years old.

Thousands of French and Spanish caves have been explored by archaeologists and speleologists, but only a tiny handful of them were decorated by the first artists in the world. It has been a while since a major site has been discovered and it is possible that all of them have been located, although this seems unlikely. Perhaps some day a lucky explorer will stumble across another spectacular cave like Lascaux, sealed from the outside world since the Ice Age.

In the meantime, archaeologists have tried to interpret the meaning of this remarkable explosion in human creativity. Even today, one can sense the mystery of the paintings. Visiting Altamira or Lascaux alone is an intense, moving experience, especially when you are carrying a candle or acetylene lamp. The animals dance and flicker in the dim light, the reds and blacks catching the moving flame. It is as if they are alive, as if the prehistoric world lives again. You emerge into daylight conscious that you have returned from a long journey into the remote past, into an unfamiliar and long-forgotten world.

Top right *The famous 'Chinese horse' from the Lascaux caves in France is so named because it resembles a style of Chinese art. In fact it displays the elongated neck, thick body and small head typical of Upper Paleolithic art about 15,000 years ago. This style was less naturalistic and clumsier than the Altamira paintings, which were produced at the very end of the Ice Age.*

Giant stags cross a stream in a brilliant example of Upper Paleolithic artistry from Lascaux, **above right**. *The artist painted a row of stags' heads from a distance, as if he or she was watching them pick their way across a stream or walk through tall grass. The animals have the branching antlers typical of giant stags.*

EL JUYO

The first French prehistorians to copy and record cave paintings and engravings were captivated by the superb naturalism of the art. Many of them argued that the artists painted the animals for the sheer pleasure of depicting them, as 'art for art's sake'. Others believed that the painted sites were sacred places where the hunters gathered in rituals to share sympathetic magic which ensured the fertility of game and the success of the hunt.

After World War II, the great French archaeologist André Leroi-Gourhan spent years recording the clusters of individual signs and motifs. He believed that the art was far from random, but part of a system of meanings that defined the hunters' world. Far from being art for art's sake, the paintings and engravings that adorned caves and individual artifacts were symbolic depictions. The selection of individual animal to paint or engrave was a deliberate symbolic act. At this remote distance, it is impossible for us to grasp these meanings. But, judging from modern hunting societies, there were probably continuities between animal and human life which carried over into everyone's social world.

Only occasionally does the archaeologist come face-to-face with the symbolism of the ancient artists. Even then the discovery is often an unexpected one that comes in the midst of a long, arduous and routine excavation. So when a student digging near the back of El Juyo cave in northern Spain exposed a ring of stones concentrated around some ash and charcoal, his supervisors were alerted to something unusual.

El Juyo is far off the tourist track, a small single-chamber cave some distance from Altamira. There is nothing mysterious or evocative about the site. Yet some 14,000 years ago, the cave was a special shrine for a band of local people, a place where they built a unique, highly symbolic structure.

Leslie Freeman and J. Gonzales Echegaray had come to El Juyo with an excavation strategy that was quite unlike those of earlier generations of cave excavators. They spent several seasons in the late 1970s dissecting the deposits of El Juyo in minute detail, scraping away the soil in thin slivers and recording the precise position of every artifact, every boulder and every animal bone. This meticulous strategy led to the discovery of a unique construction which an earlier generation of diggers with less meticulous methods would probably have missed.

Freeman and Echegaray took over the excavation of the stone circle themselves because they wanted no one else to have

The entrance to a remarkable Stone Age cave, El Juyo, before excavations began in 1978, **left**. *This cave yielded unique evidence of ritual beliefs some 14,000 years ago. The meticulous excavations recovered not only a shrine but many artifacts, shells, and animal bones. An accumulation of red ochre, fossil shells, and a whistle,* **right** *appeared after weeks of slow excavation.*

the responsibility of destroying vital evidence. The original stone circle surrounded a hearth. They soon uncovered another flat stone. At first they suspected that it was part of another hearth nearby, but as they uncovered it the surface got larger and larger. It turned out to be a slab of stalagmite 1.8m (6ft) long, 1.2m (4ft) wide and 15cm (6in) thick, weighing almost a tonne. Not only that, a team of strong individuals had at some time picked it up and moved it a distance of at least 9m (30ft) from its original resting place in the cave.

Thinking that the slab was a grave marker, the two men worked their way slowly down the sides of the stone. To their surprise, they unearthed several flat stones that had been set up to support it, together with a row of 26 complete bone points. There were no signs of a grave, just a confusion of bone fragments, charcoal, red ochre and clay chunks. With infinite care, Freeman and Echegaray worked away at the soil, tracing extremely subtle changes in earth texture and surface colour to reveal a unique, astounding structure. About 14,000 years ago, some people had built a layer of cylindrical earth columns which were fashioned by filling some form of containers and upending them, just as children today build sand castles. The builders had arranged the columns in rosettes, encircling a central column with six others, then filling in the gaps with coloured clays to create mosaic patterns.

The columns were photographed, then moved carefully. A layer of broken bones, burnt plant remains and red ochre colouring matter lay beneath the rosettes. The bones were a careful selection of body parts, perhaps the remains of sacrificial offerings. Freeman and Echegaray probed to the bottom of this remarkable archaeological 'sandwich' to reveal at least four more bone layers separated by rosette patterns, each with different mosaic designs. The entire 'sandwich' formed a mound

nearly a metre (3ft) high and was encased in yellow clay.

Later, Leslie Freeman was digging in a trench not far from the mound when he came across a chunk of rock placed vertically in the ground. The trench was a small one, so Echegaray sat on the ground above and took notes as the digging proceeded. Brush stroke by brush stroke, Freeman freed the surface of the rock from the soil, recording cracks and fissures as he went along. When the brushing ended, he was startled to find a stone face staring at him. Someone 14,000 years ago had set the rock upright and carefully embellished the

Left *The cave was excavated with infinite care, the position of each find meticulously plotted and recorded.*

natural holes and fissures in the stone with deft engraved strokes. It was an imaginary figure that stared at the archaeologists: an adult male human on the right side, complete with moustache and beard; on the left, he took the form of a large cat, probably a lion or leopard, depicted complete with muzzle, chin, fangs and whiskers.

More than two months of fastidious excavation and recording enabled Freeman and Echegaray to admire not only the details of their finds, but also to understand the overall effect that the ancient shrine must have had on a visitor. The stone face was set at such an angle that someone entering the cave saw only the human side of the countenance from 6m (20ft) away. To glimpse the feline side, a person had to penetrate the cave and examine the snarling image with a flickering light.

Freeman and Echegaray are in no doubt that El Juyo was once a sanctuary created by the combined efforts of at least ten people, in the expectation that the sacred place would be used again and again. What of the significance of the stone face? Perhaps the portrait in its mysterious dualism symbolizes the opposing forces of the world, the forces of good and evil that are powerful in hunting societies to this day.

Above *The stone face in situ at El Juyo during excavation in 1979.*

Above left *The two-sided stone face, illuminated from below, peers out of the depths of the cave. The deft strokes that delineate the features of the dual portrait are highlighted, revealing the human side, which was visible when one entered the cave, and the feline aspect, visible from inside the darkness of the cave.*

MEZHIRICH

El Juyo is but one of many Stone Age sites where archaeologists are unearthing precise, valid detail about Ice Age life, about the exciting millennia after 20,000 years ago when *Homo sapiens sapiens* mastered extremes of global climate and peopled the world. The impressive versatility and adaptability of these people took them far onto the wind swept arctic plains that stretched north and east from western and southern Europe as far as Siberia and beyond. Undulating gently, the frigid tundra steppe stretched to the horizon, occasionally dissected by a broad river valley with thickets of small trees.

To survive in this dreary environment required a brilliant ability at big-game hunting, the technology to pursue mammoth, large steppe bison and other animals large and small. You needed dwellings that would keep you snug on winter nights when the thermometer would plunge far below zero. Your clothing had to be multi-layered, tailored to fit. Only people with the ability to tolerate hardship, to co-operate with others and to live in close quarters with their neighbours could possibly survive a climate where winter lasted nine months of the year.

No environment on earth today matches the severity of the tundra steppe 15,000 years ago. Yet Stone Age people flourished in this unimaginably cold climate. Many of them lived on low promontories of land overlooking large river valleys such as the Don and Dnepr in western and central Russia. In 1965, a farmer at Mezhirich in the Dnepr valley decided to dig a cellar a few metres from his front door. He soon found several large mammoth bones. Before long, his cellar was swarming with eager archaeologists. Among those working on the excavations was one of the few American prehistorians ever to work in the Soviet Union, Olga Soffer of the University of Illinois. She found herself excavating on one of the most spectacular Stone Age sites ever found in the Soviet Union.

On this patch of ground, 15,000 years ago, stood at least five sturdy mammoth-bone dwellings overlooking the river valley. Mysteriously they were abandoned, and were soon covered by a thick layer of wind-blown glacial dust which preserved the ruins in perfect condition. The excavators trowelled and brushed away the soil from densely packed heaps of collapsed mammoth bones that sealed the hut floors below. They numbered each bone and recorded its position before removal, so that the houses could be reconstructed in the Kiev Museum.

An oval mound of collapsed mammoth bones arranged in elaborate patterns is all that remains of an extraordinary dwelling at Mezhirich in the USSR, **top**. *This important mammoth hunters' site was occupied about 15,000 years ago, probably for much of the winter months. Prehistorian Olga Soffer believes that it was an important base camp, where influential tribal leaders dwelt.*

Arching mammoth tusks interlock to form the roof and a row of mammoth limb bones stand by the entrance of a reconstruction of the hut, in the Kiev Museum, by academician Ivan Pidopichko, **above**. *Considerable communal work must have gone into collecting the bones and erecting the original house, a more permanent dwelling than many that were occupied in the valleys of western Russia 15,000 years ago.*

Each dwelling was between 4m and 6.5m (13ft and 21ft) across, covering an area of up to 79m² (850ft²). Because the builders had lived in a largely treeless environment, they relied on an alternative source of building materials – mammoth carcasses. They seem to have made a habit of saving large bones from any beast they killed and butchered, and probably scavenged parts from animals that perished of natural causes. The largest limb bones formed massive foundation walls for the oval dwellings, which supported intricate frameworks of smaller limb bones, vertebrae and other parts. Sometimes the builders arranged the bones in fine herringbone patterns. Because they lacked long timbers to use as roof supports, they employed bone uprights stuck into large holes broken through mammoth limbs. Once in place, the framework was covered with mammoth hides.

The Mezhirich houses were occupied over long periods, which was just as well, considering the great effort that it took to build the structures. Olga Soffer estimates that ten men would have needed five or six days to complete a single dwelling, without allowing for time to collect bones that may have been scattered over dozens of square kilometres. Once completed, the lodges may have served as winter bases, housing perhaps 50 people in each hut.

Soviet experts have excavated only a small proportion of Mezhirich, which may have been a large settlement occupied by several hunting bands over many generations. There was certainly enough meat around to feed them. After excavations at several sites, we know that the hunters stalked not only mammoth, but also reindeer in spring and early summer, fur-bearing animals in winter and water fowl during the short arctic summer.

Mezhirich is unique in its elaborate mammoth-bone dwellings, but we know that dozens of other hunting camps mushroomed over the central and western Russian plains between about 18,000 years and 14,000 years ago. These may have been isolated settlements, but their inhabitants maintained remarkable long-distance connections. The Soviets were surprised to find seashells from between 640km and 800km (400 and 500 miles) away in the Mezhirich houses. The people who lived there also prized amber, a yellow-brown resin which becomes charged with static electricity when rubbed. They obtained these supplies from at least 160km (100 miles) away.

SPREADING TO THE AMERICAS

To survive in the harsh arctic world meant understanding the habits of the animals that frequented the tundra steppe. The big-game hunters followed the same herds for generations, preying on individual animals as they weakened or, when circumstances allowed, capturing them. Theirs was a nomadic life, one in which the keys to survival were ingenuity, caution and opportunism.

Over hundreds of generations the nomads covered thousands of square kilometres in search of scattered herds. Sons quarrelled with their fathers and split off to settle in a neighbouring hunting territory. Daughters married outside the band, or families moved off on their own to exploit a herd of mammoth spotted some kilometres away. As time went on, *Homo sapiens sapiens* settled ever farther to the northeast, penetrating the arctic fastnesses of Siberia. In time they came to the shores of the Bering Strait, the narrow stretch of open water that separates Asia from the Americas.

Not that there was much water for them to cross. Ice Age sea levels 15,000 years ago were hundreds of metres lower than they are today, because billions of litres of water were taken up in huge ice sheets. The Bering Strait was dry land then, a low-

Above *A close-up of the intricate patterning of the mammoth bone foundation walls reveals that blades were set in pleasing herringbone patterns which also formed a strong base for the dome-like, semi-subterranean structure. This particular house was about 5m (16½ft) across, perhaps with a hide roof supported by a wooden frame with bones holding the skins in place. Five such dwellings are known, of which four have been excavated.*

Right *The site of a small encampment of mastodon hunters in Chile, at Monte Verde. Looking towards the south-east the main occupation and excavation areas can be seen in the middle ground, surrounded by woodland.*

Above *Between 25,000 and 15,000 years ago, tiny bands of big-game hunters followed Ice Age herds across arctic steppe tundra deep into Siberia. Around 15,000 years ago (the date is disputed) a few of them hunted their way across the Bering Strait when it was dry land, and the peopling of the Americas began.*

Right *Burned wood from one of the hearths at Monte Verde bears chopping marks which indicate that the inhabitants made tools with which they could break up wood.*

lying, windy arctic plain that stretched east towards the higher ground of Alaska. Very few Stone Age hunters pursued their quarry this far, wintering in tiny camps that are now buried under arctic waters. This, perhaps, was how human beings came to America.

Slowly, almost imperceptibly, the northern climate warmed up after about 15,000 years ago. Inexorably, the ice-bound sea coasts encroached on the low-lying plain. The mammoth and other arctic game gradually moved onto higher ground away from the rising water and their human pursuers followed them.

As the Ice Age ended, so the first Americans settled in a vast, unpopulated continent. Perhaps only a few families crossed into Alaska; only a handful of them appear to have penetrated south of the great ice sheets that mantled much of North America. But those that did found

themselves in a more temperate land where big game was abundant. The Paleo-Indian newcomers were so successful that they exploded throughout the Americas within a few thousand years.

Among their descendants were the bison hunters of the plains described at the beginning of this chapter. So was a small group of mastodon hunters, who camped by the banks of a small creek in south-central Chile about 12,000 years ago. Archaeologist Tom Dillehay was working at a university in the area when he came across fractured bones, worked stones and even some wood protruding from the eroding bank of a stream. The stream drains a bog in a humid forest that has been there for many thousands of years.

Dillehay found the Chilean site of Monte Verde in 1976 and realized at once that the waterlogged conditions were unique. The wood fragments emerging from the bank

hinted that normally perishable artifacts might have survived. Two years later, he returned to explore Monte Verde with a team of student helpers, in the first of several seasons of excavations that uncovered a remarkable settlement.

The site lay under a thin layer of peat that had effectively sealed wood, seeds and other perishable remains for thousands of years. Dillehay removed the peat seal very slowly, using syringes, horse-hair brushes and a water pump to recover wooden objects in good condition. He was able to

obtain samples of wood and bone for radio-carbon dating, which showed that people had been living by the stream at least 12,000 years ago.

The inhabitants had camped on both sides of the creek. Some of them lived in two parallel rows of rectangular houses between 0.8m² and 1.2m² (9ft² and 13ft²) joined by thin connecting walls. Dillehay found fragments of the wooden house frames, which rose from crude log and plank foundations. He believes that they were covered with skins. Each house had a clay-lined hearth, and the floors were covered with large quantities of seeds and other vegetable foods.

Even more intriguing was another structure uncovered a short distance away. Dillehay's trowel traced a compact sand and gravel base for two curved walls that formed a 'wishbone'-shaped structure, open on its southeastern side. Short stubs of side walls made from branches still stood vertically on the foundations. A low, semi-rectangular platform protruded from the outside of the back wall. Inside the structure and opposite the inside edge of the platform, once stood a long pole, perhaps a roof support. A burned log lay on the ground, scraped to form a semi-rectangular object. One end lay in a V-shaped

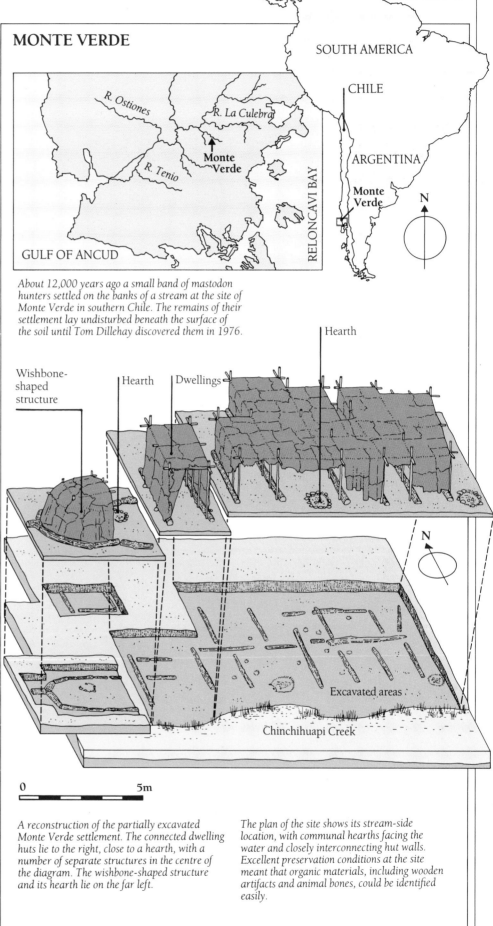

MONTE VERDE

About 12,000 years ago a small band of mastodon hunters settled on the banks of a stream at the site of Monte Verde in southern Chile. The remains of their settlement lay undisturbed beneath the surface of the soil until Tom Dillehay discovered them in 1976.

A reconstruction of the partially excavated Monte Verde settlement. The connected dwelling huts lie to the right, close to a hearth, with a number of separate structures in the centre of the diagram. The wishbone-shaped structure and its hearth lie on the far left.

The plan of the site shows its stream-side location, with communal hearths facing the water and closely interconnecting hut walls. Excellent preservation conditions at the site meant that organic materials, including wooden artifacts and animal bones, could be identified easily.

'vice', designed to hold the log in place while someone worked on it. Perhaps the builders were interrupted while completing the wishbone structure. But it had already been used, because two hearths lay on the floor inside.

Monte Verde was located in a forest, where abundant vegetable foods were to be found all year round. So Dillehay believes that it was a long-term camp site, used by people who collected many different species of forest foods, including wild potatoes, as well as fresh water molluscs. But they were also hunters, a fact that was revealed when Dillehay found the butchered remains of five or six mastodon. Because only parts of their carcasses were found, the animals may have been killed elsewhere, and portions of them brought back to the camp.

By the time he completed the first few seasons of excavation, Tom Dillehay realized that he was investigating a unique, and, by American standards, very early pre-historic settlement. The artifacts used by the people were strikingly different from those manufactured by big-game hunters far to the north. Monte Verde tools were simple and easily portable, most of them made of wood. The people who lived there hunted with wooden spears, probably used simple digging sticks to root out tubers and mounted simple stone scrapers in wooden handles. They used none of the finely made stone spearpoints used by bison hunters, or bone harpoons like those manufactured by Ice Age hunters in Europe.

The entire tool kit was simple, much of it little more than a casually modified branch or stone fragment. Yet this small settlement clustered along a Chilean stream 12,000 years ago again highlights the extraordinary ability of the first Americans to adapt not only to chilly northern landscapes or game-rich plains, but also to the depths of humid forests as well.

By the time Monte Verde was inhabited, human beings had settled nearly every

Top *Foundation logs in the residential area of Monte Verde were laid out in a rough, rectangular fashion and brought together in such a way as to form a linear settlement of small huts 12,000 years ago. Archaeologist Tom Dillehay recovered hearths, stone tools, and bone fragments from the floors of these dwellings. The wishbone-shaped structure found in the settlement,* **right,** *yielded no less than sixteen different medicinal plant species. The significance of this curiously shaped structure is yet to be discovered.*

corner of the world. They had adapted to the harsh realities of tropical deserts in Africa and to Central Asia's Gobi desert. A few bands of Stone Age people had even made their way across more than 80km (50 miles) of open water from mainland southeast Asia to another pristine continent – Australia.

No one knows quite how they managed to venture offshore, or why they undertook the journey in the first place. Perhaps they were blown into open water on a crude raft and drifted helpless, unable to return. Perhaps they spotted a tall column of smoke from a great natural bush fire far over the horizon and realized there were unexplored hunting territories in that direction. We simply do not know, nor are we likely ever to solve such mysteries, because they involve probing the deepest thoughts of people long vanished. All the archaeologist has to work with are the tangible remains of human behaviour – artifacts, dwellings, food remains and other signposts to the remote past.

BOOMPLAAS CAVE

Today's archaeologist is a specialist, working not only on a geographical area such as, say, South Australia or coastal Peru, but often carrying out prehistoric detective work. Hilary Deacon, a South African archaeologist, is not only an expert on Stone Age prehistory, but a specialist in the reconstruction of ancient environments as well. He is a firm believer in long-term research projects, designed to extract maximum information from both the excavations themselves and the finds in them.

It was Deacon who excavated the Boomplaas Cave, a prehistoric site perched above the Cango Valley in South Africa's southern Cape Province. Boomplaas is 77km (48 miles) from the Indian Ocean, a large cave with deep deposits, ideal for the kind of project Deacon had in mind. He started excavations in 1974, with the deliberate intention of combining the study of the prehistoric inhabitants with a meticulous examination of biogeographical change in the area over the millennia when the cave was in use.

To carry out such research involved time-consuming methods. Just like Freeman at El Juyo, Deacon laid a grid over the surface of the cave deposits and then excavated each layer horizontally, so that he could recover not only artifacts, but also information about activities during a particular period at the site.

Earlier excavators were content to stand on an occupation deposit as they uncovered it, but Deacon erected a framework of aluminium scaffolding traversed by planks,

so that the excavators could uncover the soft deposits without trampling on them. Because the deposits chronicled dozens of short visits over long periods of time, individual levels of occupation were impossible to identify unless the diggers used paint brushes to free such finds as humified plant remains from the clinging, friable soil.

The Boomplaas excavations took years to complete. Deacon recorded the three-dimensional position of every finished artifact and identifiable mammal bone of any size. Some randomly selected squares were sieved through a tiny mesh, so that samples of tiny mammals such as mice were obtained. When it rained, water would run off the slope above the cave and Deacon improvised storage drums to collect surplus water. This was filtered and then used to wash samples of soil collected at random. The ancient seeds in the samples floated to the top, providing statistical evidence of the vegetable diet from

each level of occupation.

As the excavation expanded, Deacon devoted more and more time to plotting ancient features such as the circles of ash that once formed hearths, pits and even postholes with the bases of wooden stakes still in place. The results from these painstaking excavations were remarkable.

Thick layers of nineteenth-century sheep dung mantled the earlier prehistoric levels at Boomplaas. This dung dates from a period when the cave was used as a stock pen to protect local herds against stock thieves. But the cave was already in use as a pen 1,600 years earlier by cattle herders, who built their hearths in the cave. Deacon believes that the cave was simply a satellite stock post, an outlying location close to seasonal grazing grounds, which was in use for short periods each year.

The excavations came into their own when Deacon probed those Stone Age occupation layers that were older than 2,000 years. Seed and animal bone samples

Boomplaas Cave lies in a spectacular setting overlooking the Cango Valley in the Cape Province, South Africa, **above and left***. The cave was occupied at least as early as 42,000 years ago. It was the site of a remarkable 'fruit farming' culture 2,000 years ago just as the valley it surveys is a rich fruit-growing area today.*

*Excavation of the upper deposits at Boomplaas Cave, **right**, revealed numerous features which were recorded with the aid of the vertical and horizontal grid, and aluminium scaffolding was used to support the weight of the diggers, **below**, so that they did not sink into the soft archaeological deposits.*

*The kernels of the wild plum Choritaenia capensis, **above and right**, were prized for their fine oil, used on the skin 2,000 years ago. They were harvested in summer and stored in storage pits.*

from these layers showed that Boomplaas had served many purposes through the millennia. At that time hunters and foragers used the cave as a base when they were harvesting and storing the oil-rich fruits of the wild plum (*Choritaenia capensis*), known to have been used historically as a skin oil. How easy were these summer fruits to harvest? Deacon experimented with modern trees and collected between 120 and 150 fruit in a minute!

About 2,000 years ago, the fruit was stored in underground pits lined with the bulbous leaves of a poisonous plant and grass. When the pits were excavated (with paint brushes) two of them were still full of harvested fruit. The other pits had been emptied, but all were marked with stone uprights ready for return visits after the harvest.

The deepest occupation layers revealed that the prehistoric chronicle of Boomplaas extends back to at least 42,000 years ago. The trenches became smaller as the diggers probed ever-lower levels. The picture of ancient life became necessarily more blurred, but even so it showed a striking change about 12,000 to 14,000 years ago.

The people who had harvested the wild plum and their predecessors were expert hunters, but they mainly pursued small and medium-sized antelope, as well as collecting wild vegetable foods. But the Ice Age inhabitants of Boomplaas before them tended to hunt larger mammals, such as the extinct Cape buffalo, a formidable quarry for them. This difference indicated a major change from Ice Age to Stone Age life, but one that defied an obvious explanation.

It was now that Hilary Deacon's environmental expertise came into play. Most of the bigger animals hunted by the earlier occupants were large grazers, species that flourished on well-watered grazing grounds. (The local mountains provided abundant rainfall during the late Ice Age, sufficient to provide ample grazing for certain seasons of the year.) But did the

Every square metre of this intricate cave was excavated with extreme care, to recover the minutest of environmental and settlement data. **Below** *An archaeologist brushes away soil from animal bones in the cave.*

Above *The stratified layers of Boomplaas Cave, with excavators working on an occupation level to a depth of ům (19½ft).*

climate change when the Ice Age ended, causing a change in the pattern of life? Here Deacon showed remarkable ingenuity. He first estimated that there are about 70 potential sources of firewood in the Cango Valley today, with thorn trees and the wild olive being the most important woods burnt in modern times.

Turning to the microscope, Deacon identified more than 350 charcoals from the deposits, with surprising results. After the Ice Age ended, thorn trees, which survive in dense bush, were the predominant source of firewood. But earlier, at the time when large mammals were hunted, the wild olive was favoured. This species flourishes in more open woodland, with plenty of grazing grass, precisely the kind of environment that favoured large mammals. Thus, argues Deacon, the Boomplaas charcoal may reflect a gradual climatic and vegetational change that forced grazing animals out and prehistoric hunters to change their habits.

Archaeology like this is on such a minute, detailed scale that it will take years to complete the analysis of the Boomplaas excavations. For instance, Deacon has spent months studying the small pellets dropped by barn owls in the cave, in the hope of confirming that their diet changed in the wake of climatic changes, which would suggest that people at that time were also forced to adapt their eating habits – and focus on smaller prey. The rewards of such research are the true treasure of modern archaeology.

THE FIRST FARMERS

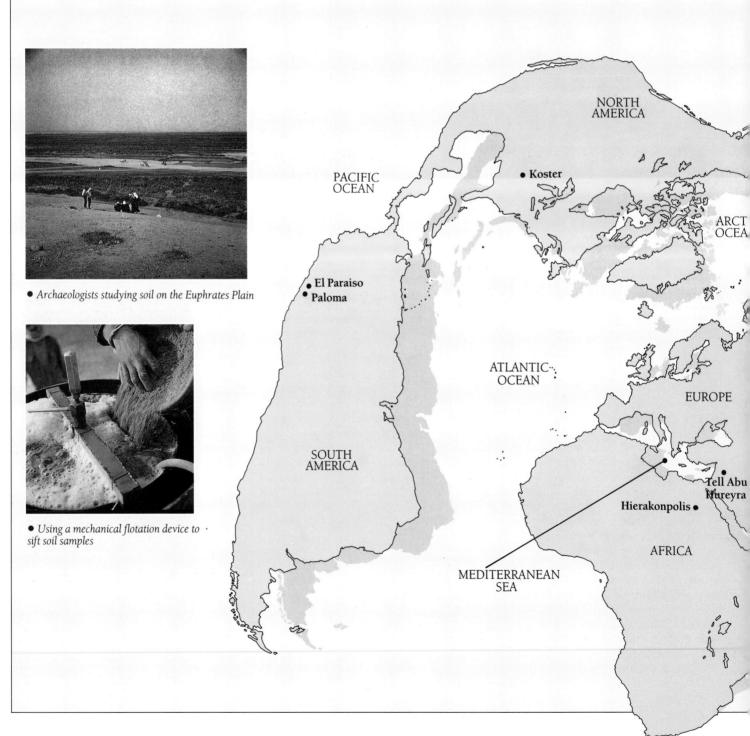

• *Archaeologists studying soil on the Euphrates Plain*

• *Using a mechanical flotation device to sift soil samples*

NORTH
AMERICA

PACIFIC
OCEAN

• Koster

ARCTIC
OCEAN

• El Paraiso
• Paloma

ATLANTIC
OCEAN

EUROPE

Tell Abu
Hureyra

Hierakonpolis

SOUTH
AMERICA

AFRICA

MEDITERRANEAN
SEA

Even the most primitive of hunters knew that seeds germinate when planted in the ground, but they rarely, if ever, put this knowledge to practical use until after the Ice Age some 11,000 years ago. In areas like the Near East, people living at the edges of woodlands, on steppes and in fertile river valleys were able to exploit a wide spectrum of different animal and vegetable resources. So favoured were these environments that population densities rose and caused shortages of key vegetable foods, such as wild wheat grasses. What more logical step than to plant such grasses for oneself to expand the available food supply? This was precisely what the inhabitants of Abu Hureyra and dozens of other small communities in the Levant did. The result was a revolution in human life that spread like wildfire to Europe and much farther afield.

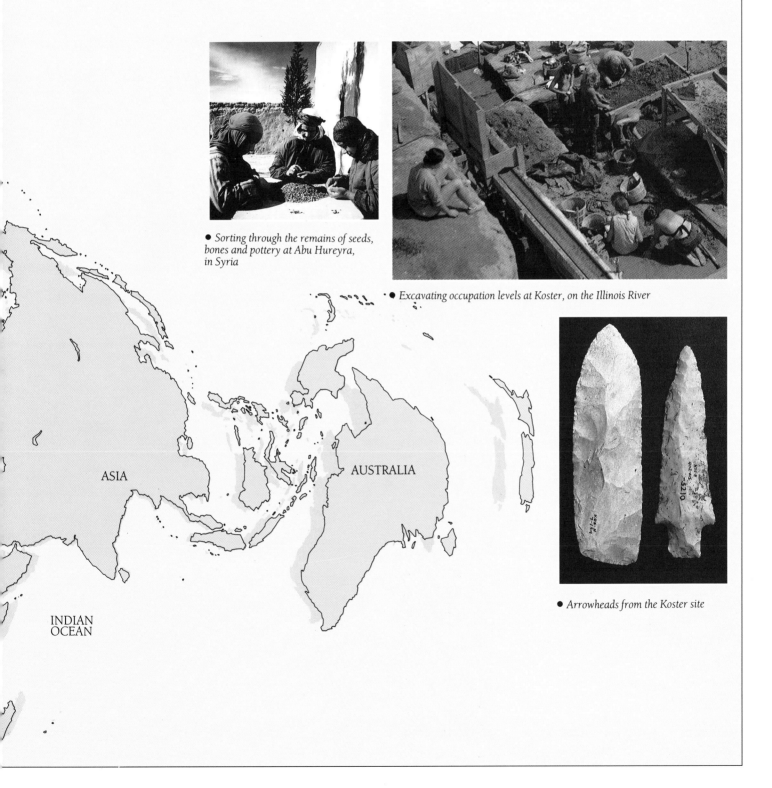

● *Sorting through the remains of seeds, bones and pottery at Abu Hureyra, in Syria*

● *Excavating occupation levels at Koster, on the Illinois River*

ASIA

AUSTRALIA

INDIAN
OCEAN

● *Arrowheads from the Koster site*

THE FIRST FARMERS

Tell Abu Hureyra once stood on the Euphrates plain, a place where people had lived for more than 10,000 years. It was a vast, artificial mountain, occupied by very early farmers for generations. The remains of their settlements covered more than 11ha (27 acres) and reached more than 7.5m (25ft) above the river. But Abu Hureyra was destined to vanish under the rising waters of the Euphrates, inundated by the construction of a dam downstream. In 1972, when archaeologist Andrew Moore picked up 8,000-year-old potsherds on the surface of the tell (the Arabic word for hill), he knew there was a good chance of finding one of the earliest farming villages in the world. However, he had only two seasons in which to find out, because the mound was due to be submerged in 1974.

Moore's excavations probed the northern end of the mound, passing through thick deposits of farming villages that dated from between 9,500 years ago and some time after 8,000 years ago. At the very base of the tell he found what he was looking for – a tiny settlement of humble dwellings dug partially into the river floodplain.

The primeval village at Abu Hureyra was far from imposing; just a hamlet of small

In 1972 a village on the Euphrates plain, occupied in the late tenth and early ninth centuries BC, was excavated; it revealed fascinating details about very early farming. The site has since vanished under the waters of the Euphrates but photographs record the finds. **Top** *The mounds of Abu Hureyra seen from the south-west, with excavations in progress.* **Above** *Two rooms of a village house dating to about 8,500 years ago were revealed with their walls standing to their original height. A broken pottery storage vessel lies on the floor of one room.*

A tiny settlement lay beneath the well-established Abu Hureyra farming village with its mudbrick houses, **left**. Its inhabitants had lived in pit dwellings dug into the underlying earth, and had hearths – visible as burned areas in the foreground.

The Abu Hureyra excavations yielded an abundance of vegetable remains, including early domesticated crops. These finds were sifted by using special froth flotation machines designed at Cambridge University. In this system piles of earth are made, **above right**, the machine is filled with water and the soil is poured into the top of the machine, **right**. The air pump then blows air bubbles up through the cylinder of water. A detergent in the water separates out the carbonized plant remains from the soil and catches them in its froth. They are caught in a fine mesh at the top of the machine, dried and saved. Meanwhile, the heavy residue is discharged from the bottom of the machine, **below right**, and washed to recover fish, birds, rodents, beads and other tiny artifacts.

circular reed and wood shelters with their floors slightly below ground level. Over the years the floor hollows had accumulated occupation debris, creating about a metre (3ft) of deposits for archaeologists to examine. Enough charcoal came from the settlement to date it with radiocarbon to the late tenth and early ninth millennia BC. The Abu Hureyra people were indeed some of the earliest farmers in the world.

The Ice Age was long over by the time Abu Hureyra flourished. The climate was

considerably warmer and wetter than it had been in earlier millennia, and the village lay on the edge of open grassland and near open woodland. Both environments abounded in small and medium-sized animals such as deer and gazelle, as well as many wild vegetable foods.

Like Deacon at Boomplaas, Moore dissected the tiny hamlet in as much detail as time would allow. He sieved all the soil from the dig through fine meshes, which yielded more than two tons of animal bones. Seeds were far harder to recover, so Moore used an ingenious mechanical flotation machine, designed by engineers at Cambridge University to pass large soil samples through water. The seeds floated to the surface, enabling him to recover large amounts of plant remains. They proved to be a rich mine of information on early farming and foraging.

When botanist Gordon Hillman identified the plant remains, he was not surprised to find large quantities of wild grasses, nuts from a tiny turpentine tree (a relative of the pistachio) and fruit from the hackberry tree, as well as caper berries. But he was surprised to find wild cereals. The most common was a primitive wheat known as einkorn, but wild barley and rye were also present in the samples. The people also collected, and perhaps even cultivated, various pulses, including a wild lentil. Hillman puzzled over a major problem: were the cereals and perhaps the pulses just being collected, or were they being deliberately cultivated?

None of these cereals is to be found in the wild close to Abu Hureyra today. The climate is now too dry. But as Hillman realized, it was not to say that they had not grown these crops earlier, in more humid times at the end of the Ice Age. The only way he could study the problem further was to examine stands of wild einkorn growing in the Munzor Mountains of Turkey, and to experiment with various ways of harvesting wild grasses and with patterns of crop rotation. He would then be able to see if simple cultivation techniques would cause natural selection in wild strains of einkorn, mutations that would eventually change the morphology of the grains. His experiments convinced him that simple farming methods would do nothing to change wild einkorn until much more intensive cultivation methods had been followed for centuries.

But these experiments in themselves did not prove that the Abu Hureyra people were farmers. Fortunately, the flotation samples yielded seeds from three humble weeds that provided the missing clue. Any form of cultivation, or clearance of land for planting, is bound to disturb the natural vegetation, allowing other plant species as well as the cherished grain to germinate on the cleared land. Hillman found a species of goosefoot, of mustard and a member of the borage family in his samples, all of them weeds that are characteristic of cultivated fields today. This proved, almost certainly, that the Abu Hureyra folk were cultivating the fertile arable land that lay near their tiny village.

Meanwhile, animal bone expert Anthony Legge found that the inhabitants were fond of eating gazelle, a small antelope that can be found in the arid Near East to this day. They also hunted wild asses, sheep and goats, as well as animals as small as rabbits. But there were no signs of deliberate herding of any animals.

ABU HUREYRA'S SECOND SETTLEMENT

After several centuries, the fledgling farmers abandoned Abu Hureyra, and it was another 1,000 years before the site was reoccupied, about 9,500 years ago. It soon became one of the largest farming villages in the area, covering nearly 12ha (30 acres). Visitors to the village would have found themselves wandering through a closely-knit rectangular community of houses built of mud brick. Narrow lanes led to small courts, passing between mud plaster walls. Small doors opened into the multi-room dwellings with their black burnished plaster floors. Some were decorated with red designs. Andrew Moore believes that each house was occupied by one family.

This was an entirely new kind of human settlement, quite different from the open camps and caves occupied for thousands of years by the Stone Age hunters and foragers of earlier prehistory. For the first time hundreds, perhaps even thousands of people, lived cheek-by-jowl in crowded dwellings. Theirs was a permanent community, not a temporary hunting camp that was abandoned after a few days, or at most a few months. In a nomadic society, if two men in a camp quarrelled badly they could solve the argument by one of them moving away. At Abu Hureyra and other such permanent communities no such solution was possible. Farmers had to live close to their fields, next to the same neighbours for years on end.

Places like Abu Hureyra may have witnessed a revolution in social organization as sedentary farmers developed new ways of settling disputes, maintaining law and order, and controlling ownership and inheritance of land. These mechanisms – village councils, kin groups, headmen and kin leaders – were to evolve into the social and political systems of the world's first civilizations within a few millennia.

Abu Hureyra gives us a glimpse of the earliest centuries of farming in the Near East. The cultivators used but the simplest of tools in their fields. Moore found tiny flint blades, which may have been mounted in wood hafts as arrow barbs for use in the chase or as sickle blades. They also used bone to make borers and needles. Stone milling tools were common in their dwellings, used for processing all kinds of plant foods. The later farmers still used a wide range of stone artifacts, including axes made by grinding and polishing stone. They stored their grain in thick, rectangular plaster vessels which were permanent fixtures in their houses.

But there is one striking difference in the later settlement – an abundance of exotic raw materials from far away. By now Abu Hureyra was a large village, perhaps a focus of trade from many kilometres away. For stone tools the villagers used pieces of fine volcanic glass from several Turkish sources. They bartered jadeite, agate and malachite, obtained soapstone from the distant Zagros Mountains in Iran, turquoise from the Sinai Peninsula and cowrie shells from the Mediterranean or Red Sea. No one knows what they gave in exchange for these imports – perhaps it was grain from their fertile fields by the Euphrates. But, as Andrew Moore points out, it was long-distance contacts like these that made hundreds of villages throughout the Near East dependent on one another for survival when farming began.

Sites like Abu Hureyra occur over a wide area of what is now Jordan, Israel and Syria – a region once known as the Levant. They show that agriculture was not a sudden invention developed by a solitary genius.

Flint arrows from the Abu Hureyra farming village, **above**, *were used for hunting a wide variety of game in the Euphrates valley and neighbouring territory. They are manufactured from chert and other fine-grained rocks. The scale is 10cm long.*

Rather, it was an adjustment to changing circumstances throughout much of the world at more or less the same time. The Ice Age ended, the global climate became warmer, and sea levels rose rapidly. The big game that had provided such reliable sustenance for humankind for millennia was reduced drastically by worldwide extinctions, probably accelerated in many areas by intensive hunting. So the big-game hunters of yesteryear turned to other forms of subsistence – foraging for wild vegetable foods, fishing and hunting sea mammals along the newly exposed coasts. The invention of the bow and arrow near the end of the Ice Age enabled people to shoot birds on the wing too, and to pursue solitary, smaller animals as well as large ones.

PERUVIAN SETTLEMENTS

The Near East was not the only place where such a transition took place. Recent excavations have identified similar developments in Southeast Asia, in China, in Central America and in one of the driest areas on earth – the Peruvian coast.

Coastal Peru is so arid that many areas receive rainfall once a decade, if then. Only about 50 rivers and streams, many of them seasonal, bring water from the Andes mountains to the coast. In addition, heavy winter fogs mantle the shore, bringing welcome moisture to the interior. Ironically, the Pacific currents bring fish in abundance to the coast. So, for thousands of years prehistoric Peruvians settled more or less permanently in favoured areas of the coast. The environment is so dry that it has preserved their abandoned villages, providing a uniquely complete picture of life at a time when the Peruvians were also beginning to cultivate the soil.

Frederic Engel has studied the archaeological sites of this desolate coast for many years. Among the most important is a series of great shrines or public buildings at El

Below left Many human graves in the Abu Hureyra farming village contained these so-called 'butterfly beads', made of serpentine and agate and imported from Turkey. They indicate that the village had regular, if not strong, trading links.

*The relatively fertile environment of Abu Hureyra contrasts with the arid surroundings of the Paloma farming settlement on the Peruvian coast, **below**. This view of the excavations of the site is taken from the south-east, with the Pacific Ocean visible in the distance.*

Paraiso, near Lima. In 1966 he uncovered seven huge square buildings constructed of stone blocks cemented with unfired clay. Hundreds of people had quarried more than 100,000 tonnes of rock from nearby hills to build this vast complex more than 3,500 years ago. What was surprising was that the builders had lived with only the simplest of possessions, in humble, scattered villages. How had they managed to survive in such a desolate environment and to amass sufficient food to feed teams of builders for months on end? The answers had to lie in earlier settlements, which were few.

Engel's search took him the length and breadth of the coastal plain, but eventually he settled on an especially promising area in the Chilca Valley, about 72km (45 miles) south of Lima. There he found dozens of ancient shell heaps. Working with the most limited of facilities he excavated a large settlement that had once lain near a reedy marsh that provided farming land as well as matting and building materials.

It looked likely that the El Paraiso inhabitants had survived on food gathered from the sea and some marginal agriculture. But Engel needed more evidence to prove this.

In the early 1970s, a geologist found another large complex of shell mounds, at Paloma, 8km (5 miles) from the Chilca River. He probed it and found not only house-foundations but numerous burial sites as well. Realizing that only a large team could investigate such a complex site, he turned to Engel and Robert Benfer, a Peruvian specialist at the University of Missouri.

If ever there was a site that needed teamwork it was Paloma – a sprawling complex of discoloured soil, shell heaps and long-abandoned, semi-subterranean houses. The most delicate of artifacts and food remains were perfectly preserved in the dry conditions; hair, skin and other soft tissue came from more than 200 burials in the 55 houses unearthed during the excavation. This prehistoric settlement was occupied between 8,000 and 4,500 years ago, a critical time when agriculture was taking hold on the arid coast. The clue to understanding this complex and long-lived settlement could come only from a minute study of the food remains in its shell mounds – and from the skeletons of the people themselves.

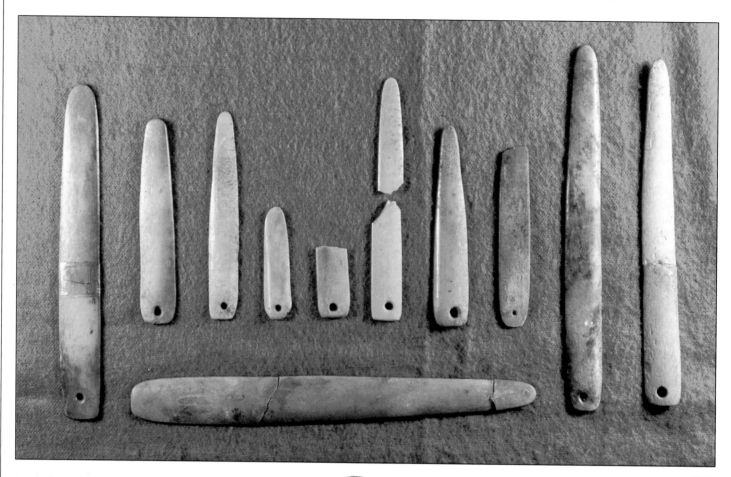

Bone bodkins, **above**, were used for twinning, or sewing together pairs of, the numerous mats found at Paloma. Textiles and weaving were an important part of Peruvian coastal culture from very early times.

The dense shell middens yielded thousands of once-edible molluscs, all of them taken from the rocky Pacific shore just less than 4.5km (3 miles) away. A fascinating discovery related to this was that many male Palomans exhibited auditory osteomas, a benign bone growth in the inner ear that can result from repeated diving in cold water.

Rich natural fisheries lay close inshore, and from the dense layers of dried fish meal found at Paloma, Engel could prove that the people had consumed thousands of small fish. Huge anchovy schools could be netted from rafts close to the shore. Sometimes the fish even stranded themselves, as the archaeologists themselves witnessed, when on two memorable days and nights thousands of anchovy leaped onto the beach close to the site. Not only did the modern local people net anchovy, they promptly used them as bait to catch the voracious jurel, a mackerel-like fish that was swarming after the anchovy. We can be sure that their prehistoric ancestors did the same. In addition, then, as now, seals mated on the local beaches in January, when it would have been easy to club large numbers of them.

If fish and shellfish were staples in the Paloma diet, so were wild vegetable foods and some vegetation which they planted deliberately, including tuberous begonias, gourds, squashes, peppers and, possibly, peanuts.

On the face of it, life at Paloma would seem to have been easy enough, with such an abundance of fish and shellfish. In addition, the lush vegetation of the fog oasis and the seasonally watered soils of the Chilca Valley would have provided alternative sources of food. However, Engel and Benfer found grass-lined pits containing both vegetable foods and cooked shellfish, stored against scarce periods. This implied that, just as at Abu Hureyra, there was

Above Sea shells found with their contents preserved testify to the extreme aridity of the Paloma site. A complex of storage pits and other features at Paloma, **right**, includes the grass-lined pit.

sufficient food for hunters and foragers to live on in one place for much of the year, but not enough when population densities increased. It seems to have been at this point when their numbers started to expand that the Paloma people began growing a handful of edible plants, probably because the supplies of natural resources were dwindling. This change from migratory to sedentary living had major effects on the health of the community.

A generation ago, Benfer would probably have been content to report the ages and sexes of individuals in the Paloma burials. Instead, he called in skeletal experts to examine the pathology of the inhabitants – tooth wear, stature changes and Harris Lines in leg bones (a classic indicator of stress in humans), even searching for mineral trace elements in bones and fragments of hair. The results were highly suggestive.

The skeletons of the earliest inhabitants display considerable stress, a factor which is common in populations that change from a nomadic life and experiment with farming. But study of subsequent generations showed improved health, with fewer Harris Lines, and during the 2,000 years of occupation, the Paloma people increased in stature.

Ironically, although the health of the Palomans improved, the pressure of their increased numbers on the natural resources caused their environment to deteriorate. It was at this time that the Paloma people may have abandoned their ancient settlement. They turned to more intensive agri-culture in the nearby Chilca Valley, using simple canals and other water control systems to irrigate their gardens. This, many centuries later, led to massive communal irrigation systems and the building of huge ceremonial complexes like those at El Paraiso.

KOSTER

Abu Hureyra and Paloma are superb examples of how much minute information about the past can be obtained from the humblest of early human settlements. Even the tiniest early farming village entails months of work for the archaeologists who probe its secrets; research even more complex than that required when examining a Stone Age hunting camp. But what about really large settlements, where thousands of cubic metres of earth have to be moved and where dozens of experts contribute their specialized knowledge to the excavation? Just such a settlement was Koster in the Illinois River Valley, in the heart of the North American Midwest.

The Koster story began in 1968, when a highly talented archaeologist named Stuart Struever was shown a large, unexcavated archaeological site in a cornfield near Kampsville, Illinois. The site was larger than anything Struever had seen before. The Illinois River Valley had long been recognized as an archaeologically-rich area, where prehistoric American Indians had lived for many thousands of years. During their long sojourn, local populations had risen to the point where some communities

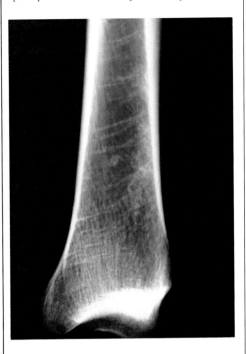

Below *A human tibia (shin bone) excavated from a Paloma burial reveals transverse, or Harris, lines. All the female tibiae from the site showed such lines, which are spaced yearly; they suggest annual stress perhaps related to seasonal food scarcity.*

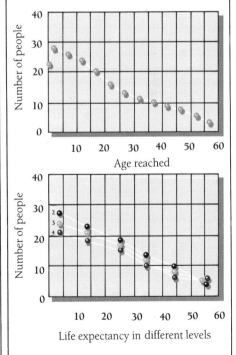

LIFE EXPECTANCY AT PALOMA

Number of people (0, 10, 20, 30, 40) vs Age reached (10, 20, 30, 40, 50, 60)

Number of people (0, 10, 20, 30, 40) vs Life expectancy in different levels (10, 20, 30, 40, 50, 60), with levels 2, 3 and 4 marked

Above *The life expectancy at Paloma could be calculated from the human skeletons found in the excavations. The upper diagram shows generalized life expectancy, the lower graph an improvement in the upper levels of the settlement. The numbers 2, 3 and 4 represent different levels excavated. Level 4 is the deepest.*

had developed into virtual towns. But no site had yet shown just how this process had happened.

Struever took one look at the site on Theodore Koster's farm and knew that this was the place where he could find an answer. In 1969, he returned to the ploughed field and sunk several test pits deep into the fertile soil. To his delight, he uncovered a series of ancient occupation levels stratified one above the other, each separated by zones of sterile soil.

Fortunately, Stuart Struever was blessed with a gift – he was a genius at fund-raising (which made him the envy of many of his

colleagues). He also had the brilliant idea of running the excavation as a summer field school, so that local secondary school and university students could gain a unique experience of hands-on archaeology. The first field school came to Koster in 1970, but Struever had no idea that he was starting work on one of the most complex sites ever found in North America.

After the first season, he discovered that he was excavating a site that had been occupied more than 8,400 years ago – more than 3,000 years before the pharaohs built the pyramids.

The only way to understand the Koster site was to open up trenches on a grand scale, to plot the distribution of artifacts, hut foundations and other features over large areas. Like a layered cake, it revealed the prehistory of the Illinois Valley in successive strata.

Above *Koster Farm, a farming settlement occupied more than 8,400 years ago, seen as you look into the Illinois River Valley towards the west. The main excavation can be seen through the break in the tree line in the middle distance. This is where the earliest occupations were found. Later settlements shifted to the higher ground at the lower right-hand corner.*

Above right *A stratigraphic profile from an early stage of the Koster excavations reveals dark occupation 'horizons'. The lighter coloured sterile soil was washed down from the bluff top during periods when Koster was abandoned.*

The very first inhabitants of the valley, about 10,000 years ago, apparently did not settle at Koster. Struever has found their distinctive stone spearpoints elsewhere in the valley. The first people to settle at Koster itself camped under the low bluffs overlooking the river – they were about 25 individuals, perhaps an extended family group. They visited the place first about 8,400 years ago, then returned again and again, perhaps because of the abundance of artifact stone and of wild vegetable foods nearby.

This seasonal settlement covered about 3ha (7 acres). The visitors hunted deer and other small mammals and ate large quantities of fish and freshwater mussels. Dozens of grinders and grinding stones lay next to abandoned hearths; these simple tools were used to grind thousands of nuts and seeds. Even at this early date, the people were eating two very beneficial dietary components: protein-rich fish and nuts rich in fats for high energy.

About 8,000 years ago, Koster was no longer a settlement but a work station. For two centuries local men came to manufacture stone tools there. They could not have chosen a better spot, because two major sources of fine-grained chert rock lay close by. There was plenty of rock for making both finished artifacts and rough blanks which could be carried back home for use later to make small tools.

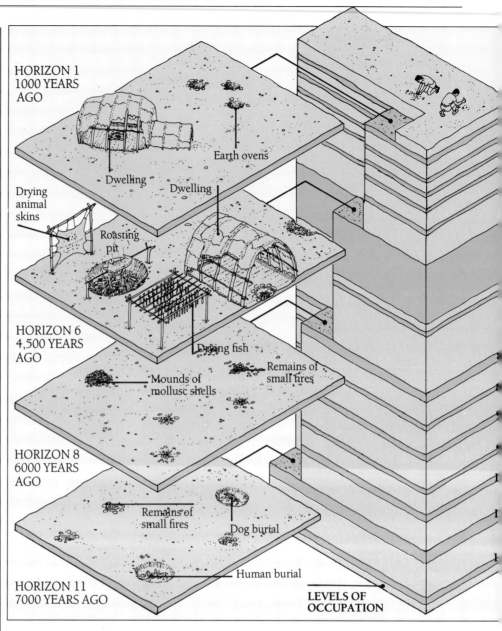

HORIZON 1
1000 YEARS AGO

Dwelling
Dwelling
Earth ovens

Drying animal skins
Roasting pit

Drying fish

HORIZON 6
4,500 YEARS AGO

Mounds of mollusc shells
Remains of small fires

HORIZON 8
6000 YEARS AGO

Remains of small fires
Dog burial

Human burial

HORIZON 11
7000 YEARS AGO

LEVELS OF OCCUPATION

Above *The excavation of the grave of a domesticated dog at Koster. Several dog burials have been found at different levels of the site, one of the earliest being on Horizon 11, which was inhabited about 7,000 years ago.*

Above *A student excavator with grinding stones from the Koster site. Stone grinders like these were found at many levels on the site and were once used to grind nuts and seeds.*

KOSTER

Left *Stuart Struever and his colleagues excavated Koster like a layered cake. At the base of the site was scattered evidence of campsites dating to earlier than 7,000 years ago.*

Horizon 1 *dating to about 1,000 years ago, was the site of a village just as the Koster people started cultivating maize and beans, crops that enabled the Koster area to support much higher population densities than ever before.*

Horizon 6 *was occupied about 4,500 years ago, when food gathering had become a highly organized team effort, involving hunting of deer and migratory waterfowl, river and swamp fishing, and intensive foraging for wild vegetable foods. The Koster settlement was probably occupied all year.*

10m
34ft **Horizon 8** *chronicles life at Koster 6,000 years ago. Piles of mussel shells, clusters of limestone blocks, and hearths mark the site of a long-term village settlement. Between 100 and 150 people lived in the village; they were much more efficient hunters and foragers than their predecessors.*

Horizon 11 *was the ground surface 7,000 years ago. Excavations revealed a dog burial and the remains of many hearths. The people survived by hunting, fishing, and foraging for wild vegetable foods, and lived in substantial wattle and daub houses with thatched roofs.*

Above *The Koster site computer laboratory, in 1974. Excavators Stuart Struever and James Brown developed an elaborate computer cataloguing and analysis system for the myriad finds from this important site.*

KOSTER'S SECOND SETTLEMENT

Stuart Struever was one of the first archaeologists to recognize the potential of the computer for cataloguing archaeological finds and analysing occupation levels. All the excavated data from Koster were fed into computerized data banks, which gave immediate access to critical information. It was with the help of the computer that many minor occupation levels were identified within the 13 major horizons at Koster. Study revealed at least four distinct settlements during this 400-year period, each of them lasting a century or so.

Between about 7,600 and 7,000 years ago, a considerably larger village thrived where the work station had lain. It covered at least 7ha (17 acres). This new settlement was much more substantial than preceding ones. The people cut down trees as much as 20cm (8in) in diameter for hut poles, and dug level terraces into the hillside to make their homes more comfortable.

Excavating these dwellings required careful scraping and brushing, to reveal the discoloured soil that marked ancient postholes. Using computers, Struever's team sorted out a confusing mass of foundation trenches which had been expanded, moved and filled in as people rebuilt their houses. Each time a home was built, a family would dig a shallow trench, set wooden posts upright in it and then fill the hole with earth and rocks to support them. Some of the houses were between 6m and 7.5m (20ft and 25 ft) long and between 3.6m and 4.5m (12ft and 15ft) across. The sides had been covered with wattle and daub (sticks and clay), but the ends were apparently open, perhaps protected with hides or mats.

These elaborate dwellings were a far cry from the simple structures of earlier times. By the time the excavation was finished, Struever had a mass of information on hearths, storage pits, artifacts and thousands of animal bones and seeds. Clearly, this was a permanent settlement, but one whose economy was based not on agriculture, as was Abu Hureyra, but on hunting, fishing and the gathering of wild

Below *Stone projectile points, the smallest of which is only a few centimetres in length, found in the 'North Field' at Koster. Similar spearpoints, dating to about 10,000 years ago, have been found in other parts of the Illinois River Valley.*

Above *Pits for refuse were found to contain the shells of mussels, gathered from the river. Such pits were dug at least 6,000 years ago.*

Above *The care with which dogs were buried at Koster indicates that they were used in the chase even 7,000 years ago.*

vegetable foods. How had the inhabitants managed to live in one place for years, whereas their neighbours outside the Illinois Valley moved constantly in search of seasonal foods?

The answer came from the seeds and animal bones. These Koster people, like everyone who lived there over the millennia, were brilliant opportunists. They lived in an exceptionally rich river valley, where fish could be caught all year. In addition, in spring and autumn migrating waterfowl would pause close to Koster. The hunters would lie in wait for the annual migrations, capturing birds by the thousand. During spring, summer and autumn, edible grasses, fruit and, above all, hickory and pecan nuts came into season, and deer and other game could be hunted for much of the year.

In short, the food base was so diverse that the people could count on some food supplies even if the nut crop failed or deer were rare on the ground. Most of the foods they exploited could be dried or stored for long periods of time, again ample insurance against lean months. The Koster people of 8,000 years ago were like settled farmers, but they did not cultivate the soil. Their environment was so diverse that they could inhabit permanent villages and enjoy a far

Left *Archaeologists excavating the levels at Koster found concentrations of stones that had obviously been 'quarried' and carried to the settlement by the inhabitants, presumably to make tools from.*

despite the exceptional richness and diversity of wild foods near the river. They had been cultivating pumpkins and bottle gourds as containers for at least 1,000 years, but it was not until about AD800 that they began to grow maize and beans. These new crops were demanding of time and took up hectares of fertile land. But the combination of protein-rich beans and carbohydrate-rich maize, both easily stored foods, made it possible to support higher population densities than ever before.

As time went on, population densities rose and food shortages developed. The Koster inhabitants' first reaction was to move to the sides of the valley, to found new villages in more marginal areas. This strategy worked for a while, but the population continued to rise. By AD800, there were some very large villages indeed in the Illinois Valley. This was the point at which the villagers turned to maize and beans, easily storable foods that were originally intended to supplement wild foods.

So successful were the new crops that the Koster people and their neighbours became dependent on them. Within five centuries, the population of the Illinois Valley and nearby Mississippi Valley had climbed by leaps and bounds. More than 40,000 people lived in one enormous complex of villages and towns at Cahokia, near the modern city of Saint Louis. Great American Indian civilizations might still be prospering in the Midwest, had it not been for the arrival of European explorers and colonists in the sixteenth century.

Abu Hureyra, Paloma and Koster boast no monumental ruins, nor are there fine temples or richly adorned houses in their occupation levels to excite a sense of romance, of long-forgotten gold. Their ancient treasures are something far more satisfying and enduring: new and exciting information about the very foundations of human civilization. All three sites show us that the most exciting clues to understanding ourselves come not necessarily from spectacular finds, but from charred seeds, crumbling potsherds and broken animal bones – the inconspicuous clues to how people lived in the past.

more elaborate material culture than their neighbours outside the valley.

Koster was virtually abandoned about 7,000 years ago, to be occupied again only about 1,000 years later, when a new, long-term village was established at the foot of the riverside bluffs. Struever's computerized data showed that at least three settlements developed over the following 1,000-year period. By this time, between 100 and 150 people were living at Koster. They were even more efficient hunters and foragers than their predecessors had been. Struever believes that they made food gathering a highly organized team effort that took full advantage of every season of the year. The hunters would 'harvest' annual crops of waterfowl, fish, hickory nuts and such wild plants as marsh elder and grassfoot, which grew in dense stands on the valley floor.

It seems as if the Koster people lived in a Stone Age form of paradise, because they enjoyed an almost unrivalled diversity of wild foods. But in fact they needed great skills to make the most of their rich environment. They had an intimate knowledge of the habits of animals, birds and fish. The seasons for collecting nuts, and especially grasses, were so short that everyone was aware of the subtle, telltale signs that the time of harvest was imminent. No one at Koster controlled the harvest date of ripe marsh elder, the foragers had to compete on equal terms with birds and other animals that fed off the fresh seeds before they fell to the ground. Timing was of the essence, so was the ability to store food for months.

Excavations like those at Abu Hureyra, Paloma and Koster tell us a great deal about the reasons our ancestors turned from hunting and foraging to the deliberate cultivation of the soil. The later Koster occupations show that the Illinois Valley people eventually turned to agriculture,

CITIES AND CIVILIZATIONS

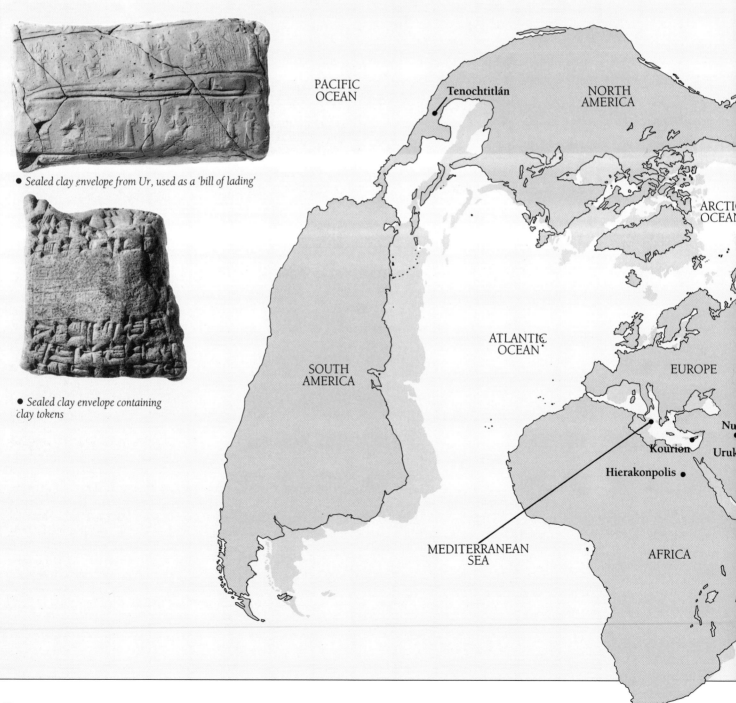

● *Sealed clay envelope from Ur, used as a 'bill of lading'*

● *Sealed clay envelope containing clay tokens*

PACIFIC
OCEAN

Tenochtitlán

NORTH
AMERICA

ARCTIC
OCEAN

ATLANTIC
OCEAN

SOUTH
AMERICA

EUROPE

Nu

Kourion

Uruk

Hierakonpolis ●

MEDITERRANEAN
SEA

AFRICA

Increasingly, permanent settlements found they could produce surplus food and, moreover, store the surplus. This meant that people could spend more time on other activities and could specialize. It also meant that they had something to trade. To regulate the surplus and to trade, people had to develop systems of production and distribution. This economic structure, together with the emergence of complex political and religious structures, signalled the emergence of more complex civilizations.

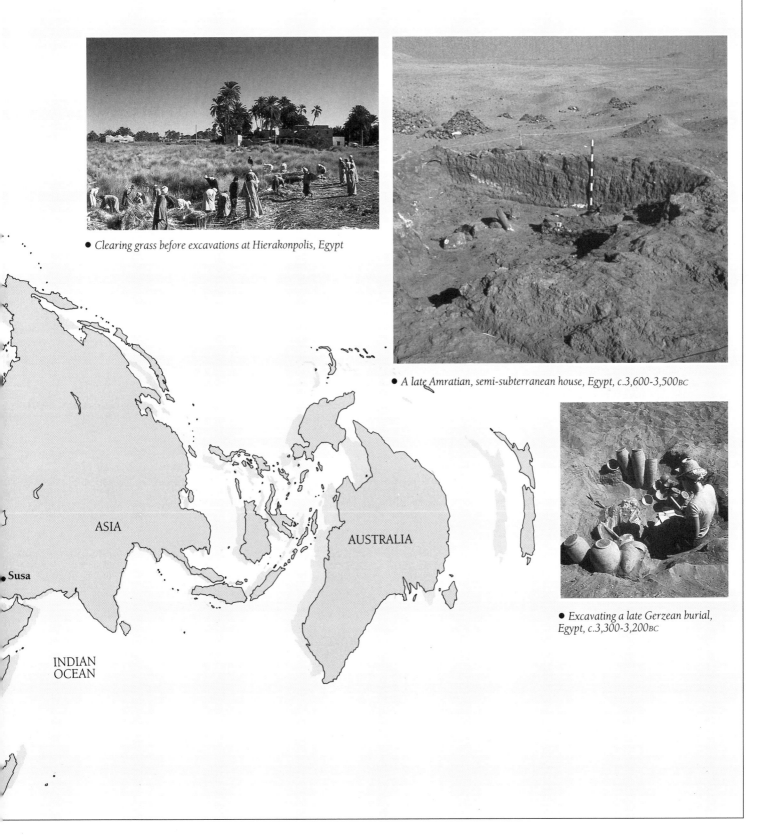

● *Clearing grass before excavations at Hierakonpolis, Egypt*

● *A late Amratian, semi-subterranean house, Egypt, c.3,600-3,500BC*

ASIA

AUSTRALIA

● Susa

INDIAN
OCEAN

● *Excavating a late Gerzean burial, Egypt, c.3,300-3,200BC*

NARMER, THE FIRST PHARAOH

His name was Narmer, which means 'Catfish', but his subjects called him Menes. He lived about 5,100 years ago and was the first pharaoh, the first man to preside over a nation rather than a tribe, an entire river valley rather than a small city-state. The civilization he founded lasted nearly 3,000 years. During Narmer's lifetime he was one of the most powerful men on earth, perhaps the earliest individual whose identity has come down to us from the mists of antiquity.

Narmer may have been a genius and a famous man, but we can be sure that he did not found ancient Egyptian civilization on his own. The first cities and civilizations, the first writing, new state-organized societies – all the elaborate panoply of early civilization – did indeed emerge in Egypt and Mesopotamia just before 3000BC But these decisive developments in human history were not the work of single individuals; they grew out of what had happened before.

Two English archaeologists, Quibell and Green, were the first to identify Narmer, when in 1898 they found a 53cm (21in) high stone palette in the ruins of ancient Hierakonpolis by the Nile in Upper Egypt. Such palettes were used for holding cosmetic pigments. This particular specimen bore fine carvings of mythical animals with long necks and lion-like heads. On both sides we see Narmer, depicted as conqueror of the two age-old lands of the Nile – Upper and Lower Egypt. On one face he wields his symbolic mace, a ceremonial club-staff, and wears the crown of Upper Egypt. His name is spelled out, complete with the symbolic sign of a catfish. The other face has him wearing the crown of Lower Egypt. He stands regally, surveying standard bearers from his allies and beheaded enemies. The palette symbolizes unity, power and the unification of the Nile valley into a single kingdom.

Ancient Egyptian legends traced the ancestry of the pharaohs to the 'Followers of Horus'. (Horus was the falcon-headed god.) They were associated with the city of Nekhen, which the Greeks called Hierakonpolis, 'city of the falcon'. Generations of archaeologists have excavated the huge pre-Dynastic Egyptian settlements around the city and have located painted tombs, perhaps of local rulers. The same scholars who found Narmer's palette unearthed a large, decorated ceremonial mace that belonged to one of Narmer's predecessors – a king named Scorpion of whom little is known. There were abundant archae-

The palette of the first pharaoh of Egypt – Narmer – was used originally for holding cosmetic pigments. **Above left** *Narmer, the conqueror of Upper and Lower Egypt, wears the red crown of Lower Egypt and stands regally while standard bearers from his allies pass before him and beheaded enemies lie in front. Mythical beasts with long necks and lion-like heads parade below.* **Above right** *On the other face of the palette, Narmer ('Catfish') wears the crown of Upper Egypt and wields his symbolic mace as he prepares to strike an enemy. His name is spelled out in the symbolic sign of a catfish.*

ological remains, but what light could they throw on the very beginnings of Egyptian civilization and on Narmer himself? It is only recently that systematic, long-term excavations have provided some clues.

Some 5,800 years ago, Hierakonpolis was a village inhabited by a few hundred people. Careful archaeological and geological surveys reveal that it lay in a protected area of the Nile floodplain, close to the river and within easy reach of fertile soils and the wooded grasslands that then covered what is now the barren desert. This was 700 years before Narmer was born.

During the next three centuries, the local population mushroomed to perhaps as many as 10,500 people. We know this because archaeological excavations and surveys have traced their settlements over about 40ha (100 acres). Many people lived in small towns, in houses constructed of mud brick or plaster smeared over a framework of saplings and reeds. Most dwellings were clustered close together, but some, which were surrounded by spacious fenced compounds, were the homes of specialist artisans and other more important individuals. Outside the tiny towns, country people lived in farming hamlets or temporary camps of small circular huts. For the first time there are signs of social and economic differences in Egyptian society.

At a time when most Egyptians lived in scattered villages, Hierakonpolis was something different. But how complex was the local society? Who ruled over the thousands of people living there? The answers came from a cemetery on the banks of a dry stream bed named Abu Suffian. Here, in the late 1970s-early 1980s, Egyptologists Barbara Adams, Michael Hoffman and Carter Lupton came across curving rows of large, sand-filled tombs. These were the sepulchres of the élite, the people who ruled Hierakonpolis and exercised economic control.

Right *Assistants clean sand from one of the oldest stone tombs in Egypt, dating to around 2,700BC. The area round this site was used as a necropolis from c. 4,000BC to c.2,700BC but few people were buried in stone tombs. This suggests that the occupant of this tomb may have been someone important.*

*An Ancient Egyptian symbol of authority – a disc-shaped mace-head of polished green and white porphyry – was found buried with someone who may have been a leader at Hierakonpolis. It dates to between 3,600 and 3,500BC, **below**. Black-topped plum-red vases were also common grave goods during the same 'Amratian' period, **right**.*

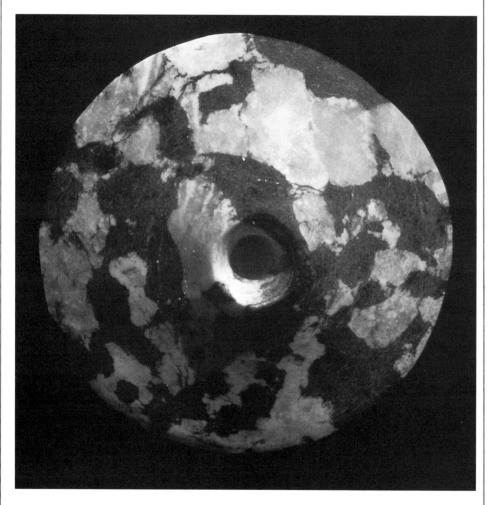

The Abu Suffian tombs were humble by the standards of those of Rameses, Seti and other later pharaohs, but they were very impressive for their day. All had been looted in ancient times, but they still contained a fascinating jumble of clues about their occupants. Beautiful, black-topped clay jars were deposited with the dead, some of them bearing complex graffiti scratched into the clay. Flint arrowheads, basket fragments, matting and pieces of furniture all offered hints of rich furnishings vandalized by tomb robbers.

The most magnificent find came from under a heap of broken grave goods – a beautiful disc-shaped mace head of polished green and white porphyry. Like Scorpion's mace, this was once a symbol of authority. But it predated Scorpion's by 500 years. Whoever carried this mace head was not a leader of Narmer's status, but he was surely an individual of great authority, perhaps one of the 'Divine Souls of Nekhen', the primeval rulers of Egypt referred to in ancient legend.

POTTERY AND POWER

Authority and political power are one thing, the economic ability to enforce such power is another. Whoever occupied the élite cemetery had to be able to pay for his imposing tomb and its contents. Michael Hoffman did not have to look far for a possible answer. The Hierakonpolis area is littered with at least 50 million pieces of broken pottery. He and his colleagues identified and mapped at least 15 large pottery kiln installations that covered more than $963m^2$ ($1,150yd^2$). The largest of them were capable of producing pots by the thousands.

Most of the pottery found in the Hierakonpolis tombs was coarse, work-a-day domestic ware, used by every household. But Hoffman noticed that all the kilns used to make fine, 'Plum Red Ware', the vessels found in the élite graves, were located in natural wind tunnels in the cliffs overlooking the cemetery. The potters used the prevailing winds to create the high temperatures needed to fire the better grade vessels. Each kiln specialized in certain types and quantities of pots, and each formed part of a well-organized industrial

*A pottery kiln for making red ware, **above**, found at Abu Suffian, was situated in a natural wind tunnel so that prevailing winds would maintain the high temperatures during firing.*

*A ring-wall type of pottery kiln dating to between 3,600 and 3,500BC, **top right**. The deep red colour on the soil is the result of intensive firing – the clay has been baked brick hard. The wares found in Abu Suffian's kilns were traded widely, as well as in local villages. Workers on a 'Gerzean' temple and town site near Abu Suffian sort pottery dating from 3,400 to 3,200BC, **above right**.*

machine that produced far more vessels than could ever be sold locally. Michael Hoffman believes that these products, and other manufactured objects, were traded up and down the nearby river to neighbouring communities.

This, he believes, was the key to power in this the first of Egyptian cities. The local pottery lords traded high-grade pottery, which was used in burials as prized offerings for the dead. In this way they profited from the preoccupation that everyone had with life after death, and with the idea that wealth accompanied one into the afterlife. These lords became rich, prestigious members of the community, 'big men', if you will, with contacts with other communities near and far. These were the primeval leaders, perhaps the 'Divine Souls of Nekhen'.

So far so good, but disaster eventually struck. About 3500BC the fragile ecological balance of desert and grassland collapsed. Perhaps the climate became drier, but the people themselves may have contributed to the breakdown. Egyptian botanist Nabil El

Hadidi of Cairo University's Herbarium has identified vast quantities of carbonized acacia and tamarisk wood in the Hierakonpolis kilns. Once, both these trees thrived on the ancient savanna and along the valleys where the kilns lay. Perhaps the potters contributed to the deforestation by felling thousands of trees for their insatiable fires. Another strong possibility is that herds of grazing sheep and goats, whose bones have been found in the hundreds in every settlement, must have degraded the local pastures. There was only one way the Egyptians could respond to the crisis, and that was by moving closer to the Nile.

Undoubtedly, many of the powerful men who controlled the pottery trade were ruined by the disaster. However, Michael Hoffman believes that some of them grabbed a unique opportunity and invested their money in the land by helping to develop and expand irrigation agriculture. The Egyptians had always used the annual Nile floods to water their fields, but now the leaders of Hierakonpolis used their wealth to enlarge irrigation canals and develop water management systems under their control. Their investments were crowned with brilliant success. Harvests were larger and more reliable, yielding much greater grain surpluses, which were stored under the watchful eyes of those who controlled canal building and flood works. New villages came into being.

The élite became increasingly powerful and invested their capital and grain surpluses in temples, palaces, town walls and ever more imposing tombs, which set them apart even further from the common people.

THE CEMETERY AT HIERAKONPOLIS

For three centuries, local leaders in dozens of kingdoms along the Nile vied for power, wealth and trading opportunities with neighbours near and far. The rulers of Hierakonpolis were deeply involved in the ebb and flow of Egyptian politics as battles flared and valuable territory changed hand, until Narmer eventually unified the Nile Valley under a single pharaoh – himself.

They were troubled times, but the ambitious rulers of Hierakonpolis never forgot their ancient roots. They built their tombs in the same cemetery as the pottery barons had used centuries earlier. Egyptologists had long known of the existence of this cemetery, but had always attacked it with picks and shovels, the coarsest of digging methods. Hoffman and his colleagues used a subtler approach, excavating

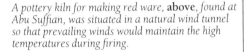

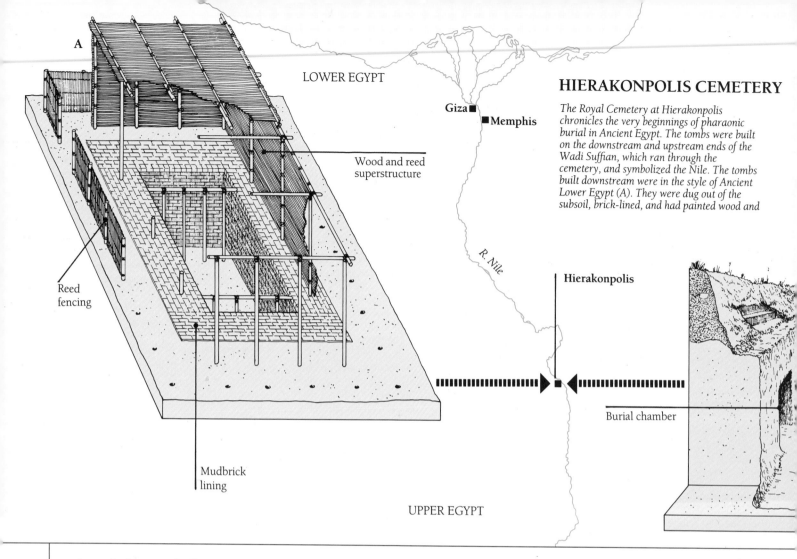

A

LOWER EGYPT

Giza ■
■ Memphis

HIERAKONPOLIS CEMETERY

The Royal Cemetery at Hierakonpolis chronicles the very beginnings of pharaonic burial in Ancient Egypt. The tombs were built on the downstream and upstream ends of the Wadi Suffian, which ran through the cemetery, and symbolized the Nile. The tombs built downstream were in the style of Ancient Lower Egypt (A). They were dug out of the subsoil, brick-lined, and had painted wood and

Wood and reed
superstructure

R. Nile

Hierakonpolis

Reed
fencing

Burial chamber

Mudbrick
lining

UPPER EGYPT

each tomb, however badly ravaged in the past, with brushes, trowels and the most accurate recording technology. To their surprise, they found that the cemetery was far more than a burial ground. It was a piece of political propaganda, a symbolic map of a dream – a new, unified Egypt.

The ancient Egyptians called their homeland 'Tawy' ('two lands'). The two lands were Upper and Lower Egypt: the territories upstream, and the delta lands by the Mediterranean downstream. The royal cemetery at Hierakonpolis straddled the dry Wadi Suffian. This represented a symbolic Nile. The tombs to the left of the wadi, at the downstream end, were in the ancient Lower Egypt style, lined with mud brick. Hoffman found groups of three to five graves in this part of the cemetery, as if close members of the family or the royal court were buried near the ruler. They were quite sumptuous sepulchres, the largest and perhaps the latest being 6m (20ft) long and 3.5m (11½ft) wide. All the tombs had been robbed of their splendid furnishings in antiquity. Only a few clues remained – some fine pottery and the remains of a finely carved sycamore bed, the legs carved in the form of bull's legs.

When the diggers scraped the soil around the tomb pits, they located circular brown discolorations, the only traces of long-rotted wooden posts. They showed that the cemetery had once been a small city of brightly painted model palaces and shrines, each covering a tomb and separated by reed fences. The excavators even found the holes for the surveyors' posts that were used to align the graves.

The upstream portion of the cemetery contains tombs of a quite different design, sepulchres excavated into the bedrock. These stone tombs were trenches, with burial chambers set off to the side, a design favoured in Upper Egypt upstream of the delta and of Wadi Suffian. An assemblage of wild and domestic animals was buried around the rock-cut tomb. Hoffman believes that the sometimes mummified animals were symbols of gods associated with the various provinces of Egypt.

The ancient Egyptians never lived in the great walled cities, that later became a powerful symbol of political authority. Because their intricate religious beliefs involved the gods of the dead in the world of the living, royal cemeteries and great temples became the symbols of political power instead of cities.

It was the genius of Narmer and his predecessors that turned Egyptians from being pottery merchants to divine rulers.

reed buildings built over them. The structures resembled those depicted in later Egyptian art. The Upper Egyptian-style sepulchres upstream were cut into solid rock (B), with the burial chamber at one side. Archaeologists believe the Royal Cemetery was a propaganda device devised by King Narmer to legitimize the union of Upper and Lower Egypt.

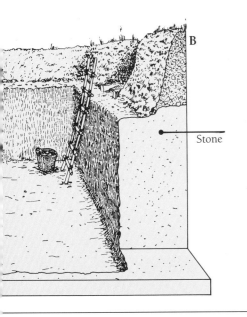

Stone

They did so both by sheer economic power and by harnessing the Egyptian preoccupation with the afterworld to create a symbolic map of their kingdom in the most sacred place of all – a royal cemetery. The experiment was so successful that their successors ruled Egypt for the next 2,500 years.

TOKENS AND TRADE

The Hierakonpolis excavations show us just how important trade was to early civilization – just as it is today. The farmers of Abu Hureyra in Syria traded fine obsidian and sea shells from hundreds of kilometres away. Their successors expanded this trade and bartered basic commodities such as metal ores and grain, as well as luxuries, over deserts and mountain passes, down turbulent rivers and eventually the length and breadth of the Mediterranean. At first this trade was informal and personal. Everyone involved knew everyone else. For generations families would regularly exchange gifts between villages, visit their neighbours to barter hut poles for deer meat and obtain their basic needs through familiar contacts.

But the pattern of trade changed rapidly as village populations rose and more and more people became involved in trading as a full-time activity. Some of them were expert artisans, who travelled from village to village to practise their craft. Others became professional merchants who carried copper ingots, sea shells, beads and a myriad other commodities along what soon became regular trade routes. Trading became so complicated that it was almost inevitable that some form of recording system would come into use. As University of Texas archaeologist Denise Schmandt-Besserat has shown, this system was to become the ancestor of one of Western civilization's most revolutionary and profoundly important inventions – writing.

Schmandt-Besserat is an expert in very unspectacular archaeological finds – small clay tokens. In 1969 she started researching early uses of clay by studying figurines and other Near Eastern artifacts in dozens of museum collections. Then she noticed a category of humble objects that had been excavated but had so far been ignored. These artifacts, which dated from between 8,500 and 3,000 years ago, came in spheres, discs, cones, triangles, rectangles and many other shapes, and most were little more than 0.6cm (¼in) across. Schmandt-Besserat was so intrigued that she started cataloguing them by size and shape. When she discovered that there were distinct groupings within different

Left *Now reduced to a muddy pit this tomb was once one of the largest in the Lower Egypt section of the cemetery at Abu Suffian. Dating to c.3,100BC it consists of a rectangular pit lined with thick mud walls. The pit was 6.5m (22ft) long, 3.5m (11½ft) wide and 2.5m (8ft) deep. The floor would have been lined with wooden planks. Wooden columns once supported the roof and a wooden temple originally covered the tomb.*

Above *The precursors of Sumerian pictographic writing, these complex clay tokens from Tello in Mesopotamia, dating to about 3,300BC were once used for trading. Denise Schmandt-Besserat believes that they each stand for a single commodity. Top left: one metal ingot; centre top: meaning unknown; top right: one ewe; bottom right: one sheep; bottom centre right: unknown; bottom centre left: one unit of 'sweet', perhaps honey; bottom left: one jar of oil.*

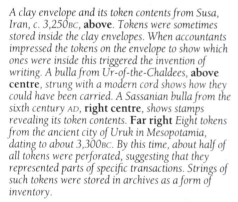

A clay envelope and its token contents from Susa, Iran, c. 3,250BC, **above***. Tokens were sometimes stored inside the clay envelopes. When accountants impressed the tokens on the envelope to show which ones were inside this triggered the invention of writing. A bulla from Ur-of-the-Chaldees,* **above centre***, strung with a modern cord shows how they could have been carried. A Sassanian bulla from the sixth century AD,* **right centre***, shows stamps revealing its token contents.* **Far right** *Eight tokens from the ancient city of Uruk in Mesopotamia, dating to about 3,300BC. By this time, about half of all tokens were perforated, suggesting that they represented parts of specific transactions. Strings of such tokens were stored in archives as a form of inventory.*

shapes – large and small cones, for example – she realized that the mysterious objects had once been trading tokens.

Earlier, in 1958, cuneiform expert Leo Oppenheimer of the University of Chicago's Oriental Institute had studied the palace archives from Nuzi, a city that flourished in Iraq about 1500BC. He had argued that there were two accounting systems in the city – the palace scribes' elaborate cuneiform archives recorded on tablets, and a much simpler inventory based on tokens. The tokens were tiny clay models that were counted and shifted from place to place as they were needed. Oppenheimer's theory was confirmed by the discovery of a hollow clay tablet inscribed with a list of 48 animals. The tablet rattled, so the translator opened it, to find 48 tokens inside. Unfortunately the tiny objects were mislaid before they could be examined closely. Perhaps, argued

Oppenheimer, the hollow tablet was a record of the transfer of animals from one palace department to another.

Subsequently, in 1964, French archaeologist Pierre Amiet found similar hollow tablets at the ancient Elamite city of Susa in Iran, this time dating to about 3000BC. He called them 'bullae'. Each bulla contained collections of geometric tokens.

But Schmandt-Besserat's research, aided by radiocarbon dating, proved that her tokens were much earlier, far earlier in fact than the earliest known cuneiform tablets of the fourth millennium BC. By the time she had completed her museum studies, she had established that they were found all over the Near East, from Turkey to Pakistan, even in Egypt and the Sudan, as long ago as the eighth millennium BC.

The earliest tokens came from sites in the Zagros mountain region of what is now Iran, from settlements dating back to about

10,500 years ago, to the very earliest centuries of farming. These farmers used at least 20 different token symbols. The same system remained in use for more than 5,000 years with surprisingly few changes. Schmandt-Besserat believes that the tokens first came into use as a way of keeping track of crop yields and food surpluses stored in houses and grain bins, as well as individual animals in farmers' herds.

What she has found is a hitherto unknown accounting system which used 15 major classes of clay tokens, divided into at least 200 subclasses. Each shape had a meaning of its own: some of the spheres, for example, were marked by quarters,

halves or three quarters, presumably to denote fractions of a unit. Some represented animals, others numbers.

BULLAE AND THE BIRTH OF WRITING

The first major changes in the token system came between 3500BC and 3100BC, when the first cities were appearing in Mesopotamia. At that time, many more shapes came into use. About 30 per cent of the large sample that Schmandt-Besserat examined from this period were perforated, and many of them bore incisions or punched impressions. Schmandt-Besserat believes that these changes came about in response to new complexities, both in the production of artifacts such as metal tools and in trade itself. She believes that individual transactions were recorded with strings of perforated tokens rather than individual symbols, which could be lost.

It is at this moment, too, that the clay envelopes, or bullae found by Pierre Amiet first appear. The exterior surfaces of these hollow containers were first smooth, marked only with the seals of both parties, and the tokens were sealed inside with a patch of clay. Pierre Amiet believes that his Susa bullae were bills of lading which accompanied shipments from, say, a rural village to a city. The sealed clay envelope and its contents provided evidence that there had been no tampering with the merchandise. All the recipient had to do was to break the bulla to count the tokens. It was not long before someone hit on the idea of marking the surface of the envelope with symbols representing the tokens inside as well. Sometimes they even impressed the wet clay with the very tokens that were to be stored inside.

This was the way in which writing was invented, Schmandt-Besserat believes. The new bulla/token system was so convenient that it was inevitable that two-dimensional signs on a solid clay tablet replaced the tokens and the hollow envelope. It is no coincidence, she notes, that some of the written signs on very early clay tablets found in the ancient city of Uruk, reputedly the oldest city in the world (fourth millenium BC), are exact copies of the token symbols in two dimensions. For example, the Uruk symbol for a sheep is a circle enclosing a cross; the age-old token is disc-shaped, incised with a cross. So one of humanity's most important inventions was no dramatic innovation, just the logical development of a simple recording system that originated about 11,000 years ago.

KOURION

Archaeologists of prehistory study the material remains of the past – artifacts, food remains, abandoned houses, graves. The intangibles of human existence such as religious beliefs, ethical ideals and legends can be inferred and surmised only from surviving material objects, and then only in vague and general terms. From the time of the development of writing in which events have been recorded, the guesswork is made a little easier. For example, as early as 5,000 years ago, people were recording commercial transactions on clay tablets. Later, Sumerian literature gave us the Epic of Gilgamesh, and an insight into philosophical values and legends that have shaped western civilization itself.

But most historical documents immortalize the deeds of rulers or deal with the broad sweep of events. Only rarely does one hear the anonymous voice of the common citizen, the humble farmer or fisherman, the artisan or the slave. This is where archaeology comes in, for the excavator's spade probes domestic rubbish, house foundations and the utterly commonplace – the fabric of daily life. Sometimes, however, a combination of documents and excavation forms a spectacular way of understanding the past, as happened recently at Kourion in Cyprus.

Early on the morning of July 21, AD365, a terrible earthquake shook the island of Cyprus in the eastern Mediterranean. Huge tidal waves devastated nearby coasts. One of the eyewitnesses was the Syrian historian Ammianus Marcellinus, who wrote: 'A little after daybreak, preceded by heavy and repeated thunder and lightning, the whole of the firm and solid earth was shaken and trembled. The sea with its rolling waves was driven back and withdrew from the land . . . Many ships were stranded as if on dry land.' When the dust settled, thousands of people lay dead, many of them drowned while gathering dying fish on the exposed sea bed. Dozens of villages were levelled to the ground. The port of Kourion in southwestern Cyprus collapsed within minutes under several metres of rock and dust.

More than sixteen centuries later, classical archaeologist David Soren and a team of scientists from the University of Arizona probed under Kourion's rocky mantle. After eight years of excavation they have exposed a remarkable time capsule of late Roman life. Thousands of insignificant clues from the past have helped to reconstruct life in a thriving fourth-century port moments before it perished.

Just how massive was the Kourion earthquake? Soren enlisted geologists Reuben Bullard and Frank Koucky to make a geological profile of the great earth movement. The tidal wave must have been of great magnitude, because Marcellinus reported widespread damage not only in Cyprus, but throughout the eastern Mediterranean. Bullard and Koucky came up with an estimate of nine on the Modified Mercalli Scale, a standard measure of earthquake strength. Their estimate left no doubt that this was a powerful quake.

Meanwhile, Soren tried to confirm the date that Marcellinus had given for the disaster. Previous estimates were vague. They were based on disputed passages in literary texts, and had dated the catastrophe to between AD321 and AD342. But Soren's excavations pinned the date down precisely. He unearthed a cache of coins in a jar dating to the reign of the brother emperors Valens and Valentinian I, which began in AD364. So the earthquake could not have occurred any earlier than that year, and since no later coins were present, it must have happened within a year or so of the coins' minting.

Where was the epicentre of the earthquake? Soren turned to Kourion's roof tiles for help. They lay exactly where they had fallen. All had tumbled to the north and east, which meant that the seismic waves

CYPRUS

Kourion

48km (30 miles)

○— Epicenter

Above *Archaeologists excavating a house destroyed by the earthquake at Kourion. They dug five-and-a-half rooms of this dwelling, which dated to the second century AD. It showed astounding resemblances to contemporary stone and mudbrick village architecture on Cyprus.*

Right *Lying next to the stone trough to which it was tethered when the earthquake struck is the skeleton of a horse, and near it, the remains of the girl who went to calm it. From evidence like this archaeologists have pieced together a remarkably detailed scene of the events during the earthquake which struck the eastern Mediterranean in AD365.*

KOURION

Kourion was a small, coastal port with few distinguished public buildings, **below**. The Acropolis with its Basilica and small Theatre is where the current excavations are taking place. **Below left** The epicentre of the great earthquake which devastated Kourion in AD365, here indicated by shock rings, has been calculated to have been close enough to level the small town.

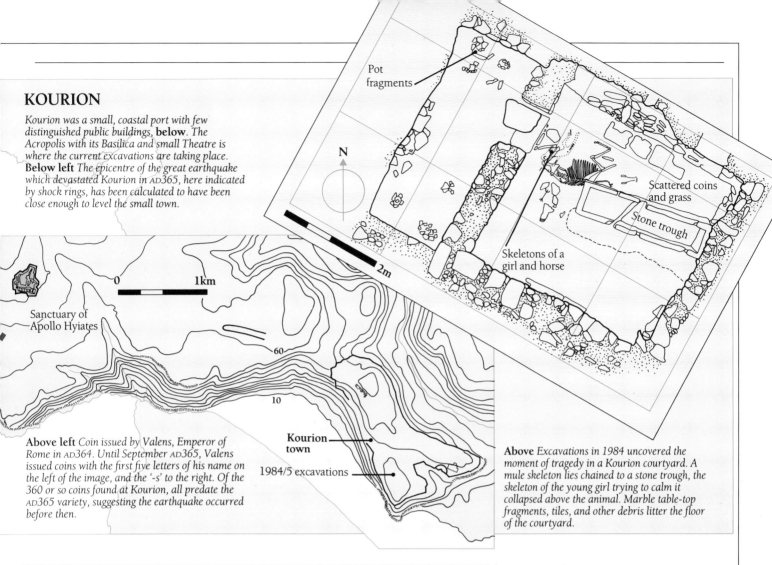

Pot fragments

N

2m

Scattered coins and grass

Stone trough

Skeletons of a girl and horse

Sanctuary of Apollo Hyiates

0   1km

60

10

Kourion town

1984/5 excavations

Above left Coin issued by Valens, Emperor of Rome in AD364. Until September AD365, Valens issued coins with the first five letters of his name on the left of the image, and the '-s' to the right. Of the 360 or so coins found at Kourion, all predate the AD365 variety, suggesting the earthquake occurred before then.

Above Excavations in 1984 uncovered the moment of tragedy in a Kourion courtyard. A mule skeleton lies chained to a stone trough, the skeleton of the young girl trying to calm it collapsed above the animal. Marble table-top fragments, tiles, and other debris litter the floor of the courtyard.

had come from the southwest. This gave him one reference point. A second came from the port of Paphos in western Cyprus, which was also destroyed by the earthquake. Here the tiles lay towards the northwest. A simple triangulation gave him the epicentre point, about 48km (30 miles) southwest of Kourion, where the African and European tectonic plates meet.

Kourion was not a spectacular Roman city, unlike Herculaneum and Pompeii. It was a quiet port community, inhabited by ordinary people rather than rich merchants and officials; it had none of the fine public buildings found in the shadow of Vesuvius. Kourion's humble dwellings lay 3.2km (2 miles) from a modest sanctuary dedicated to Apollo, the only large temple around. Stone by stone, wall by wall, Soren and his colleagues are dissecting one of Kourion's houses, a dwelling with a central courtyard surrounded by living areas and store rooms, and one which has revealed a vivid scenario of unexpected disaster.

The earthquake caught the inhabitants by complete surprise. It was just after dawn, so only a few people were astir. The first tremor woke a 13-year-old girl. She heard the horse that was tethered to a stone trough outside stirring and slipped out to calm the animal down. Just as she gripped

the tether chain in her hand, another great tremor struck. Inside the dwelling a glass vessel full of coins crashed to the ground. A heavy roof column collapsed, and tumbling stones buried the girl and the horse alive. Some time later, a rodent burrowed through the debris and fed on the girl's body. The rodent, too, was buried, this time by subsidence.

The young girl and the horse were not the only casualties. The collapsing house buried a 19-year-old mother and an 18-month-old child clutched to her chest. As the tremor struck the bedroom, she raised her hands to protect the child's head. Her husband desperately shielded his family with his body. Frantically, he stretched his left hand and leg across his wife and held the child's back, but to no avail. Falling plaster and stones broke the mother's neck. Stone blocks weighing 227kg (500lb) crashed into the husband's skull and spine and buried the family for 16 centuries. Perhaps they were Christians: the man wore a copper ring inscribed with the Greek letters Chi Rho, a symbol of Christ.

At least seven people died in this one house, among them a man in his fifties, crushed in a nearby doorway. Two family members perished in a room next to the courtyard where the horse was stabled. One woman crouched in a foetal position among the storage jars and bronze pitchers. Both she and the 13-year-old girl wore identical bone pins in their hair; perhaps they were mother and daughter.

The Kourion excavations are remarkable not only for their intimate picture of a terrible disaster, but also for their meticulous detail. David Soren is no conventional classical archaeologist concerned with great buildings and fine statuary, although he enjoys these as much as the next scholar. He has applied to Kourion the sophisticated analytical techniques developed by North American archaeologists. He is fascinated not only by details of daily life, but also by the diseases that can be identified from the bones of Kourion folk. So he enlisted the services of forensic experts, who established that the 13-year-old girl had bones the size of a 10 year-old. Her bones contained high concentrations of lead and other heavy minerals, which indicate that she may have been poisoned by the lead pipes that carried water throughout Kourion. Many Roman skeletons from elsewhere display the same

Three unfortunate victims of the Kourion earthquake huddle together for protection. A man, top, shields a woman with his left arm and leg. She, in turn, desperately clutches a small child.

chronic poisoning from such plumbing.

Kourion is another kind of Pompeii, a unique window into the lives of ordinary citizens of the Roman Empire. Pompeii was buried by the ash of exploding Vesuvius, ash that literally choked the town, leaving even tiny objects intact and in perfect condition. Kourion is a far more demanding archive, because preservation conditions there are very poor. So David Soren has had to rely on fragmentary historical accounts and a host of inconspicuous archaeological clues to complete his ancient jigsaw puzzle: tiny rodent bones, bone pins, copper pitchers, even the angles of fallen tiles. The time capsule comes alive in the creative, ingenious hands and minds of a team of scientists who, by means of archaeology and written records, probe the past on a minute scale.

TENOCHTITLAN

Historical records from a more recent era have proved to be a priceless asset for archaeologists studying the Aztec civilization of highland Mexico. Hernan Cortes and his Spanish conquistadores came to the great city of Tenochtitlan in 1519. Fifty years later conquistador Bernal Diaz recalled his first sight of the Aztec capital as vividly as if it had been the day before. 'We were astounded,' he wrote, 'these great towns . . . and buildings rising from the water, all made of stone, seemed like an enchanted vision.' The market was even larger than that in Seville.

Hardened soldiers who had visited Constantinople were amazed by Tenochtitlan. But two years later, Tenochtitlan was in ruins. 'Today all that I then saw is overthrown and destroyed . . . nothing is left standing,' wrote Diaz. Only now are archaeologists unearthing the wonders of this ancient city.

Today, the urban sprawl of Mexico City covers what remains of the Aztec capital. Even so, the Aztec city pops up from time to time. Thousands of Aztec artifacts came to light during tunnelling for the city's subway system, for example. Then some urban renewal works close to the fifteenth-century Catholic cathedral revealed one of twentieth-century archaeology's most impressive finds – the great temple of the sun god Huitzilopochtli, a structure described with awe and dread by the stunned conquistadores in 1519.

By fortunate chance, the archaeologist chosen to investigate the Templo Mayor was Eduardo Matos Moctezuma, a descendant of the Aztec ruler who had greeted Cortes. He was confronted with a huge

task. Bernal Diaz described how the 46m (150ft) high, stepped pyramid rose from Tenochtitlan's central plaza, with two brightly painted temples on the summit, the one dedicated to Huitzilopochtli, the other to the rain god Tlaloc. Cortes and his conquistadores climbed 114 steps to the shrines. Huitzilopochtli's idol was girdled with huge snakes made of gold and precious stones. The floor and walls of the shrine were black with dried human blood. The priests would tear out the heart of the sacrificial victim with a stone knife, offer the still pulsing heart to the god and tumble the corpse down the slippery steps.

Above *A detail of the serpent wall (Coatepantli) which surrounds the whole of the temple precinct of the Aztec city Tenochtitlán. The serpent is Quetzalcoatl (feathered serpent) and serves to delimit the sacred space inside the wall around the temple from the profane space outside it.*

Eduardo Moctezuma was faced with excavating a minor mountain, even though the conquistadores had quarried the pyramid for building stone and levelled much of it to the ground. It stood at a sacred place, the spot where Huitzilopochtli himself had ordered the early Aztec priests to build his shrine.

Arguing that successive Aztec rulers had 'stacked' even larger structures against earlier ones, Moctezuma decided on a high-risk gamble that turned out to be an archaeological masterstroke. He peeled off successive stone and mortar façades to reveal at least seven building phases. The earliest and most intact temple dated to about AD1390. Huitzilopochtli's sacrificial stone was still in place, exactly where Cortes found its successor 150 years later.

The Templo Mayor excavations yielded a superb array of Aztec ceremonial artifacts – and gruesome reminders that their priests practised human sacrifice. The skulls of prominent victims were carefully adorned

and displayed. Sometimes the priests left the stone sacrificial knife in place, replacing the eyeballs with shells. One sacred pit contained the skulls of 34 children between three months and eight years old. They had been sacrificed to the rain god, their bodies dismembered before their heads were buried with painted stone effigies of Tlaloc the rain god.

The Mexican Government has opened the Templo Mayor to the public. You can walk through sacred precincts that were alive with colour and bustling with people centuries before the conquistadores set foot in the New World. Close your eyes for a moment, and you can visualize the scene. The priests chant, the great drum sounds and a line of richly adorned sacrificial victims passes you on their way to eternity. A long-forgotten civilization comes alive – a civilization that has become part of the national legacy of the nation that rose from its ashes.

Below *Lining a colossal stairway which links one of the many levels of the Templo Mayor are stone figures, which were probably placed there as dedicatory offerings when the next level was built on top of this one. The holes in the chests of these figures indicate that they represent sacrificial victims whose hearts were torn out and offered to the gods.*

Below *Flanking the main entrance to a small temple dedicated to the Eagle warrior society are two eagle heads, one of which is shown here.*

Above *A cross-section through the various building stages of the temple, and in the background, buildings from the Spanish colonial era. Much more of the temple lies beneath these colonial buildings, some of which were torn down to excavate the temple, but it is unlikely that any more will be destroyed.*

Right *A detail from the gruesome Tzompantli, or skull rack. This is an imitation of the real thing which was an abacus-like structure on which heads were threaded once the flesh had been pulled off them. The Spanish destroyed most of these structures and their stone replicas, but obviously missed this one.*

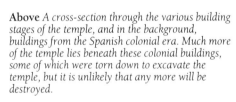

PART TWO
NEW PERCEPTIONS

DECODING
MAYA SIGNS

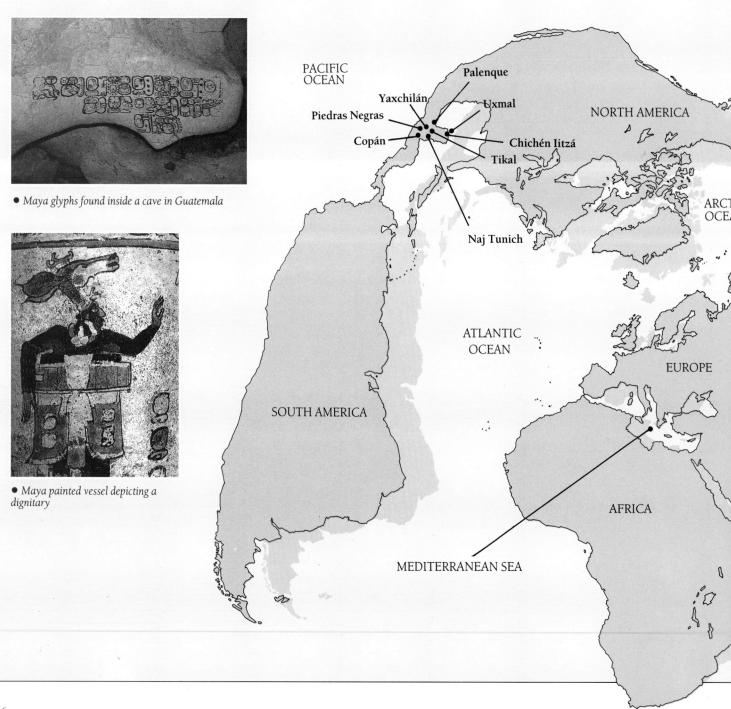

• *Maya glyphs found inside a cave in Guatemala*

• *Maya painted vessel depicting a dignitary*

PACIFIC OCEAN

Palenque

Yaxchilán

Uxmal

Piedras Negras

NORTH AMERICA

Copán

Chichén Iitzá

Tikal

ARCT OCEA

Naj Tunich

ATLANTIC OCEAN

EUROPE

SOUTH AMERICA

AFRICA

MEDITERRANEAN SEA

Some of the most spectacular archaeological discoveries of recent years have come not from dramatic excavations, but from hours of patient work in the laboratory, among archives or from quiet study. Perhaps the greatest triumph of all is the decipherment of the ancient Maya script, which has led us to an image of Maya life hitherto undreamed of.

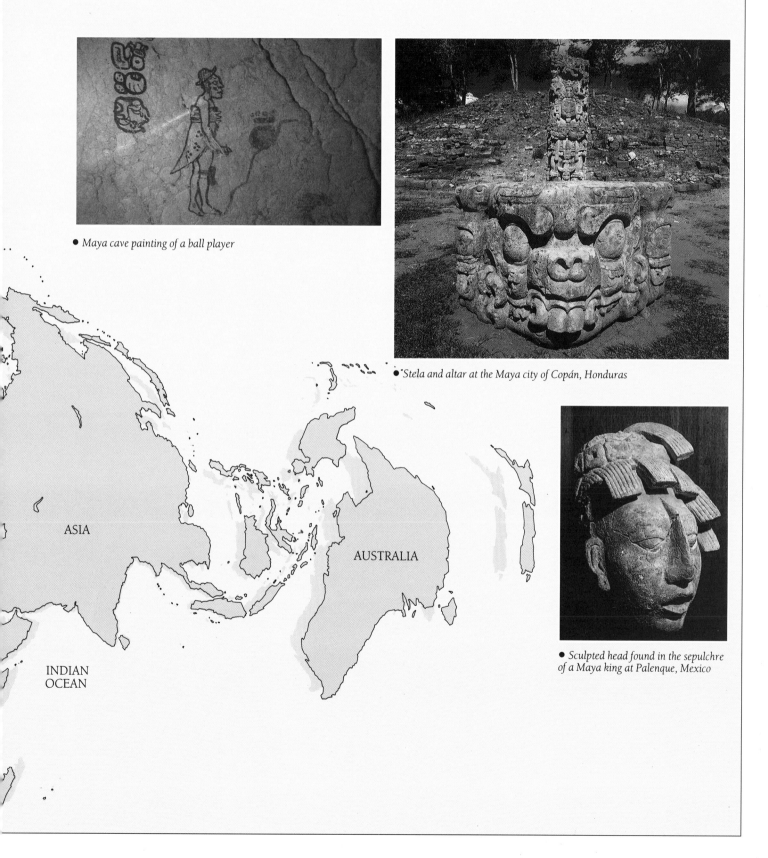

● *Maya cave painting of a ball player*

● *Stela and altar at the Maya city of Copán, Honduras*

● *Sculpted head found in the sepulchre of a Maya king at Palenque, Mexico*

ASIA

AUSTRALIA

INDIAN
OCEAN

Deep in the forests of Mexico, one of a group
of Maya temples called Bonampak (meaning
'painted walls') contains a brilliantly naturalistic
sequence of frescoes. Running right round the walls
and up into the vaulted ceiling the frescoes describe
with awesome realism the preparations for a raid
for sacrificial victims, the raid itself, and the
following sacrificial ritual. The example shown here
is a reconstruction from one of the walls, in which
Maya nobles gather for the ceremony.

A MYSTERIOUS SCRIPT

'It lay before us like a shattered bark in the midst of the ocean, her masts gone, her name effaced, her crew perished, and none to tell whence she came ... The only sounds that disturbed the quiet of this buried city were the noise of monkeys moving among the tops of the trees, and the cracking of dry branches broken by their weight. They moved over our heads in long and swift processions, forty or fifty at a time ...'. John Lloyd Stephens – writer, traveller, archaeologist – was not often at a loss for words, but the ancient Maya city of Copán left him speechless with wonder when he discovered it in 1839.

He wandered for days among miles of jungle-wrapped ruins, courts and temples, through plazas and up pyramids. Intricately carved stelae peered down at him, covered with bizarre faces and elaborate hieroglyphs. His artist friend and companion Frederick Catherwood stood ankle-deep in mud, dripping with sweat and perennial rain, sketching the stelae and measuring buildings. This lavish, completely forgotten city was unlike anything either man had seen in Egypt or Greece.

Stephens realized at once that the builders of Copán were the dimly remembered ancestors of the modern Maya Indians who live in this part of Guatemala. 'These cities ... are not the works of people who have passed away ... but of the same great race which ... still clings around their ruins,' he wrote in his brilliant best-seller, *Incidents of Travel in Central America,* published in New York in 1841. The publication of this book marked the beginning of a scientific quest that continues today – the study of ancient Maya civilization.

This triumphant quest has resurrected a long-forgotten civilization from almost complete historical obscurity. But perhaps the greatest triumph of all is the decipherment of the ancient Maya script; which has totally altered our perception of Maya life and society.

Stephens and Catherwood were completely baffled by the Maya hieroglyphs, which bore no resemblance to any known ancient script. Generations of gifted linguists after them were also at an impasse, for no Jean Francois Champollion, Henry Creswicke Rawlinson or Jules Oppert, who had deciphered ancient Egyptian hieroglyphs and Assyrian cuneiform, emerged to unlock the mysteries of Maya writing.

It seemed that they were getting close to an answer when the great British Mayanist J. Eric Thompson discovered that Maya priests had used an elaborate calendar of repeating cycles of days. The calendar with

Top *Copán is one of the great centres of the Maya civilization. Shown here is a small sample of the many altars and stelae which dot the Great Plaza.* **Above** *A sculpture on the façade of a temple, possibly representing a Maya deity.* **Right** *Temple XXII at Copán with a stela depicting one of the Copán rulers, and an altar.*

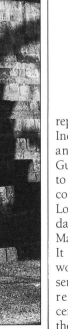

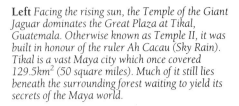

Left *Facing the rising sun, the Temple of the Giant Jaguar dominates the Great Plaza at Tikal, Guatemala. Otherwise known as Temple II, it was built in honour of the ruler Ah Cacau (Sky Rain). Tikal is a vast Maya city which once covered 129.5km² (50 square miles). Much of it still lies beneath the surrounding forest waiting to yield its secrets of the Maya world.*

Below *The so-called Leiden Plate, a Maya jade plaque found in 1864. It was removed from the tomb of Jaguar Paw, an early but very important ruler of Tikal. On the left, a Maya lord tramples a captive underfoot. On the right, are the glyphs which relate the 'Long Count' date for the event – 8.14.3.1.12 – which corresponds to a day in the year AD320. The plaque is 21.6cm (8½in) long.*

repeating cycles of 52 years was used by Indian societies all over Central America, and survives to this day in parts of Guatemala and Mexico. What was unique to the Maya, however, was a cumulative count of days, known to Mayanists as the Long Count. This begins on an arbitrary day in August 3114BC, long before the Maya emerged as a distinct cultural entity. It may represent the latest creation of the world in Maya mythology, but in any case served as a baseline for a dating system that remained in use for more than six centuries, from as early as AD200. During these classic centuries of Maya civilization,

the people erected hundreds of monuments inscribed with glyphs that dated them to the day.

In 1549, a fanatical friar named Diego de Landa arrived in the Yucatán. Landa was an austere, forbidding friar, who had a single-minded obsession – to rid the Maya of their pagan ways. But, like so many fanatics, he was a contradiction. He was profoundly interested in the very Maya life and customs he worked so hard to destroy. Landa visited Maya ceremonial centres, such as Chichén Itzá and Uxmal, and described their elaborate hieroglyphs, even translating some. But his observations were not published

Below *Epigrapher Heinrich Berlin dusts down glyphs in the tomb chamber of Burial 48 at Tikal. The significance of these glyphs is not yet understood but it is thought that they depict astronomical phenomena. They also record the 'Long Count' date 9.1.1.10.10.4 (March 19, AD457).*

until 1863. Even then it was a generation before Maya dates, expressed in a system of bars and dots, were first deciphered by a German librarian named Ernst Forstemann in the 1880s. Then Joseph Goodman, the American newspaper publisher who first recognized the talents of Mark Twain, used de Landa's account of Maya writing to link the Mayan calendar to the Christian one.

For years, Maya specialists believed that the hieroglyphs at Palenque, Copán, Tikal, Chichén Itzá and other great ceremonial centres were mainly calendrical and astronomical records of religious significance. They were impersonal records that, aston-

ishingly, never commemorated the names of rulers. Yet excavations and survey work at the great centres were revealing an ancient civilization in which great rulers at competing ceremonial centres had vied with one another for political and economic power, ruling over thousands of humble farmers scattered in small villages over the Maya lowlands. And still no one knew who these rulers were.

The picture changed dramatically between 1958 and 1960, when epigrapher Heinrich Berlin showed that a range of Maya glyphic signs had restricted geographical distributions. Berlin called them

emblem glyphs, and wondered if they represented place names or the identity of a ruling dynasty. If this was true, then Maya hieroglyphs were far more than just calendar inscriptions.

While Berlin was working on emblem glyphs, another brilliant scholar, Tatiana Proskouriakoff, noticed that a series of stelae at a Maya centre named Piedras Negras, on the Usumacinta River, formed a consistent pattern. They were in groups. In each case the earliest showed a seated figure at the top of a ladder, with footprints indicating that the individual had just ascended to his seat. Were these, then, the

portraits of the powerful secular rulers of the Maya world, she wondered?

Proskouriakoff recorded seven successive groups of monuments that dated to between AD613 and 795, and documented reigns that lasted for an average period of about 30 years. She showed that each ruler erected an accession monument on the fifth anniversary of his assuming the throne, adding fresh stelae every five years thereafter.

This was a major breakthrough. But Proskouriakoff did not rest on her laurels – in 1964 she turned her attention to Yaxchilán, upstream of Piedras Negras, where she identified at least two long-forgotten Maya rulers. One of them she named Shield-Jaguar, after the form of his name glyph. He was a remarkable man, who was born about AD647, became ruler of Yaxchilán by AD682 and lived beyond his 90th birthday. Shield-Jaguar was a successful warrior. Proskouriakoff theorized that he may have taken the throne of Yaxchilán by force. Her researches showed beyond all doubt that some Maya monuments were not calendars at all, but documented important personal and political events.

Above *Maya stelae from Piedras Negras, on the Usumacinta River, which are thought to depict the accession of secular rulers. The stela on the left depicts an unknown young Maya ruler. At the foot of the platform where he sits stands a middle-aged woman, perhaps his mother. The monument commemorates the date of his accession in AD761.*

PACAL, THE SHIELD

Proskouriakoff and Berlin started a revolution in Maya epigraphy, a revolution that has taken dramatic hold in the past decade. In the early 1970s, experts could read about 10 to 20 per cent of Maya glyphs. Now they have deciphered more than 80 per cent, revealing all the startling complexity of the ancient Maya world. For the first time, we can identify individual rulers, grapple our way to at least some understanding of Maya rituals, philosophies and beliefs, and give meaning to spectacular archaeological discoveries made by earlier scholars. At Tikal in Guatemala, epigraphers such as Proskouriakoff and Clemency Coggins have placed in order a dynastic succession of four centuries of rulers from the late fourth to late eighth centuries AD, reigns that can be linked with some of the buildings in this great centre. At Palenque, a centre visited by John Lloyd Stephens and studied sporadically ever since, even greater triumphs awaited the epigraphers.

In 1952, the great Mexican archaeologist Alberto Ruz Lhuiller began clearing the jungle-entangled Temple of the Inscriptions at Palenque. His workmen laboriously cleaned the nine-tiered pyramid and the imposing temple at its summit. Working painstakingly across the flagstone floor, Ruz discovered a hidden entrance leading to a staircase into the pyramid below. So much rubble was packed into the stairway that it took an entire season to clear 23 steps. After 71 steps, the sweating work-men reached a landing sealed with a rubble wall. They broke through it, only to find yet another wall. In front of it, like an offering, lay pearls, jade ornaments and pottery. It took a week to break through the 3.7m (12ft) thick barrier. Beyond it lay six young sacrificial victims, in a masonry box.

At last the men came to a huge triangular stone slab that sealed a chamber 3.9m by 8.8m (13ft by 29ft) with a vaulted ceiling 7m (23ft) high. A huge limestone slab adorned with hieroglyphs and reliefs almost filled the floor. Ruz and his work-men carefully pried open the five-tonne slab. Inside lay the bones of an aged Maya lord smothered in jade ornaments and buried with a superb jade mosaic mask.

But who was this important ruler? At the time Ruz discovered the grave, no one could read the inscriptions on the lid of the sarcophagus. Then, in 1974, epigraphers Peter Mathews and Linda Schele used the dramatic research of Proskouriakoff and others to identify the man as a ruler named

Top *The city of Palenque, Mexico, with the Temple of the Sun on the left, Temple XIV at the centre, and the Palace on the right. The ruler of this city from AD613 was Pacal, or Shield.* **Far left** *is his jade mosaic burial mask and* **left** *his burial chamber in the Temple of Inscriptions with the engraved sarcophagus lid. Made of limestone, this lid is 3.6m (12ft) long and weighs five tonnes.*

Left *A richly robed woman kneels before the formidable Yaxchilán ruler 'Shield Jaguar' in a bloodletting rite in which she draws a thorn-lined rope through her tongue. The woman has been identified as the ruler's wife, Lady Xoc. This relief from Yaxchilán, Mexico, was dedicated in AD709, shortly after 'Shield Jaguar' had captured his enemy 'Death'.*

Pacal, or Shield. Patiently, they traced the dates along the sides of the sarcophagus lid and established that his reign at Palenque began on July 29, AD613, and ended in AD672. He died at the age of 38-40.

Fortunately for archaeologists, Pacal was passionately interested in the deeds of his predecessors. His sarcophagus records the accession and death dates of seven rulers, including two women, who held the throne of Palenque before him. Some of his successors associated important events in their lives with those in their ancestor Pacal's life. So the Temple of the Inscriptions, his mortuary temple, became an important symbol during Palenque's second century of power from AD700 to AD800.

Palenque's scribes used wall panels instead of stelae to record not only contemporary events but also the historical and mythical contexts in which they were seen. It was the same mythical context that caused a later ruler named Kan-Xul to enlarge the Palace at Palenque. He made the accession monument of Pacal the focal point of a complex of buildings that included a four-storey tower. A priest could gaze over the roofs of Palenque at the winter solstice and watch the sun set. This was the day when the sun would seem to enter the underworld through Pacal's tomb

– the Temple of the Inscriptions.

The brilliant research of Maya epigraphers has brought Maya civilization to life in unique ways. We can watch powerful rulers such as Pacal expand their control through trade and timely marriage alliances, and build lavish temples and public buildings which reinforce their political and religious authority. Dynasties pass from generation to generation, their deeds commemorated on stelae and wall panels. The epigraphers are still grappling with fundamental problems, but they can begin to trace the spheres of influence of different centres by studying the distribution of emblem glyphs.

Just occasionally we come across an individual event from the Maya past. In the 1970s, a burial of a middle-aged woman came to light at Altar de Sacrificios, a small Maya centre. She lay in her grave accompanied by another woman, perhaps a sacrificial victim, surrounded by painted pots, some imported from Tikal and Yaxchilán, many miles away. A painted scene depicts what may be mourners at her funeral – a Bird-Jaguar from Yaxchilán dancing in jaguar-skin trousers and a mask, and a member of the Sky dynasty from Tikal also in jaguar costume. One figure is of a young woman killing herself with a stone knife like the one found beside the

Left *The Temple of the Sun at Palenque, a late Classic structure built in the late seventh century* AD. *A carved panel inside the shrine commemorates the ascension of Chan-Bahlum, son and successor of Pacal in* AD684. **Above** *A watercolour by the Guatemalan artist Antonia Tejeda of a wall painting from Room 2 at Bonampak dating to about* AD800. *The ruler of Bonampak stands on a terraced platform with his subordinates. At his feet lies a sacrificial victim.*

younger body in the grave. Does this scene represent a mythical scene from the Maya underworld, or is it a depiction of the funeral of an important middle-aged woman, perhaps related to an important dynasty by marriage ties? The mystery remains unsolved.

A MAYA 'BOOK OF THE DEAD'

As settings for elaborate public ceremonies and religious festivals the great Maya temples were built to dazzle and impress; apart from their awesome size they were adorned with colourful murals that depicted battles and ceremonies, both actual and mythical. Unfortunately, the damp lowland climate has destroyed many of these murals. The same artists who created murals also painted clay vessels or vases, some with a skill that rivals the finest work of the classical Greek painters. Hundreds of these vessels have come from the graves of the Maya élite, but unfortunately many more have been found by looters, so we know little of their significance. However, they do give us some clues to the intricate symbolic world that surrounded the Maya.

Some of the vases depict rituals performed in the presence of gods: the taking of hallucinogenic drugs, and human sacrifices accompanied by dancing. They display an elaborate pantheon of gods: there was Itzam Na (iguana house), the creator of the universe, who was a deity with four parts assigned to different compass directions and colours; there were the gods of the sun and moon; there were the *chaacs,* or rain gods, who sent the rain that maintained life; and the *bacabs,* the supporters of the sky. All the deities reflected the forces of nature. Corn was so important that it too was a god – a handsome young man with corn leaves rising from his hair. The jaguar was the symbol of power and rank.

Left *The hook-nosed and toothless God 'L', one of the supreme gods of the Maya underworld, sits on his throne surrounded by beautiful women, on this 20cm (8in) high Maya vase. Also in attendance is the Rabbit God who appears to be painting a codex. Scenes like these on this and other Maya vases are being deciphered at the moment and revealing hitherto unknown myths in Maya religion concerning the underworld.* **Below** *A Maya dignitary.* **Right** *Francis Robicsek's rollout photographs of vase paintings placed in proper order read like a comic book with elaborate scenes and short texts. Note the identical artistic style, the same characters, and the movie-like sequence of action.*

Francis Robicsek is a surgeon by profession and an archaeologist by avocation, a scholar with a passion for Maya painted vases. He has spent much of the past decade studying these intricate vase paintings, using a novel photographic technique that takes roll-out pictures of the vessel by rotating it. Robicsek remembered the writings of Bishop Diego de Landa, who in the sixteenth century saw Maya codices, hieroglyphs written 'on a long sheet folded up'. Landa was so terrified of idolatry among the Maya that he supervised the destruction of dozens of these codices. Only a handful survived his depredations, much to the frustration of modern epigraphers, who realized what a priceless archive of Maya life had been destroyed.

Then, in the mid-1970s, Yale Mayanist Michael Coe realized that the same techniques used to paint the codex drawings were used on clay vessels. Robicsek took Coe's ideas still further. After undertaking a lengthy study, Robicsek believes that the painted vases are just like pages of codices, except that the images are recorded on clay rather than bark paper or skins. Unfortunately, the ceramic codex is not yet complete because some of the vases were looted, others destroyed during the past centuries and many more have not yet been found. But the complex, formalized scenes he has managed to retrieve reveal fragments of Maya religious thought in a unique 'Book of the Dead'. Since the publication of this book Robicsek has assembled several complete chapters of Maya mythology using his method.

Little Maya mythology survived the Spanish Conquest, except for the *Popol Vuh* from the Guatemalan highlands, an oral saga written down after the Spanish Con-

quest. This saga tells how two heroic brothers, the children of the old goddess Xmucane, played a ball game. The rulers of the underworld challenged them to a series of magical contests and defeated them. The brothers were sacrificed, their heads hung on trees. One of the heads spat on a passing daughter of an underworld lord. She became pregnant and gave birth to Hero Twins. They were also challenged by the lords of the underworld, but prevailed. The triumphant twins and the brothers became celestial bodies. Robicsek believes that some of his vase codices depict scenes from the *Popol Vuh*.

One vase depicts an idyllic palace scene, in which a lord of the underworld disports with women. Next the painter depicts an execution scene. The bound victim is attended by two executioners: one bends over the victim, with long deer ears; the

other wears a monster mask on which a jaguar paw serves as the nose. Perhaps this represents the execution of one of the hunter brothers in the *Popol Vuh*:

'And when they were sacrificed
And they were buried
At Dusty Court, as it is called,
They were buried then
1 Hunter's head was cut off.
Only his body was buried with his younger brothers . . .'

Other vessels also depict scenes that may appear in the *Popol Vuh*. The old god seen in all his glory in the first vase is humiliated by young lords, who stamp on him and break his regalia. There are mythical beasts, such as the Great Bearded Dragon, a Water-lily Jaguar and the Uinal Monster, a toad-like creature associated with the Maya calendar. Deciphering this elaborate iconography of beasts, underworld deities, humans and executioners is almost impossible.

Even so, Robicsek draws attention to other parallels between the *Popol Vuh* and the codex vases. On one dish, the painter shows one of the Hero Twins, Jaguar Deer, dancing between two beasts. He swings an axe and decapitates himself. Robicsek remembers the Maya epic:

'And they marvelled,
The lords.
"And now sacrifice yourselves in turn,
So we can see it.
Truly our hearts are delighted with this dance of yours,"
The lords repeated.
"Very well, oh Lord,"

They said then.
And they sacrificed themselves . . .'

Robicsek believes he has untangled the message of several of the vessel 'codices'. These codices are like a highly abbreviated, Maya equivalent of the Egyptian Book of the Dead. Each clay codex, each vessel, repeats highlights of great mythological importance to the Maya in this world and the next. For generations, Mayanists have lamented de Landa's savage destruction of Maya codices, but now it seems very likely that many of them were under our noses all the time.

NAJ TUNICH

Clay pots, codices and inscriptions are not the only gateways to the forgotten Maya world. The Maya themselves worshipped their gods and performed important rituals at thousands of locations. The élite worshipped in lavish public buildings that proclaimed their great power. But the humble farmers and less prestigious nobles performed the same ceremonies far more modestly, often in the bowels of the earth. A chance discovery in Guatemala in 1980 provided dramatic proof that caves were an important part of Maya ritual.

The dogs of Bernabé Pop, the Kekchi Maya Indian, were hot in pursuit of a peccary down a forest trail. Bernabé followed the dogs down the dark, overgrown path and found himself in an enormous chamber, the entrance of a long-forgotten cave. The shadowy daylight revealed a tunnel hung with stalactites and petroglyphs of human faces on the walls. The

Below *A design from a famous Maya vessel, the Chama vase, which depicts a scene from the underworld. The main figure seems to be a combination of two of the supreme gods of the underworld, God 'L' and God 'N'; he is paying host to the Merchant God.*

Above *View of the balcony in Naj Tunich with people on the cave floor and the first level. This balcony is the largest artificial structure ever found in a Maya cave and may have been the site of sacrificial rituals.*

NAJ TUNICH CAVE

Naj Tunich cave is entered through a long passage (1) that leads to the Passage of Rites (2), with its bloodletting scene. The West Terminus (3) leads to the Hall of Balam and the Chamber of Crystal Columns. The other passage (4) extends more than 800m (874yds). The Bearer of Fire Room (5) contains several figures and glyph texts that have helped to date the cave's use as a shrine. The passage to the Silent Well (6) is at the very end of the passage, 470m (513yds) further along.

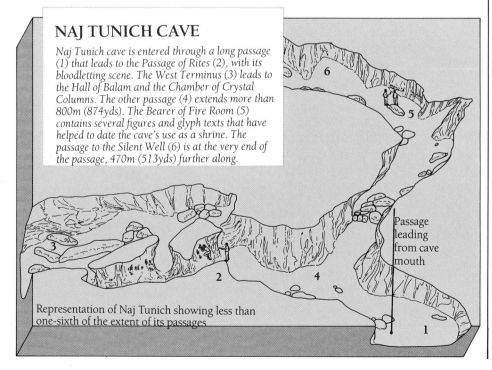

Passage leading from cave mouth

Representation of Naj Tunich showing less than one-sixth of the extent of its passages

young man hastened home to fetch his father. The two men explored the cave several times and found ancient inscriptions and glyphs quite unlike anything they had ever seen before. In June 1980 a Yale University linguist, Pierre Ventur, visited the cave. He named it Naj Tunich, which means 'stone house' in the local Maya dialect. Maya archaeologists have been studying this cave ever since.

You approach Naj Tunich along a narrow ravine. Two low mounds run on either side of it for about 49m (160ft) before you reach the entrance. Perhaps they served as a gateway to the sacred precinct. The entrance hall of Naj Tunich itself is an enormous chamber nearly 30m (100ft) across and running almost 152m (500ft) east to west. A tunnel system about 15.2m (50ft) in diameter extends off the entrance chamber before it branches into two. There were major clusters of drawings in each fork, and two standing pools that once functioned as ceremonial centres.

The entrance chamber, filled with subdued dappled sunlight, contains no paintings. The stalactite-covered ceiling rises nearly 30m (100ft) above the muddy floor. On the eastern side of the hall the Maya fenced in a natural rise with retaining walls, filling the space behind them to form a balcony that rises in two tiers as much as 14m (45ft) above the entrance. (This balcony is the largest construction in a Maya cave ever reported.) This was one of the most sacred areas of the cave, the place where sacrifices may have taken place. A shaft leads from the lower level down to six chambers, where the remains of at least two children lay, perhaps sacrificial victims.

The chambers contained ritual paraphernalia – miniature vessels, incense burners and dozens of sharp bone needles. Naj Tunich may have witnessed a considerable number of human sacrifices, because the bones of at least 20 people, mainly children and youths, have come from the excavations in its chambers and galleries. The most complete skeleton is that of a child about five to six years old buried in a shallow grave. The skull bears three holes from wounds that were inflicted in life and that never healed. Naj Tunich is the only Maya cave in which tombs have ever been found.

The upper tier of the entrance balcony was once a burial ground for at least six important people. All their graves had been looted in the distant past. The tombs were either masonry structures or simple alcoves. At least one had a wooden roof or ceiling. Jade beads, some fragmentary bones and incomplete clay vessels came from one of the excavated graves. The incomplete rim of one of the vessels bears two glyphs that are known to be associated with Maya kingship. Roughly translated, they mean 'lord of the office, lord of succession'. Unfortunately, the looters had done their work too well. They left no trace of the identity of the owner.

This upper level was sacred not only because of its burials but also because of a small chamber there that once contained a shallow pool, formed by damming the chamber with a stone wall. The Maya considered pools of water sacred. Places such as the celebrated Sacred Well at Chichén Itzá in the Yucatán are so hallowed that people made pilgrimages to it from miles around, to throw offerings in their muddy waters. The excavators of Naj Tunich found some potsherds that had been cast into the long dried-up pool, cemented to its bottom by stalagmite.

About 40m (130ft) inside the tunnel system, which leads off the entrance hall, lies another sacred area – a second pool that still holds water and is associated with an earthen platform with steps, a crude altar and some alcoves in the wall. Large quantities of pottery that could be dated on the basis of the designs to between 100BC and AD250, lay on the edge overlooking the pool. A third sacred area was found at the very end of the eastern branch of the tunnel system, a deep shaft more than 4.9m (16ft) across, which has still to be explored. The approach was so muddy that bare footprints could still be seen in the floor. The cave explorers who first located this pool called it the Silent Well. Nearby, a deep midden of broken pots and a jade mask, probably an offering, lay under a projection in the cave wall. Presumably offerings were cast into the mysterious pool, just as they were into the other pools in the cave.

Naj Tunich was used for centuries, from as early as 100BC to as late as AD550 and probably much later. It was an important religious shrine, for generations before elaborate paintings were executed on its walls. It differs from other Maya painted caves in the sophistication of the drawings – more than 500 hieroglyphs, paintings and rock engravings appear on its walls. The petroglyphs depict human faces. One hieroglyphic inscription contains two dates that correspond to August 25, AD744 and August 20, AD772, but the meaning of the dates is uncertain.

The paintings depict some men drinking from a bowl, others engaged in the act of autosacrifice, piercing themselves with sharp instruments and dripping the blood on paper to be burned. Another seated man wearing a deer headdress accepts a bowl from a kneeling dwarf. Perhaps he is about

Above *An individual performs an act of genital mutilation to draw blood with which to feed the gods. This was sometimes done with the spine of a sting ray.*

Above *In probably the most sexually explicit scene in Maya art, a copulating couple have been drawn on the walls of Naj Tunich. The woman is thought to be the Moon Goddess, the first woman to have had sexual intercourse, and a symbol of fertility.*

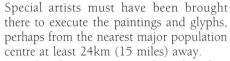

to drink an alcoholic beverage made from fermented honey, water and the bark of the balche tree, a drink well known for its mind-altering properties. Two scenes show musicians playing drums and wind implements. (Bone flutes and broken whistles were found in the excavations.)

What do these paintings mean? Enough is known about Maya rituals from deciphered hieroglyphs and modern ritual to know that caves were important as sites for rain-making and agricultural fertility ceremonies. Many such caves have been discovered, decorated with crude petroglyphs that resemble human faces or figures, but Naj Tunich is unique in its elaboration.

*Few Maya caves contain sophisticated art, but Naj Tunich is an exception. This fine example of inscriptions, **left**, contains two dates, which correspond to August 25, AD744, and August 20, AD772. **Below** These paintings are thought to depict the hero-twins of a Quiché Maya epic, Hunahpu and Xblanque.*

Special artists must have been brought there to execute the paintings and glyphs, perhaps from the nearest major population centre at least 24km (15 miles) away.

Archaeologists James Brady and Andrea Stone, who work at Naj Tunich, point out that caves were always a symbol of the open mouth of the jaguar, serpent or earth monster. The same motif appears again and again at major ceremonial centres where great rulers exercised their divine authority and political control. Although the rulers made their offerings at grandiose temples, in the depths of little-known caves in the countryside, the humble farmers and local élite celebrated similar fertility and rain-making rites with much the same motifs.

Fertility rites would account for the scenes of autosacrifice, the deliberate mutilation of one's body to draw blood for feeding the gods. The Naj Tunich paintings depict richly clothed male figures holding bloodletting instruments at their waists. A seated figure painted on a fine vase found in the entrance chamber is shown scattering drops of blood from his hand, blood that will provide nourishment for the gods. The bloodletting scenes flank a painting of a man and woman locked in sexual embrace. The Maya associated sexual union with fecundity, with the moon goddess, the ancestral deity who was the first woman ever to have sexual intercourse. The moon goddess was also the patron of the month named Ch'en, a name meaning a hole in the ground like a cave or deep pool.

So Naj Tunich was a sacred place associated with fertility and bountiful crops. The dates from the glyphs tend to cluster near the summer and winter solstices. The summer dates coincide with the beginning of the rainy season, when the rain god would have been propitiated. Interestingly, these summer glyphs are found close to the scenes of bloodletting and copulation, and corn grinders and corn cobs have been found in the cave. The child skeletons show that the Maya went to extreme lengths to find favour with the rain god. These age-old beliefs still persist. During the 1982 excavations, a group of Maya came to the cave and wanted to make offerings for a plentiful harvest. They suspected that Naj Tunich was still the abode of the god of corn.

NEW LIGHT ON OLD WORLDS

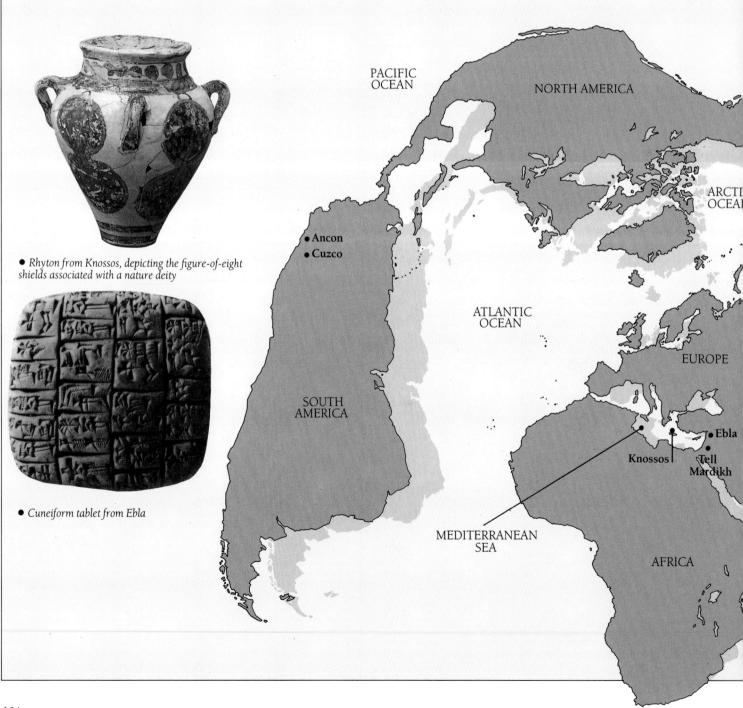

• Rhyton from Knossos, depicting the figure-of-eight
shields associated with a nature deity

• Cuneiform tablet from Ebla

PACIFIC
OCEAN

NORTH AMERICA

ARCTI
OCEA

• Ancon
• Cuzco

ATLANTIC
OCEAN

EUROPE

SOUTH
AMERICA

• Ebla

Knossos

Tell
Mardikh

MEDITERRANEAN
SEA

AFRICA

After more than a century of spectacular discoveries and intricate, often brilliant, research, the past continues to amaze us, to provide new insights into human civilizations, so that only now are we beginning to understand how some of them came into being. In some cases we are having to revise completely our old ideas about well-known civilizations. The Near East, for example, has yielded marvellous archaeological discoveries for centuries, to the point that one might think that little of any importance remains to be found. Nothing could be farther from the truth, as each excavation season brings new revelations.

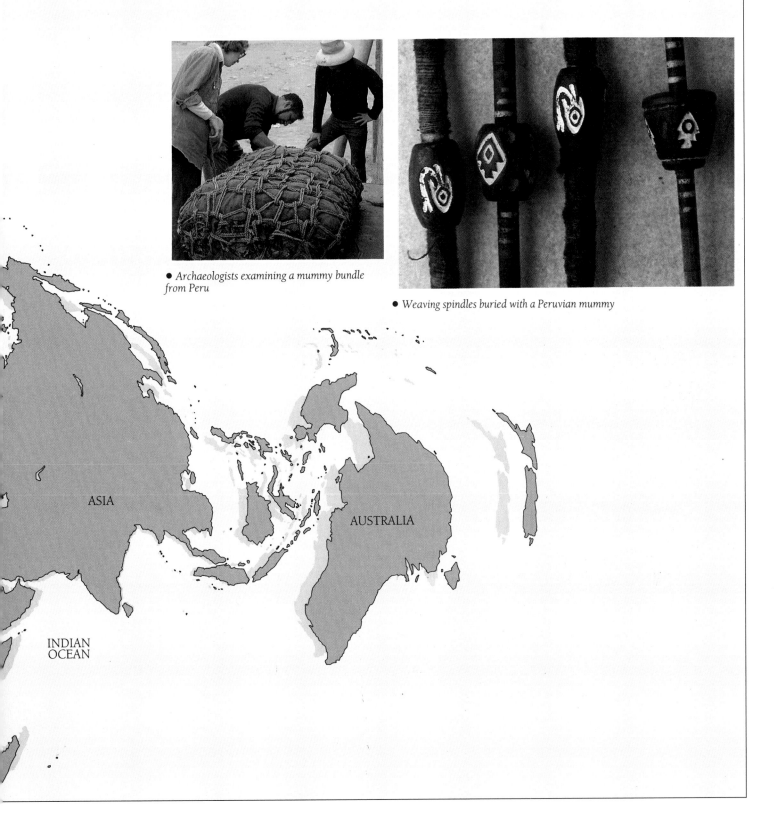

● Archaeologists examining a mummy bundle from Peru

● Weaving spindles buried with a Peruvian mummy

ASIA

AUSTRALIA

INDIAN OCEAN

TELL MARDIKH: THE EBLA TABLETS

Generations of archaeologists had read of a mysterious state named Ebla, on tablets from Sumerian and Akkadian cities in Mesopotamia. But the location of the ancient city was lost, except for vague references to a military campaign by the Akkadian monarch Naram-Sin, who ruled between 2254BC and 2218BC. His armies defeated 'Amanus, the Cedar Mountain, and the Upper Sea . . . Naram-Sin the mighty has won Armanum and Ebla, and beyond the Euphrates bank, up to Ulisum . . .'. Then, in 1968, Italian archaeologist Paolo Matthiae recovered the basalt torso of a votive statue in the occupation levels of Tell Mardikh, southwest of Aleppo in northern Syria. The figure had been dedicated by Ibbit-Lim, son of Igrish-Khep, ruler of Ebla. This statue was the key to one of the most important Near Eastern archaeological discoveries in recent memory.

Matthiae's excavations soon established that Ebla had flourished between 2400BC and 1600BC. But the most important discovery came in 1974, when his workmen uncovered some imposing mud brick structures – part of the Royal Palace of Ebla. Inside these structures the excavators found 42 cuneiform tablets, written in a hitherto-unknown Semitic language. The following seasons not only showed that the palace had been destroyed by Naram-Sin around 2250BC, but also led to the discovery of Ebla's State Archives. More than 15,000 clay tablets came to light in 1976, and many more still in subsequent years.

Ebla's Royal Palace was a complex structure, enlarged by several generations of monarchs. A monumental gateway was the main entrance to the palace and perhaps to the city's fortified citadel as well. A tower enclosed the ceremonial staircase at the intersection of the northern and eastern façades of a large audience court. This was a wide courtyard with wood-columned porches along the façades. The court was a vast open space 52m x 20m (170ft 6in x 65ft 6in), and separated the private houses of the lower city from the royal precinct. The king sat in audience on a podium on the north side.

The palace had a northwestern wing that was built on terraces on the steep slopes of the city mound. The wing consisted of two long rooms, which had been burned when Naram-Sin sacked the city. One room once contained a fine wooden table and armchair richly carved, engraved and inlaid with shell. A frieze of lions assaulting bulls, of fights between heroes and lions and of duels between warriors also once adorned

*Cuneiform tablets from the Palace of Ebla (Palace G) with lexical texts, **left**, and undeciphered texts, **below**. The few texts that have been deciphered tell of expanding international relations and a successful military campaign in Ebla against Mari, some detail the distribution of spoils from victory, and others contain book-keeping records.*

Left *View of the Monumental Gateway, seen from the west. It was the main entrance to Ebla's Royal Palace 'G', which flourished between 2,400BC and 1,600BC.* Below centre *The Palace Archive Room, or Library, seen from the south. It contained the biggest and most complete archive of tablets ever found from the third millennium.* Bottom *The fire that destroyed Ebla baked the tablets so hard that many of them remain intact to this day.*

the table. The southern room in the north-western wing was where the original 42 tablets were found, as well as cylinder seal impressions on clay 'envelopes' that once belonged to the high officials of the palace.

The administrative wing, in the southern area of the palace, had its own entrance with a wide vestibule. The north end of the vestibule led to the palace library, a room 3.5m x 5.5m (11ft 6in x 18ft) with wooden shelves on three walls. In the library, Matthiae found about 14,000 tablets, which had once been stacked on these shelves. He ingeniously traced the design of the bookshelves from the holes left by the supports in the floor and walls.

When fire destroyed the palace, the square tablets collapsed onto the floor into several levels. The tablets had originally been stacked next to one another with their faces towards the walls, in series separated by large wedges made of broken tablets. Many smaller, rounded tablets lay under the shelves on the floor, together with much larger clay documents that contained as many as 30 columns of cuneiform with 50 lines on each face.

All the Ebla texts are written in an archaic Semitic language, a language with significant connections to Ugaritic and Phoenician. Many of the tablets hold long reports of Ebla's important international trade in textiles and clothes with neigh-bouring states and cities. There are ad-ministrative tablets dealing with taxes and salaries paid to high officials. Some texts list the rations and drink supplied to diplo-matic missions and officials who travelled on Ebla's business. The diplomatic and pol-itical tablets offer fascinating perspectives on the relations between Ebla and other Syrian and Mesopotamian cities. Matthiae has reconstructed a complete dynasty of five or six Eblan kings. Most important of all, one group of tablets listed 3,000 Sumerian words and their Canaanite equivalents – the language of the Ebla tablets. Canaanite is a direct ancestor of modern Hebrew.

Epigrapher Giovanni Pettinato, who deciphered many of the tablets, was able to piece together from them an idea of Ebla's constant negotiations with dozens of other states as far away as Cyprus and the Euphrates. No fewer than 30,000 people lived in Ebla at the height of its prosperity, with as many as 12,000 of them serving the palace in various functions, presiding over a regional population of more than 250,000 people.

Pettinato identified a great king named Ebrium, who ruled Ebla about 2400BC, and also discovered that the city's inhabitants worshiped a god named Ya, a name that seemed to him to resemble the name for God in the Hebrew Bible (Yahweh). Carried away with enthusiasm, Pettinato claimed that there was a clear connection between the civilization at Ebla and that of Israel and the Hebrew Bible. Ebrium, he claimed, bore a name that was similar to that of Eber, a Hebrew patriarch who was a direct ancestor of Abraham. These Hebrew Bible connections raised a storm of protest, for most experts violently disagreed with Pettinato. Today, most scholars concur that there is a solid linguistic connection between Ebla and the Bible, but Pettinato's more specific Biblical claims are almost certainly unsubstantiated.

Even without these connections, the Ebla discoveries are among the most important of this century. They reveal a hitherto unknown language and an almost unknown civilization that was a powerful force in the Near East 4,500 years ago.

A PALACE SACRIFICE

The Minoan civilization of Crete was first discovered in 1900 by the great British archaeologist Sir Arthur Evans. He devoted much of his life to excavating the Palace of Minos at Knossos, a great palace that was a royal residence, commercial centre and ritual complex all in one. Perhaps this was the home of the fabled Minotaur – half human, half bull – commemorated in Athenian legend centuries after the Minoan civilization declined, after 1500BC.

Evans believed that the Minoans were a gentle peaceful people, who traded the length and breadth of the Aegean. They were skilled farmers, who cultivated a fertile countryside and brought their produce to great centres like Knossos. Indeed, the image of the Minoans as 'civilized' people persisted long after Evans' death at the beginning of World War II. But recent discoveries have produced evidence that the Minoans may have engaged in child sacrifice and perhaps even ritual cannibalism, a far cry from the pastoral religion attributed to them by Evans three quarters of a century ago.

Peter Warren of the British School of Archaeology at Athens has been excavating areas to the northwest of the palace since 1978. His main objective was to document the emergence of Knossos as an urban centre farther back in time even than 2000BC. But instead, his excavations revealed something quite different – traces of sophisticated rituals.

One of the purposes of the Warren dig was to excavate an area on the west side of the Knossos Stratigraphical Museum, some 350m (383yds) northwest of the palace,

before the museum was enlarged. But the rescue excavation soon turned into a spectacular discovery. Warren uncovered a substantial structure, soon called the North House, with basement rooms and an open court. He also revealed a paved road that ran along the south façade of the North House. This was probably the royal road to the palace, which the newly excavated building faced.

Judging from both the architecture and potsherds in the rooms, the North House was built about 1500BC and was destroyed in a violent earthquake some 50 years later. The house burned as it fell. The first floor and basement ceilings collapsed, burying the contents of both ground floor and basement underground. Later, a new building rose on the site, sealing off the site for more than 3,000 years.

No one knows what purpose the North House served, but it was clearly an imposing and important building with fine plastered and masonry walls and floors. Frescoes adorned some rooms, and large clay pots (known to archaeologists as *pithoi*) held collections of ritual vessels. A large basement room still contained what appears to be a stone bench. Perhaps it was a cult room. Two smaller basement rooms were separated from this chamber by a

north-south passage. One of these yielded children's bones.

Warren was confronted with an intricate archaeological jigsaw puzzle. He pieced together the complex pottery fragments – the remains of at least 37 vessels, most of which had originally been stored in large *pithoi*. They had once stood in a ground floor room, but the earthquake had toppled them into the basement. Many of the smaller vessels were *rhytons*, vessels used for pouring ritual libations. All of them had a small hole in the base through which the liquid could be allowed to drip slowly. Many years before, in the palace itself, Arthur Evans had excavated a frieze in which pairs of men sit opposite one another performing drinking rituals in the presence of a priestess or a deity.

Some of the *rhytons* were exquisite vessels, bearing figure-of-eight shields and squills, as well as a depiction of a *gorgoneion*, a mythical creature with wild eyes, large nose and protruding tongue. Warren realized that this was an important discovery, because he knew that this was the great Minoan goddess of nature, often shown as a snake goddess.

Other scenes on the vessels showed shields in figure-of-eight designs. He knew from finds elsewhere that shields were

Left *View of the basements of the North House, in Knossos, Crete, which was destroyed in about 1450BC. The Cult Room Basement is the large room on the upper left part of the picture. The room at the bottom centre of the image is where the childrens' skulls and other bones were found.*

Below *The reconstructed skulls of two children, aged about 8 and 11 years respectively found in the Childrens' Room of the North House. They also date to about 1450BC, which suggests that children were sacrificed, possibly in a ritual to evoke the goodwill of a nature deity and ensure bountiful crops.*

Above right *A miniature amphora, or rhyton, depicting figure-of-eight shields which were a symbol of possession by the Minoan goddess of nature. This vessel came from the Cult Room Basement and dates to about 1450BC.*

often symbols of the nature goddess, sometimes associated with ecstatic dancing and nature rituals.

Some 304 unburned human bone fragments came from the carbonized levels of the small room close to the cult chamber in the basement. Warren and his colleagues pieced the bones together and reconstructed the skulls of two children aged about 8 and 11 respectively. A set of ritual drinking vessels lay in an adjacent room. The children were in good health at death, their bones bearing ample signs that the flesh had been cut away, just as a priest would do with a sacrificial animal. Warren also found the remains of a slaughtered sheep with the children's bones. There was even a knife mark on one of the neck vertebrae, as if the sheep's throat had been cut. Warren reached a startling conclusion: that the two children had been killed and their flesh was cooked and possibly eaten in a sacrificial ritual for a nature deity – perhaps to ensure the fertility of crops and soil.

What had happened in the North House? All Warren had to go on were the fragmentary bones and broken pottery vessels in the burned room. He ruled out simple murder, because the bones of the victims were unlikely to have received such elab-

orate cutting treatment. Nor do the children seem to have been killed during an attack on Knossos, for there are no signs of wounds or of a siege of the city. Nor had the children's bones been carefully prepared for burial long after they died – a common practice in Minoan civilization. It seems almost certain that the two bodies were cast into the basement a very short time before the earthquake toppled the North House.

Did the Minoans sacrifice children? Warren remembered a Minoan ring impression found at another Minoan site. It shows a large seated goddess with a girl in a skirt standing in front of her. A hilted sword is held over the child, perhaps held for the sacrifice. It is, of course, almost impossible for archaeologists accurately to reconstruct ancient religions. But there are some early Greek myths that might have originated in ancient Minoan beliefs and that may reveal something of the Minoan religion. One of the myths concerns the young god Zagreus, a deity connected with fertility, who was carefully guarded during his early years. But the Titans lured him away with toys and Zagreus was torn to pieces and eaten. He subsequently reappeared and was brought to life again. Warren wonders whether the children in the basement were sacrificed and their flesh perhaps eaten as a ritual re-enactment of the killing and devouring of the youthful fertility god Zagreus. Perhaps the Minoan priests identified themselves in this way with the reborn god, and with the Earth Mother – Zagreus' consort and the ultimate source of all fertility. Certainly the dramatic finds in the North House at Knossos give us a completely different view of the Minoans, one quite unsuspected in Arthur Evans' pioneering days.

THE INCA OF PERU

We tend to think of the past in terms of spectacular discoveries such as the royal library at Ebla. But some of the most exciting advances in archaeology have come from combining modern archaeology with neglected information from long-forgotten archives. Such research has given us new insights into the mysterious Inca empire of Peru.

When Francisco Pizarro and his conquistadores penetrated the central Andes in AD1532, they found themselves at the heart of a vast empire controlled by the Inca from their capital in the southern highlands of Peru. Their great empire – they called it *Tawantinsuyu*, 'Land of the Four Quarters' – extended from the southern frontiers of Colombia, southward along the coasts and highlands of Ecuador and Peru, then inland to highland Bolivia and northwestern Argentina. It measured more than 4,300km (2,672 miles) from end to end. But for all its size and splendour, Tawantinsuyu lasted only a century. It was brought down in a few months by a few hundred Spanish adventurers. For generations, archaeologists and historians have puzzled over the meteoric rise of the Inca empire. It is only recently that they have begun to understand how Tawantinsuyu came to be.

The Inca themselves stated grandiloquently that the Andean world was in a state of chaos before they mastered it. In fact, nothing could be farther from the truth. Complex Peruvian civilizations had emerged at least 4,000 years before the Inca Empire, between 2700BC and 1800BC. We know that Peruvian civilization alternated between periods of great diversity and times when there was far greater cultural and religious unity. The last of these unifying phases was the so-called Late Horizon, the period of Tawantinsuyu, between AD1438 and AD1532. The forces that brought the Peruvians together were predominantly religious, one of them a deep veneration for ancestors.

Throughout the Andean world, everyone believed in the power of the spirits of the dead, of the ancestors. In every village, every town, the ancestors of one's kin group were venerated as the protectors of life – and their bodies were treated as sacred objects. One seventeenth-century Catholic priest wrote that 'their [the Indians'] greatest veneration is for their *mallquis* . . . which are the bones or mummies of their pagan progenitors'. The ancestors spoke through these mummies and there were special priests who interpreted their oracular pronouncements.

The Peruvian obsession with the dead dates to long before Inca times. When

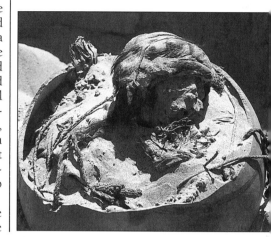

individuals died, some of their personal effects were destroyed; others were buried with them. Their descendants would return to the grave at intervals to make offerings. The ancestors' bodies took part in processions and other festivals. To neglect sacrifices and other rites for the ancestors was to invite the wrath of the spirits.

This cult of the dead in Inca society bound people to their kinsfolk, to the land owned by their kin group and to acceptable bounds of behaviour. But the demands of the dead were relatively small. Their shrines were tended by old men, no longer capable of heavy manual labour. Plots of farming land were reserved to feed ancestral mummies, but these demands did not place excessive strains on their kin.

All this changed when an Inca ruler named Viracocha embarked on an ambitious campaign of conquest in the early fifteenth century. He extended Inca boundaries by adroit political marriages and systematic conquest. One of his sons named Pachakuti, 'He Who Remakes the World', came to power in 1438 and continued his father's aggressive policies, bringing the broad expanse of Tawan-tinsuyu into being. In the process, he remade the royal ancestor cult in such a way that it forced its successors to conquer more and more territory.

Pachakuti was the *Sapa Inca,* the 'Unique Inca'. He had the right to govern, wage war and impose taxes, powers that passed to his successor, one of his sons. But the new Inca order was so arranged that all Pachakuti's residences, lands, servants and belongings were still his property, vested in a social group that comprised all his male descendants *except* his successor. This social group, known as the *panaqa,* served

Left *The pitted surface of a prehistoric cemetery in Peru relates a sorry tale and dramatizes the difficulties archaeologists face in reconstructing ancient burial customs in many countries. Looters destroy such burial grounds in search of well-preserved textiles, mummies, pots, and precious metal objects.* **Above left and right** *The heads of two mummies from the Ica Valley near Nazca, Peru, dating to between AD600 and AD800. Many Peruvian mummies, especially those of the earlier Paracas culture, were buried with richly decorated textiles,* **above right***. They are known for the woven cotton masks tied on the outside of the mummy bundles. The Inca of the highlands revered their mummified rulers, parading them in public at festivals such as the 'Feast of the Dead' each November. One such festival was recorded by the seventeenth-century Spanish chronicler Guaman Poma de Ayala,* **right***.*

Right *The Inca Emperor Pachakuti drawn by the seventeenth-century chronicler Guaman Poma de Ayala. Pachakuti was the first Inca ruler to foster expansionist ambitions among his people, in about the year AD1438. He was also intent on establishing Cuzco as a great Inca capital. It was he who founded the royal mummy cult that was to play such an important part in the expansion of the Inca Empire.* **Below** *The Tomb of the Inca Emperor Pachakuti, at Kenko, near Cuzco.*

as the dead ruler's court, maintained his mummy and perpetuated his court. Later chroniclers describe how the rulers' mummies would attend religious ceremonies, take part in rain-making rituals, even visit one another. 'They sat them down in the plaza in a row, in order of seniority, and the servants who looked after them ate and drank there . . . The dead toasted one another, and they drank to the living and vice versa; this was done by their ministers in their names', wrote chronicler Bernabé Cobo in 1653.

The Inca did not think of their past rulers as 'dead' in the western sense. They were maintained in state at vast expense, as symbols of continuing life. The royal mummies were the visible links between the Inca people and the gods. So important were they to Inca religion that it took the Spaniards 27 years to find and destroy the last royal mummy.

This system of 'split inheritance' left each new Inca ruler rich in privilege but poor in property. The existing tax revenues came in the form of labour to cultivate public lands, man the armies, or work on public works projects. Under age-old notions of reciprocity, the ruler or the beneficiary of the labour had to feed and entertain those who worked. This meant having the land from which the food could come to feed them. But the proceeds of taxes imposed by a deceased ruler remained his after death. So a new ruler could accumulate his own property only by increasing revenues through new taxes – and that meant additional people to donate their labour.

Every ruler had two options: either to increase the tax obligation for existing subjects, which meant that he had to have more land with which to support them, or to conquer new territories, add them to the empire and impose taxes on his new subjects. Without land an Inca ruler could not build a loyal following and could not govern; above all his cult would not be sustained after his death.

After combing through thousands of complicated Spanish colonial legal documents dealing with land titles, archaeologists are convinced that split inheritance was a major cause of the rise of the Inca empire within a brief century. And the brilliant rulers who headed the empire were superb propagandists. They constantly reminded everyone that they were gods, that their interests were everyone's interests and that the welfare of every citizen of the empire, however humble, depended on the prosperity of all Inca rulers, past and present. The result was a grandiose, volatile empire that controlled the destinies of millions of South Americans.

A PERUVIAN MUMMY

Thousands of Peruvian mummy bundles have been looted and excavated on the dry Pacific coast of that country, but only a handful of them have been described or unwrapped with scientific care. Some 500

Reyno has ta chile y se to dasu cor se lleca

pacha qui

Right *Spinning and weaving equipment found in a basket buried with an Inca mummy from Ancon, Peru. The woman was probably buried about 500 years ago.*

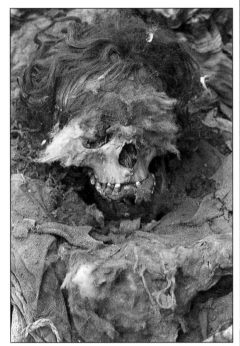

Above *The head of the mummy from Ancon. The woman was buried with her hair loose, in a cross-legged position. The numerous spinning and weaving artifacts buried with her,* **right***, testify to the importance of weaving to coastal peoples of the time – it was the primary work of women.*

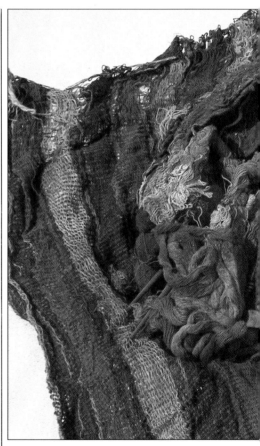

Above *The contents of a cloth bag buried with the mummy included additional weaving spindles, maize cobs, thread, beans, and pods.*

years ago, a woman died in a small coastal village near the modern town of Ancon in central Peru. Her body was ceremonially prepared for burial, wrapped in a mummy bundle and then buried. The dry sand of the desert desiccated and dried the mummy. It lay undisturbed until 1976, when a bulldozer unearthed the long-forgotten woman. Fortunately, archaeologists Rogger Ravines and Karen Stothert were able to unwrap and photograph her.

By unwrapping the body, Ravines and Stothert were able to tell what happened during the funeral, who was buried and when the ceremony took place. First, the body was dressed in a sleeveless tunic of plain cotton fabric, fastened over the shoulder with a copper pin. The woman was laid out on a large piece of cloth, with feet bare and hair loose. The fabric served as the first shroud. Next, her head was placed on a roll of woven cloth stuffed with cotton and vegetable matter, and a piece of silver was inserted between her teeth. Perhaps her relatives believed that valuable possessions like this would mean that she would not have to work in the afterlife.

A layer of cotton and what appears to

Left *The mummy bundle, which included layers of cloth as well as weaving implements, was finally enclosed in a knotted and woven rope bag. It was then wrapped in a woven reed mat and buried with offerings of food.*

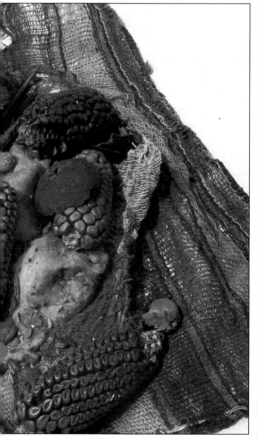

have been a mantle covered the woman's face and her chest. Her ring-adorned hands were wrapped and tied in cotton, her arms arranged across her chest. A wicker basket containing her weaving kit was placed on top of her body, as close to hand in death as it had been in life. Next her legs were drawn up into a cross-legged position with her feet tucked into her lap. Raw cotton was packed into the space between her thighs, together with small gifts. More offerings wrapped in cloth, perhaps her personal possessions, lay near the head and shoulders. The shell of a *Spondylus*, for thousands of years a Peruvian food of the gods, lay wrapped in cloth beside the pillow. It came from coastal Ecuador, more than 1,000km (621 miles) away.

The first beige shroud – a coarse cloth with green and maroon stripes – was then folded tightly over the body from both sides and ends and sewn tightly in place. The body was tied at the neck, around the chest and at the hips with rope, then lifted onto a square of maroon cloth. Large quantities of leaves were stuffed around the body, so that the second shroud could be drawn over the corpse to form a rectangular bundle. This was sewn and bound into a net bag 110cm (43⅓in) long and 50cm (19½in) wide.

The mourners then laid out another piece of cloth. They set the bundle on top and arranged additional gifts around and on the bundle. These included cotton distaffs, another *Spondylus* shell, vegetables, weaving tools, even brightly decorated miniature shirts that substituted for larger garments. A beautiful wicker basket on the

centre of the bundle contained coloured thread, dyeing materials, and still more weaving implements. When the third shroud was sewn in place, the bundle was crammed with maize offerings, nets and other gifts. The completed bundle was lashed to the supports of a loom, perhaps the woman's own, probably to make it more rigid and easier to move, for it weighed more than 68kg (150lb).

A fourth and final white cotton shroud made up of several lengths of cloth was drawn over the bundle, stuffed with more leaves and sewn tight. The entire mummy bundle was then enclosed in a knotted and woven net bag of twisted plant fibre rope, probably made on a simple loom laid out on the ground. Two workers – they had different techniques – pegged out 15 rows of knots for the bottom of the bag. Then they placed the bundle on the ground and removed the stake, weaving the bag into place around the bundle. The completed mummy, 120cm x 90cm (47¼in x 35½in), was now ready for transporting to the burial ground, where it was interred in a reed mat with gourds and jars containing food offerings.

The mourners used more than 17m (56ft) of textiles for the shrouds alone. Using a local loom, this work would have taken more than 500 hours. Cloth was the most important status symbol in ancient Peruvian society. It was the commodity that the Inca rulers used to reward their loyal subjects, to worship their gods and to pay their armies. It was even more vital in death, a symbol of social status that was to follow the wearer into the afterlife.

FROM IRON AGE TO IRON BRIDGE

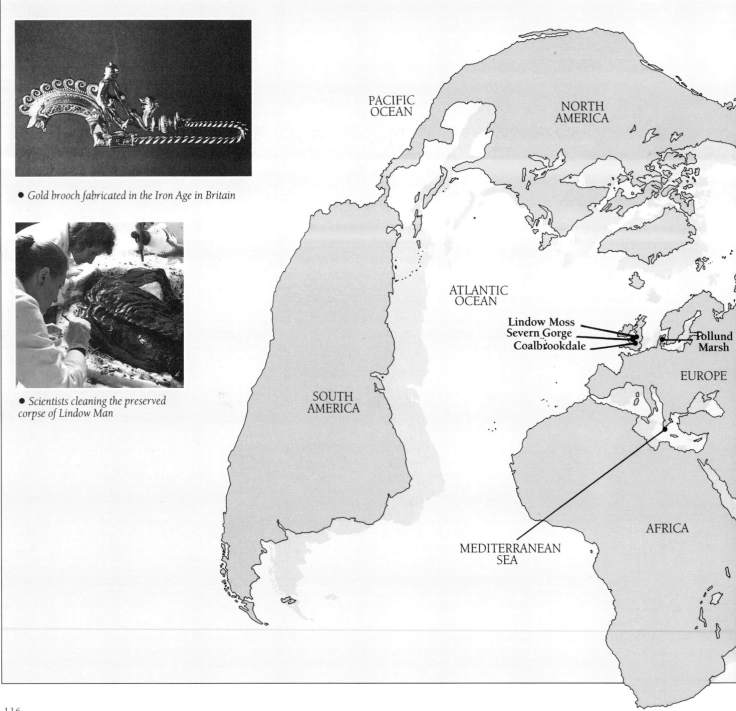

• *Gold brooch fabricated in the Iron Age in Britain*

• *Scientists cleaning the preserved corpse of Lindow Man*

PACIFIC
OCEAN

NORTH
AMERICA

ATLANTIC
OCEAN

Lindow Moss
Severn Gorge
Coalbrookdale

Tollund
Marsh

EUROPE

SOUTH
AMERICA

MEDITERRANEAN
SEA

AFRICA

In the last twenty years archaeologists have come across some astounding discoveries. Among the most amazing are the well-preserved bodies found in the bogs of England and northern Europe. Faces from prehistory . . . these are the special moments when the archaeologist gazes on an ancient countenance, or excavates not a blurred impression of the past but a specific incident that changed history. But archaeology is not only concerned with prehistory; it spans the entire spectrum of human history, from the places visited by our earliest ancestors and the early cities that they founded, to the places where modern history was made.

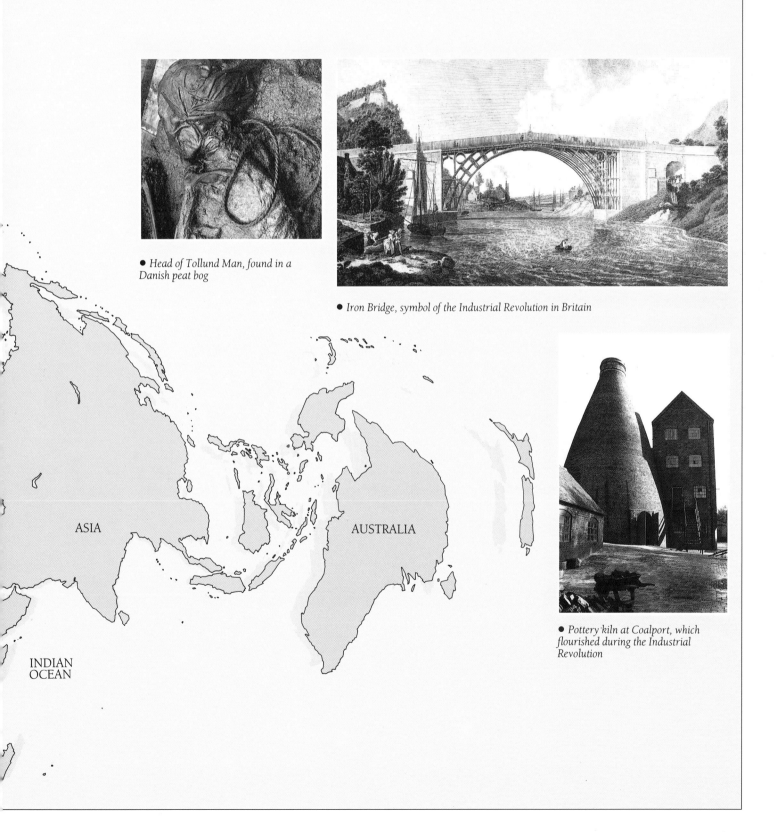

● Head of Tollund Man, found in a Danish peat bog

● Iron Bridge, symbol of the Industrial Revolution in Britain

● Pottery kiln at Coalport, which flourished during the Industrial Revolution

ASIA

AUSTRALIA

INDIAN OCEAN

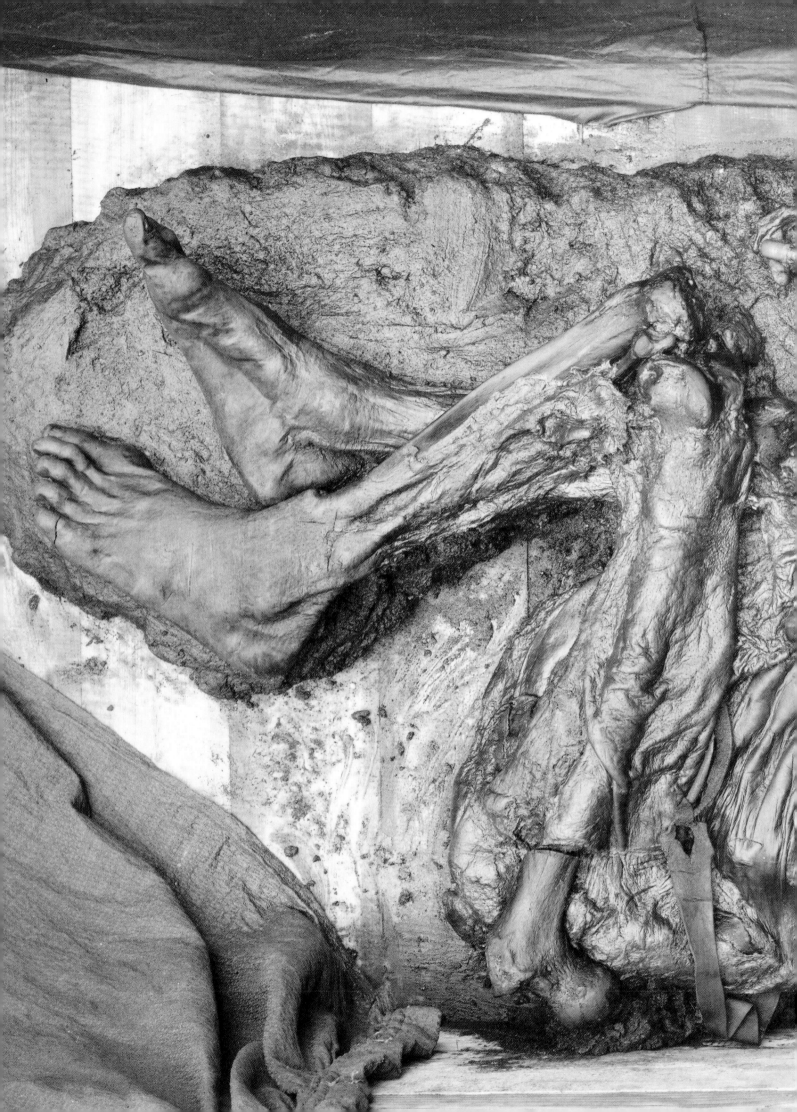

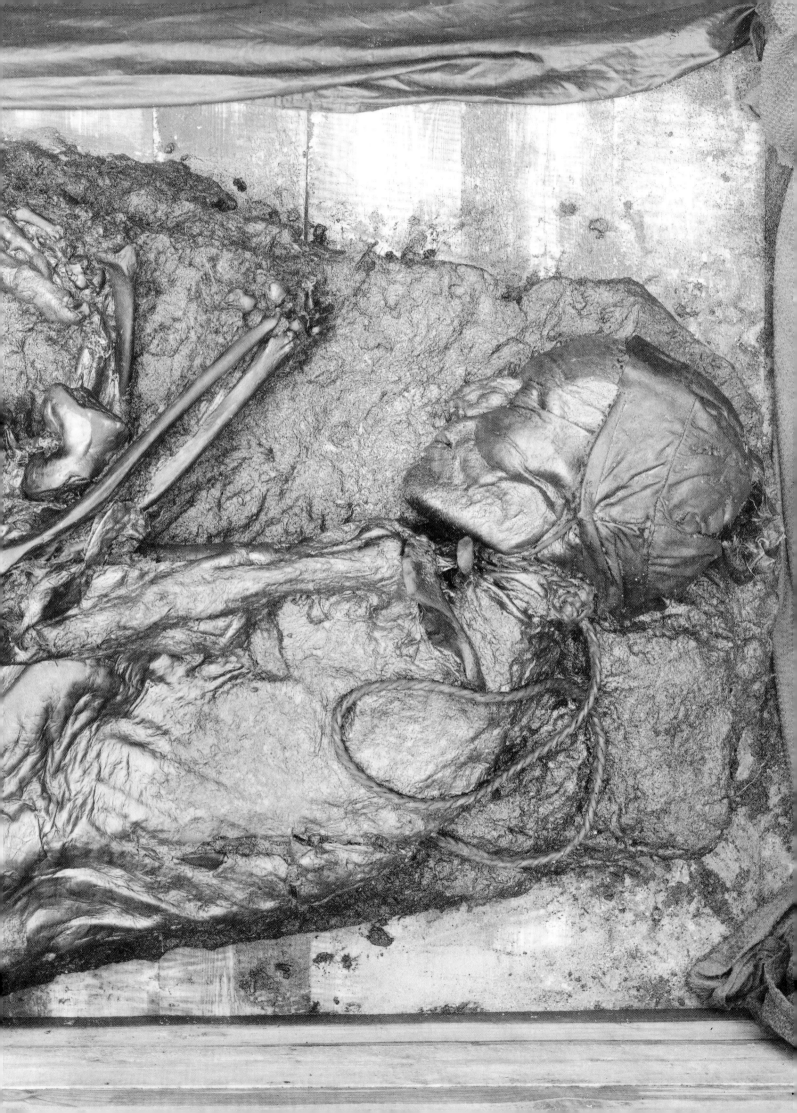

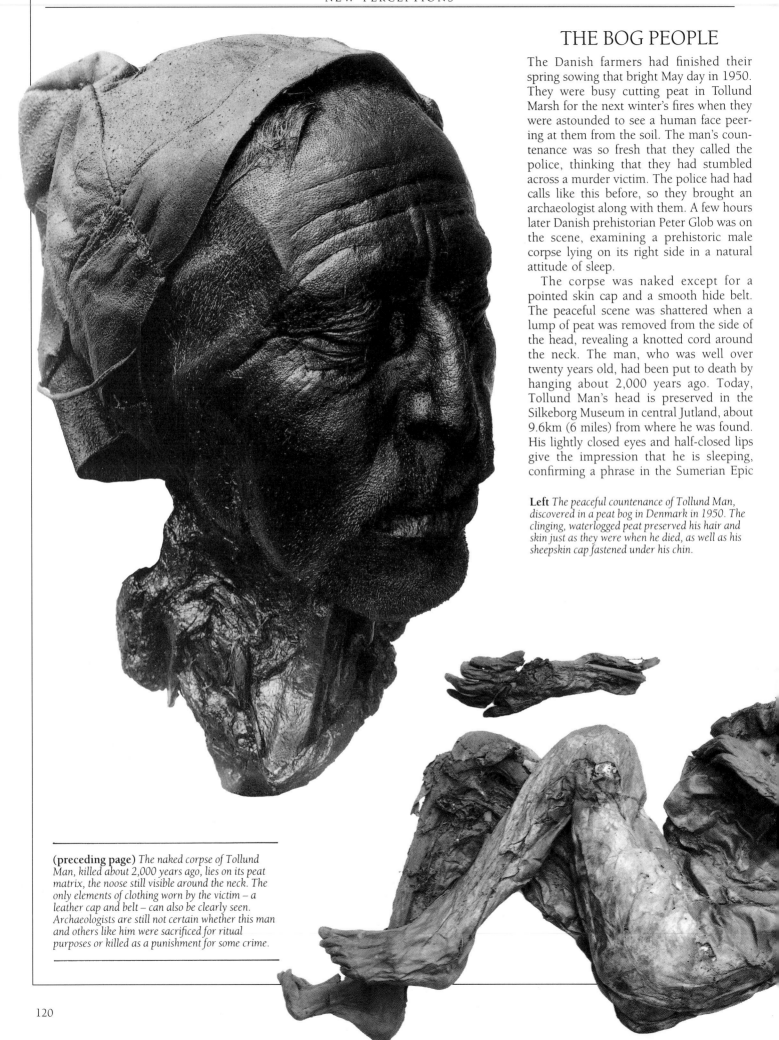

THE BOG PEOPLE

The Danish farmers had finished their spring sowing that bright May day in 1950. They were busy cutting peat in Tollund Marsh for the next winter's fires when they were astounded to see a human face peering at them from the soil. The man's countenance was so fresh that they called the police, thinking that they had stumbled across a murder victim. The police had had calls like this before, so they brought an archaeologist along with them. A few hours later Danish prehistorian Peter Glob was on the scene, examining a prehistoric male corpse lying on its right side in a natural attitude of sleep.

The corpse was naked except for a pointed skin cap and a smooth hide belt. The peaceful scene was shattered when a lump of peat was removed from the side of the head, revealing a knotted cord around the neck. The man, who was well over twenty years old, had been put to death by hanging about 2,000 years ago. Today, Tollund Man's head is preserved in the Silkeborg Museum in central Jutland, about 9.6km (6 miles) from where he was found. His lightly closed eyes and half-closed lips give the impression that he is sleeping, confirming a phrase in the Sumerian Epic

Left *The peaceful countenance of Tollund Man, discovered in a peat bog in Denmark in 1950. The clinging, waterlogged peat preserved his hair and skin just as they were when he died, as well as his sheepskin cap fastened under his chin.*

(preceding page) *The naked corpse of Tollund Man, killed about 2,000 years ago, lies on its peat matrix, the noose still visible around the neck. The only elements of clothing worn by the victim – a leather cap and belt – can also be clearly seen. Archaeologists are still not certain whether this man and others like him were sacrificed for ritual purposes or killed as a punishment for some crime.*

of Gilgamesh written about 5,000 years ago: 'the dead and the sleeping, how they resemble one another.'

In August 1984, another team of peat-cutters, this time at Lindow Moss in Cheshire, England, accidently unearthed another well-preserved prehistoric body, once again that of a man. Again the police were called in, but soon archaeologists were summoned. They gathered together a team of medical specialists and environmental experts to study this Iron Age corpse that had been preserved from decay in oxygen-free, waterlogged conditions. Back in the British Museum, the corpse was freed from the peat, then dissected with infinite care. There were no artifacts or funerary pots with the body, so the archaeologists had to rely on radiocarbon dating and pollen analysis to date the man. Lindow Man is believed to have died during the Iron Age, just over 2,000 years ago.

Lindow Man was about 25 years old and about 1.7m (5ft 6in) tall. He was red-headed, and his hands showed that he was not accustomed to manual labour. Perhaps he was a noble. His stomach contents revealed that he had eaten a meal of bread or millet porridge shortly before his death and that he had suffered from worms. The un-

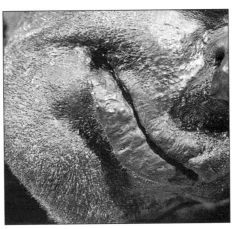

The chin of Lindow Man, **left**, who was found in Cheshire, England in 1984, was so well preserved that you can still see two or three days' beard growth on it. Grauballe Man, **below**, another Danish find, was buried in about 55BC. He was found naked, with his throat cut.

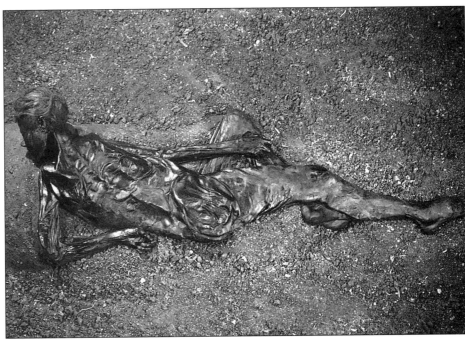

Below Another peat body from Denmark, this time a woman from Huldre Fen, discovered more than 100 years ago. Her right arm may have been hacked off in life. She was buried in AD95 with garments which included a lambskin cape, a checked shirt and a scarf, as well as a comb made of horn and a necklace with two amber beads. These suggest a high position in society.

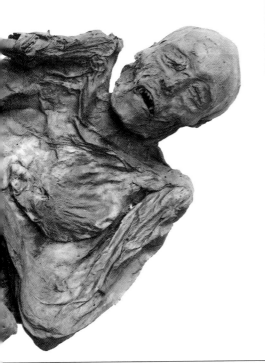

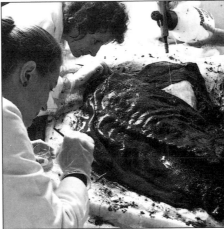

Above Distilled water was sprayed onto Lindow Man's skin to keep it moist. Beetle expert Maureen Girling, at the top of the picture, searches for insect debris close to the body surface.

Above A portrait from prehistory. This is an expert reconstruction of Lindow Man's face based on careful measurements and an evaluation of his probable appearance before decay set in.

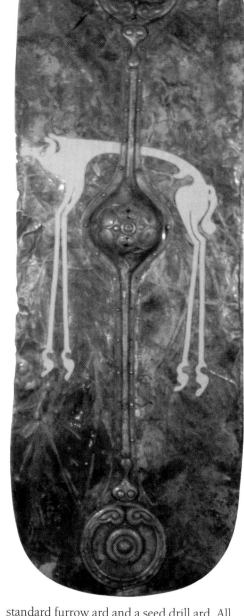

Evidence of ancient diet is revealed by the microscope. Scientists were able to identify a fragment of cereal chaff, probably barley, from Lindow Man's gut, **right**, *and* **below**, *a fragment of either wheat or rye. These may have been eaten in the form of a cereal 'gruel'.*

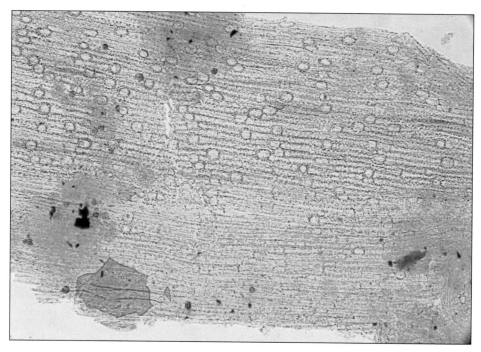

fortunate man had met a brutal end. He had been felled with a savage blow to the head, then been garrotted and his throat was cut before his body was thrown into the bog. His gruesome death seems more than a simple murder. Perhaps it was a ritual killing, conceivably an offering to a Celtic war god, not an uncommon practice in Iron Age society. For all the teamwork and all the minute pathology research, Lindow Man's end remains a tantalizing mystery.

IRON AGE TECHNOLOGY

In Britain, the time of Lindow Man, in the centuries immediately before the Roman invasion in AD43, was a period of relative stability and success founded on a sound agricultural base. Classical documentary sources, confirmed by archaeological excavation and field work, refer to a heavily populated landscape not only in the south, but on a countrywide scale. Both good and poor land was exploited for arable agriculture, traces of which survive in many areas in the form of field systems despite subsequent agricultural activity.

The principal cereals of the period were emmer and spelt wheats and barley, although the farmer had at his disposal a wide range of crop plants including the legumes, peas and beans, as well as oats and probably rye. Farming was necessarily labour intensive, as it continued to be right up to and beyond the Industrial Revolution. However, the farmer had a full range of agricultural implements, many of them forged from iron. The most important of these was the plough of the period, called an 'ard'; it lacked a mould board and therefore stirred rather than inverted the soil. There was also a 'sod buster', which enabled the farmers to make virgin or old fallow land arable. In addition they used a standard furrow ard and a seed drill ard. All these implements were pulled by cattle.

A number of tools remain from this age, although not as many as one might hope because of the corrodible nature of iron. Among those that have been found are a complete carpenter's tool kit, with chisels, mallets, hammers and saws, all using iron. Smiths at that time forged on relatively small hand forges, about a third of the size of the modern anvil. But they did not restrict their skills to making agricultural and carpentry implements. Their remarkably fine metalwork included torcs, shields, swords, equestrian equipment, jewellery and the like. Many pieces are beautifully inlaid with enamel and all exhibit the brilliant Celtic art form based on the open-ended curve. As well as iron, the metals employed by the smiths were gold, silver and bronze. The creation of such beautiful pieces demonstrates a complete understanding of the technology involved and a

*Beautifully worked metal testifies to expert Iron Age technology in the centuries before Julius Caesar invaded Britain in 55BC. Celtic artisans lavished their bronze-working skill on ornate brooches, like this one from Blandford, Dorset, **left**, and on shields: **below**, the Wandsworth circular shield dredged from the River Thames; **far left** the rectangular Witham shield with a metal inlay. Gold torcs such as,the Snettisham torc, **bottom**, were prized ornamants. Gold artifacts like this are often found in Britain today when the ground is being ploughed, or during quarrying work, and may suggest that their original owners abandoned them in times of trouble.*

remarkable sympathy with the metals.

The space of time from the Iron Age to the Iron Bridge, a period of some 1,800 years, is in a sense a brief technological span. Despite invasions, wars, peaks and troughs in population figures, and demographic development, basic technology changed little other than in scale. It was not until the Industrial Revolution, of which Iron Bridge is the epitome, that technology actually changed and fundamentally altered society from a primarily agricultural base to an industrial one.

IRON BRIDGE AND THE INDUSTRIAL REVOLUTION

British archaeologists have recently turned their attention to decaying factories and furnaces built during the early years of the Industrial Revolution. We often think of the Industrial Revolution in terms of squalor – grinding poverty, sooty factories, decaying terrace-housing and ever-present smoke. In fact, historians have discovered that this landscape was regarded with something close to awe in the years before the great social crises of the 1830s and 1940s. Eighteenth-century tourists enjoyed not only the countryside but also the dramatic scenes at Josiah Wedgwood's potteries and the Derbyshire cotton mills. But perhaps the most spectacular attraction of all was the Iron Bridge that spanned the Severn Gorge, close to the place where the Industrial Revolution began.

The Iron Bridge is close to Coalbrookdale Ironworks, the place where coke was first used to smelt iron ore. Before 1750, the English iron industry was scattered far and wide in the countryside, especially in places where water power or charcoal were in plentiful supply. But the discovery of coke smelting changed all this. Ironworks began to concentrate around the Severn Gorge, where iron ore and coal were readily available. Blast furnaces lit up the sky all around Coalbrookdale. By 1788 this area produced about a third of all Britain's iron.

Coalbrookdale exported steam engines and iron cookware to North America. New coal-making industries moved in, among them glass and china factories, and porcelain manufacturers. The curious tourist was rewarded with spectacular sights and sounds. Blazing furnaces, smouldering piles of coke and iron ore were everywhere to be seen. Steam engines wheezed and puffed, moving wagons along rails. The steep cliffs and dense woodland of the gorge added to the dramatic effect. At the centre of this unique landscape stood the

Below *The Iron Bridge restored. This dramatic symbol of the Industrial Revolution, built in 1781, is now a pedestrian bridge.*

Right *William Williams painted this dramatic morning view of Coalbrookdale in 1777. It was still a romantic view of the countryside but one in which the beginnings of smoke pollution and industrial devastation of the landscape are evident.*

very symbol of the Industrial Revolution – the Iron Bridge.

An architect named Thomas Farnollis Pritchard suggested an iron bridge in 1773. His ambitious ideas appealed to the hard-nosed iron masters of Coalbrookdale, one of whom, Abraham Darby, supervised the construction of the bridge between 1778 and 1781. The Iron Bridge was an immediate sensation, described by one anonymous diarist as 'an elegant Arch in some ancient cathedral'. The famous and not-so-famous flocked to Coalbrookdale to admire the bridge and to watch iron furnaces being 'tapped', as they were twice every 24 hours. The visitor could see as many as 11 cannon being bored at once. None other than Thomas Jefferson purchased a print of the Iron Bridge, which hung in the White House during his Presidency.

The Iron Bridge was not an engineering miracle for long. The railway and its stupendous works soon superseded Coal-brookdale, as the Industrial Revolution came to stand for quite different phenomena – disillusionment with uncontrolled industrial growth, exploitive working conditions and smoke pollution in places like Manchester. Tourists interested in economics and business now visited great industrial cities rather than rural backwaters like Coalbrookdale. The Shropshire iron industry gradually collapsed. Its unique factories fell into neglect and disuse until the 1960s.

It was 1955 when archaeologist Michael Rix pointed to Coalbrookdale as a place of special importance to students of the Industrial Revolution. In 1959 the 250th anniversary of the first smelting of iron with coke was commemorated with the excavation of the old blast furnace at Coalbrookdale. Then, in 1968, the Ironbridge Gorge Museum Trust was formed to preserve as many industrial monuments in the area as possible. Apart from taking over several buildings of historical interest as a Museum

(preceding page) *Coalbrookdale by night, painted by Philip de Loutherbourg in 1801 at the height of public fascination with the Industrial Revolution. Although the factories and forges were later to become highly unpopular, what remains of them today provides fascinating details of the technology at that time.*

of Iron and a visitors' centre, the Trust has played a major role in restoring the Iron Bridge itself to its former glory. The north abutment was completely rebuilt, and in 1973-74 an invert concrete slab was installed in the river bed to keep the two abutments apart. The bridge was closed to vehicles in 1934, but is now a pedestrian crossing, from which you can enjoy the unique beauty of the area, just as eighteenth-century tourists did.

The Trust has done far more. It is excavating the Bedlam Furnace, which operated from 1757 to the 1830s. The excavations move slowly, because each dig requires a lengthy period of conservation before more digging can take place. Two of the three furnaces have been excavated. Each still contains the remnants of its large 'charge' of coke, iron ore and limestone, partially fused by the heat. The archaeologists have shown that air was blown into the furnace from three sides. They found the walls of an engine house which once housed the steam engine that pumped water from the river to power the bellows.

At the Blists Open Air Museum you can see the most ambitious results of the Trust's work. A 17ha (42-acre) site is devoted to ironworks, brickworks, mines, railways and a nineteenth-century canal preserved in situ. The eastern boundary of the museum is formed by an inclined canal plane that once lifted canal boats 64m (210ft) down the side of the Severn Gorge, over a gradient of one in five, using iron rails. Three blast furnaces have been restored, and many buildings and machines have been transferred to the site, including a steam winding engine which was used to raise and lower miners in a pit shaft. The Trust plans to operate a wrought iron furnace at the museum, using the very types of steam hammers and steam-powered rolling mills that were used in Coalbrookdale in the early days of the Industrial Revolution.

Today, the Ironbridge region is quiet and peaceful. No flames leap into the night sky, the air is no longer smoke-filled, the masts of coasting vessels no longer crowd the banks of the Severn. But an inspiring, long-term archaeological project tells us much about the roots of twentieth-century industrial civilization.

Top *The Ironbridge Gorge Museum Trust has reconstructed many of the buildings and ironworks at what was once the heart of the Industrial Revolution. In the foreground is an iron canal boat of the type that once plied the waters of the Severn canal system. Many of the factories and industrial centres of the nineteenth century lay along the River Severn.* **Above** *Volunteers dressed in contemporary costume roll wrought-iron the way it was done in the early nineteenth century.*

Above *A Victorian public house offers refreshment in the reconstructed township at the Blists Hill Open Air Museum.*

Top *The pottery kiln at the Coalport China Museum. Coalport china was produced here until 1926; now the kiln serves as a museum for its old manufacturing techniques.*

Above *The chemist's shop in the Blists Hill township with all the original fittings and jars.*

UNDERWATER ARCHAEOLOGY

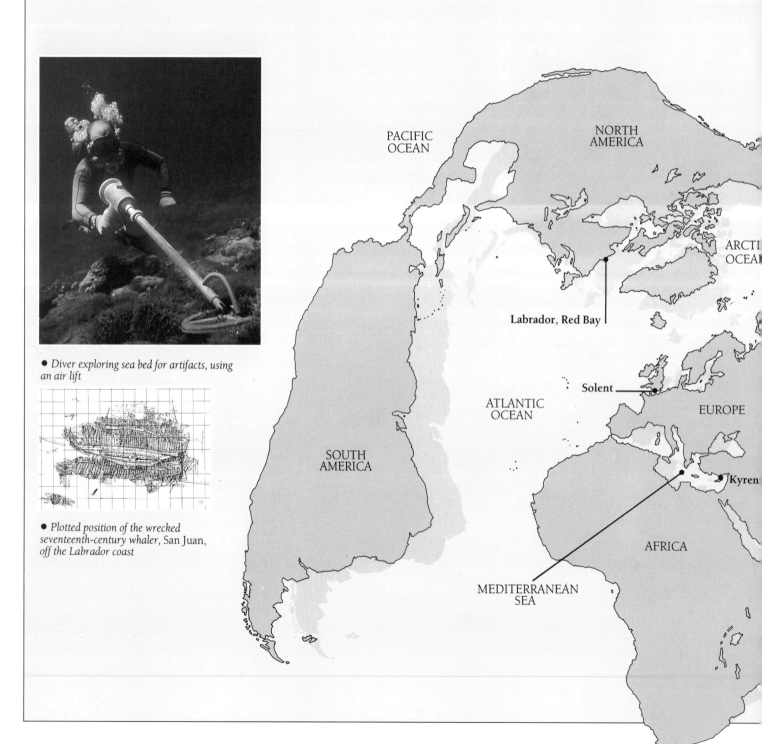

• Diver exploring sea bed for artifacts, using an air lift

• Plotted position of the wrecked seventeenth-century whaler, San Juan, off the Labrador coast

PACIFIC OCEAN

NORTH AMERICA

ARCTI OCEA

Labrador, Red Bay

Solent

ATLANTIC OCEAN

EUROPE

SOUTH AMERICA

Kyren

AFRICA

MEDITERRANEAN SEA

Archaeologists do not restrict their studies to the land, but also search under water for information on human societies. Archaeology under water is no different from archaeology on land, except that the excavation technology and recording methods are adapted so that they can be used beneath the surface of lakes and oceans. The insights that ancient wrecks can give us into life on land are priceless. Much of what we learn comes from months, even years, of patient work in quiet laboratories far from the wreck, piecing together clues from all over the world. Underwater archaeology is as fully scientific and demanding as archaeology on land and has the same objective – understanding the past.

• Red Bay, Labrador, site of a seventeenth-century whale oil tryworks

• Hull of the Mary Rose *preserved in moist conditions to prevent the timbers from drying*

• Porcelain figure salvaged from the Nanking cargo

(preceding page) *The glaze of eighteenth-century Chinese porcelain glimmers on the sea bed under the South China Sea where it lay for two centuries, ever since the Dutch East Indiaman that was transporting it to Europe was wrecked. Most of it has been salvaged and it was auctioned in 1985 by Christie's.*

THE POINT CLOATES EAST INDIAMAN

On a fine day in 1974 four skin divers hovered over a wreck off Point Cloates, a remote promontory on the coast of western Australia. The ship on the bottom rested on her starboard side, half buried in the sand. The four excited men spotted a mound of ballast stones, then a collection of silver coins lying slightly forward of the stern. Within a few hours they had gathered up 6,000 Spanish coins, as well as copper hull fastenings and glass and clay vessels.

This deserted coast was a promising place for such discoveries. In the early nineteenth century, the regular route for outward bound East Indiamen was round the Cape of Good Hope at the southern tip of South Africa, and across the Indian Ocean to a landfall on the coast of Western Australia, close to where the wreck lay. 'Proceed with caution,' warned the sailing directions of the time. (Uncharted coral reefs and the treacherous Tryal rocks make the landfall a hazardous one.) Sometimes mariners failed to heed the dire warnings. An English and a Dutch ship were stranded on the rocks within a month of one another in 1622. Other vessels shared their fate in the following century. A Portuguese ship was wrecked in 1816, as was an American Indiaman some time in the second decade of the nineteenth century. The position of this wreck was unknown until the skin divers came across its coin cache in 1978.

Fortunately for archaeology, the divers reported their exciting find to the Museum of Western Australia in Perth. Within weeks, archaeologists and volunteers led by Graeme Henderson were on the scene. The logistic problems they faced were formidable. The wreck lay off an exposed, uninhabited, barren coast. Henderson had to import drinking water in a fire truck from a town 110km (68 miles) away. His diving tender was towed up from Perth over 1,000km (621 miles) of rough roads to a small port on the coast, and then sent by sea over another 157km (97 miles) to the wreck site. Luckily, he could borrow a sheep-shearing shed close to the beach for his camp. The archaeologists slept on the floor in shearing enclosures and sorted and studied their finds on fleece-sorting tables.

The work began with the arduous task of

Left *Beneath the sea off the coast of western Australia lies the wreck of the American merchantman* Rapid, *found by divers in 1974. So that archaeologists could reconstruct the ship rather than remove it from the sea bed, the hull structure was labelled systematically in preparation for photogrammetric and manual recording.*

keel and port-side timbers were in good condition because they had been buried in the sand, but the stern had disintegrated. Every timber was photographed in place, forming part of a master plan of the ship, which was created from the photomosaic.

When all the timbers were exposed, Henderson calculated that he was dealing with a wooden vessel about 30m (98ft) long. She had white oak ribs, and was planked partly in spruce. Two mast steps were still in place, as was the main bilge pump, just aft of the main mast. Henderson carefully reburied the timbers under the sand and weighted them with ballast stones. But the many artifacts from the wreck were taken to the Maritime Museum in Fremantle (near Perth) for conservation and identification. The artifacts would also help him to identify the wreck.

The identification involved both simple deduction and archaeological detective work. Henderson was certain that the ship was outward bound. She was in ballast, carrying worthless stone to keep her in trim. The ballast would be thrown out at her destination and replaced with valuable pepper. The ship carried 19,000 Spanish dollars (worth about 4,750 Australian dollars in 1980). Henderson believes that the crew salvaged most of the money aboard when they abandoned ship, perhaps more than US$50,000.

When they were cleaned, the coins proved to date between 1759 and 1809 (most of them to 1802-4) and were minted in Mexico. There were some Peruvian, Guatemalan and Spanish coins, too. Some of the latter had been overstamped with the head of Britain's George III, a move by the Bank of England in 1797 to alleviate a coin shortage. The presence of Spanish coins aboard did not mean that the vessel was from Spain. Spanish dollars were the major international currency of the time. Perhaps more revealing were 13 American dollars, as well as coins of smaller denominations, found in the bow where the crew's quarters once lay. These included six copper US one-cent coins (two dating to 1805), and a single Chinese coin. Perhaps the ship had been to China before.

Was the ship American? An unexpected clue came from the provisions that had been carried aboard. Ships of the time had

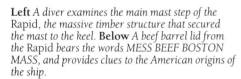

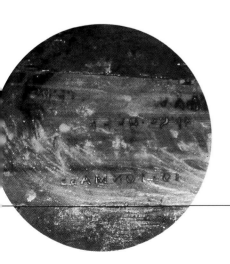

Left *A diver examines the main mast step of the* Rapid, *the massive timber structure that secured the mast to the keel.* **Below** *A beef barrel lid from the* Rapid *bears the words MESS BEEF BOSTON MASS, and provides clues to the American origins of the ship.*

clearing more than 100 tonnes of ballast stone from the centre of the wreck, a pile of rubble up to 1.2m (4ft) thick. The volunteers used baskets and lifting barrels. Some of the ballast had washed ashore soon after the wreck foundered. It was used by local aborigines for grinding stones, and was then abandoned on an ancient camp site nearby.

Time was short, so the diving proceeded in morning and afternoon shifts, each lasting about four hours. Henderson laid out a survey grid over the wreck so that every find could be recorded in position before being dislodged from the bottom and lifted to the surface. Pairs of divers used two airlifts made of plastic drainpipe and fuelled with compressed air to provide suction. One diver would operate the lift, and the other record the positions of small artifacts within the grid, while the air removed the coral and sand from the ship's timbers. The divers soon found that the

Right *Salt beef and pork were standard foods on board the Rapid because fresh food would not last long. Graeme Henderson, Archaeological Director of the Western Australian Maritime Museum examines a pig skull from a barrel of salted pork found in the ship;* **below,** *an intact beef barrel is uncovered under the hull and prepared for removal from the site.*

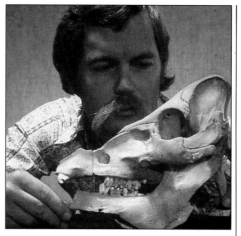

no refrigeration and carried little fresh food, so the crew on the Indiamen relied on salt beef. Henderson's divers found a beef barrel lid with the words MESS BEEF BOSTON MASS burned into the wood. In addition to this clue, there were copper dovetail fittings, used for strengthening major joints in the wooden hull, that bore the name J. DAVIS. This was perhaps Jonathan Davis of Bath, Maine, a merchant and ship chandler who built 22 ships between 1785 and 1819. Davis enjoyed connections with merchants in Boston and Salem and his son was connected with the spice trade.

So the wrecked vessel may have come from the United States and been outward bound with a cargo of silver coins. But how big was she? Henderson located three anchors near the wreck, one 4.23m (14ft) long. This was exactly the same length as the main anchor of *H.M.S. Sirius*, the flagship of Britain's first colonizing fleet to New South Wales, wrecked off Norfolk Island. That anchor weighed 1.2 tonnes. Henderson knew that in 1800 the US Navy used anchors weighing 2.26kg (5lb) per tonne of vessel. If the wreck's anchor was the same weight as that from the *Sirius*, then the ship would have displaced about 490 tonnes, making her a larger vessel than most American East Indiamen of the early

nineteenth century.

None of these clues actually identifies the specific ship wrecked off Point Cloates. Nor do the clues necessarily mark her as American, particularly since she was carrying British cannons. All East Indiamen of the early nineteenth century had to be well armed against pirates and warships. Eight guns came from the wreck, and are still being cleaned. One weighs 1.8kg (4lb) and bears King George III's monogram and the manufacturer's mark of Joseph Christopher, a well-known British gun founder from 1760 to 1820. There were five other cannon and two carronades often used by Indiamen to repel boarders.

Above *Concreted silver coins from the* Rapid *recovered from the site after their original location was recorded. After conservation,* **left**, *experts identified the silver coins as Spanish and United States dollars.*

But the fact that there were British cannons aboard does not mean that the ship was not American. Henderson points out that the British held a virtual monopoly on cannon manufacture even after the American Revolution, so one could logically expect American shipbuilders to rely on British weapons until local supplies became available.

After the diving was over, the real business of archaeological and historical detective work began, especially the search in historical archives for records of a major wreck in western Australia. Henderson narrowed the date of the wreck to 1810-11, on the basis of the coins in her hold, the latest of which dated to 1809. Another event narrowed the chronological 'window'. The War of 1812 reduced American and European trade with the East, making a voyage of this scale after that date less likely. The loss of such a large Indiaman must have had serious economic repercussions at home, and Henderson hoped that he could identify the mysterious ship in insurance and other official documents far from the remote shore where she broke up. His research paid off; recently he identified the ship as the *Rapid*, which sailed from Boston to Canton in 1811.

THE KYRENIA SHIP

Consider the example of the Kyrenia ship, a humble Greek merchantman that sank off the north coast of Cyprus in the late fourth century BC. The doomed ship settled on her port side in 30m (100ft) of water and split open along her keel. Her cargo of 400 amphorae and other artifacts formed a low mound on the muddy sea bed. There she lay until a sponge diver spotted the amphorae in the late 1960s.

The archaeologists of the Institute of Nautical Archaeology, at Texas A&M University, maintain close ties with sponge divers in Cyprus and Turkey, because they are usually the first people to spot wrecks on the sea bottom. There are telltale signs – piles of amphorae, heaps of ballast stone, sometimes a cargo of copper ingots. The Kyrenia ship was located in just this way and then excavated by an international team of scuba divers under Michael Katzev in 1968 and 1969. Work on the artifacts and the ship itself has gone on ever since; it takes that long to piece together all the clues from the sea bed.

After months of arduous work, the archaeologists recovered about 25 tonnes of cargo from the merchantman. She carried nearly 400 wine and olive oil amphorae, staple commodities of eastern Mediterranean trade at the time. There were some millstones from the island of Nisyros, too, the remnants of a consignment that must have been sold off at various ports. The remainder were serving as useful ballast.

As the overburden was removed, Katzev was delighted to find that many of the ship's timbers were still intact. The archaeologists plotted the precise location of more than 6,000 wooden fragments on the sea bed, covering an area of 6m × 12m (19½ft × 39ft). They then brought them to the surface and preserved them in polyethylene glycol so that the ship could be reassembled in a museum.

About 60 per cent of the hull and many isolated fragments survived. Enough remained to show that there once had been two cabins aboard, fore and aft. They held four place settings of wood and pottery. The crew had used portable grills for cooking. Katzev believes that the crew may have cooked on beaches ashore and only eaten raw food when they were afloat. Sufficient artifacts came from the wreck to reconstruct the ill-fated merchantman's voyage, using the origin points of the cargo as clues. She had sailed from Samos to the islands of Nisyros and Rhodes before arriving in Cyprus, where she was attacked by pirates and sunk. The divers found eight iron spearheads under the hull.

Above Wine and olive oil amphorae from the Kyrenia ship provided clues to the route of her voyage: in the centre of the foreground is an amphora from Rhodes, and to the left of it a vessel from the island of Samos. **Right** The hull of the Kyrenia ship lying on the sea bed, seen from the bow, with an archaeological recording grid superimposed on the undisturbed timbers.

Dozens of ancient wrecks have yielded fascinating information about life on the water centuries, even thousands, of years ago. But the Kyrenia ship is especially important because we know so much about her construction – thanks to the work of Richard Steffy, an expert in ancient ship construction. Steffy was a modelmaker for years before he joined the Katzev team to study the Kyrenia wreck. He applied his unique skills and vast knowledge of wooden shipbuilding to the jigsaw puzzle of timbers that were stored in a Crusader castle at Kyrenia.

With a computer you can easily reconstruct the lines of modern ships from relatively small fragments of the hull. The same is not true of ancient merchantmen, which were built without plans or even scale models. Each ship was approximately the same, but varied according to the idiosyncrasies of the men who built her. So Steffy reconstructed the ancient hull timber by timber, built models and pieced together the lines from detailed drawings and photographs. Thanks to his painstaking research, you can visit the reassembled ship in Kyrenia castle.

So accurate was Steffy's reconstruction of the merchantman that Greek craftsmen in Piraeus, the port of Athens, are building a modern replica of the ship using the same construction methods employed by the original builders. A scale model replica sails surprisingly well, even to windward, displaying many of the design features that persisted in the Aegean until the first century AD.

We can imagine the builders setting up shop on a sheltered beach near their village. First, they selected a single log of straight-grained Aleppo pine. This they hewed with adzes into a slightly curved keel 9.33m (30½ft) long. Stem and stern were carefully mortised or scarfed to the completed keel. The men would then have inserted wooden pegs into the keel to support it until the hull form was complete. At this point a

Left The waterlogged wood from the raised Kyrenia ship soaks in a freshwater bath, awaiting preservation treatment with polyethylene glycol.

Left Finds from the ship allow archaeologists to piece together an idea of the trade it carried. A pair of grain milling blocks, far left, may have come from the island of Nisyros; left, crockery includes an oil jug, bowls, a wine pitcher, and plates.

Left *A triumph for underwater archaeology. The reassembled hull of the Kyrenia ship with its original timbers (here viewed from above the starboard bow) is exhibited in the Crusader Castle of Kyrenia, Cyprus.* **Below** *Richard Steffy's meticulous studies of the Kyrenia merchantman have enabled experts to build this full-scale replica of 2m (6½ft) of the hull of the original ship, from aft amidships.*

modern boat builder would erect frames and stringers to form a skeleton for the hull planking. Our team followed a different practice. They fitted the planks first, starting with the bottom timbers, then the floors and side planks, half frames and topsides. The work took many months, because every plank was joined with tenons and wooden pegs. The result was an immensely strong hull capable of withstanding beaching and every kind of hard use for many years.

Steffy calculated that the Kyrenia ship was 14m (46ft) long and about 4.6m (15ft) across. She was a small merchantman, displacing only about 25 tonnes, with a convex midsection to her hull that gave her ample strength. The ship was very old and worm-eaten when she sank. Many planks were thin and rotting away at the edges, and there was woodborer damage throughout the hull. The owner had hauled her out at least twice for major repairs, once when the keel was cracked. After replacing several planks, and countless patch jobs, he sheathed the aging hull with thin lead sheet to keep out the borers. Only a few patches of lead remained on the wreck, so Steffy traced the sheeting pattern by plotting the tiny tack marks in the wood.

This kind of archaeological research is like peering into a microcosm of ancient life, reconstructing the life of an aged seagoing workhorse kept afloat as long as possible. Just as she neared the end of her working life, pirates attacked, She slipped beneath the waves for archaeologists to resurrect her 23 centuries later.

BASQUE WHALERS IN LABRADOR

Some of the most dramatic underwater discoveries of recent years have come not from tropical waters, but from North America and northern Europe. Southern Labrador may seem an unlikely place for underwater archaeology, but thanks to a

Red Bay, Labrador has yielded rich information on ancient Basque whaling, such as the remains of this barrica, **right**, *an oak case used to transport the valuable whale oil. The inside of the cask would have been rounded with a cooper's adze,* **below right**. **Below, far right** *A head vice or cask hook (the larger object) was screwed into a hole bored in the cask with the gimlet (the smaller artifact). The coopers used cask hooks to lift the last head piece of the barrel into place.*

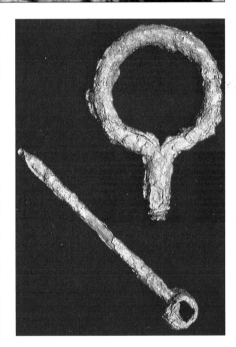

persistent historian it has proved a treasure trove of vital information about whaling more than four centuries ago.

Selma Barkham was a historical researcher for the Canadian government in 1965. She was familiar with general monographs on the Basques and whaling in Canada in the sixteenth and seventeenth centuries, but many of the details were missing, partly because all the documents were in Spanish and buried deep in European archives. With single-minded dedication, Barkham moved to Mexico, where she taught English and studied Spanish until she felt qualified to work on original documents. Even then she had to master the archaic form of Spanish used in sixteenth-century documents. Ten years of patient digging in centuries-old commercial and legal documents followed, years that took her to more than ten archives. Her painstaking research produced evidence of 12 Basque whaling centres along the southern Labrador coast.

In 1977 archaeologist James A. Tuck followed up Selma Barkham's historical clues at Red Bay, Labrador – today a small community of 300 people. Her documents recorded how, between about 1540 and 1610, hundreds of whalers had descended on the strait of Belle Isle each year for the five short months of the whaling season. They processed whale carcasses on Saddle Island, opposite where Red Bay village now lies, from where day and night thick columns of oily smoke would have risen into the summer sky. In early winter the Basque ships sailed for home with as many as 50,000 barrels of whale oil in their holds, a cargo as lucrative as the vaunted gold trade of the Indies.

Tuck soon located on Saddle Island a low wall encrusted with a black substance. A veteran of archaeology in the Arctic, he identified the substance as charred whale blubber. The wall had once been part of a tryworks, a place where the Basque whalers rendered blubber into oil. In eight seasons

of excavations Tuck has dug up not only tryworks, but places where coopers re-assembled the knocked down oak barrels that were carried from Spain to Labrador.

There were probably temporary camps ashore, too, places where the open whale-boat crews waited until whales were sighted offshore. Tuck found the whalers' cemetery in 1982, where he excavated 125 male skeletons, almost all individuals between their early 20s and early 40s. There were multiple graves, too, perhaps the burial places of whaleboat crews who perished during the chase.

Selma Barkham's historical researches revealed that in the year 1565 a sudden autumn storm swept down on Red Bay, catching at anchor a fully laden whaler, named the *San Juan*. The ship's anchor lines parted and the whaler was driven ashore and pounded to pieces close to land. Her keel soon split and she sank less than 27m (30yd) from shore. In 1978 Parks Canada marine archaeologist Robert Grenier located the wreck preserved under layers of fine silt. After seven years of research, he has found two more sixteenth-century wrecks of whalers in Red Bay, as well as the remains of four smaller boats. But most of the underwater excavators' efforts have concentrated on the *San Juan*.

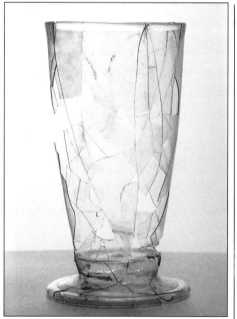

A one-piece drinking glass brought from Spain to Red Bay by one of the whalers. Now restored with epoxy resin, it stands 15cm (6in) high.

Above *A typical late sixteenth-century Iberian majolica jug, restored by Judith Logan of the Canadian Conservation Institute. Finds such as these are a small sample of what archaeologists may yet uncover at similar stations.*

Left *One of the many mass graves from the Red Bay whalers' cemetery recalls a long-forgotten accident. The skeletons are probably those of a boat crew killed while pursuing a whale.*

Diving in such cold conditions was a challenge until the archaeologists hooked up flexible hoses that pumped water warmed to 40°C (105°F) into their suits. This enabled each diver to spend long hours beneath the water tracing the position of the split timbers of the whaling ship and recovering dozens of artifacts from the wreckage. The ship emerged from the excavation like a blueprint. She was a three-master, very much a work-a-day vessel, a bulk carrier designed for years of service in a brutal trade. Her keel was nearly 15m (50ft) long, and she could carry a burden of between 250 and 300 tonnes; she was certainly capable of carrying a heavy cargo of full oil barrels through autumn gales far offshore.

The wreck could not have come at a worse time for the shipowners. The *San Juan* was fully laden, about to sail for home with the season's profits, a cargo of barrels estimated to be worth now between US$4,000 and US$6,000 each. Whale oil can literally be described as the lubricant of sixteenth-century European society, a commodity as precious then as Middle Eastern oil is today. Selma Barkham's documents revealed that the *San Juan* had been carrying around 1,000 barrels of oil. As far as we know there was no loss of life; perhaps only a skeleton crew was aboard. At least half the precious cargo was recovered. The whalers used grappling irons to pull open hatches and planks apart. Many barrels (*barricas*) then floated to the surface; whale oil has a lighter specific gravity than water. But the archaeologists recovered shattered fragments of at least 450 barrels trapped in the ship's ballast, beyond the reach of the whalers' hooks.

The *San Juan* was not embellished with fine carving, nor did her wreck contain the fine possessions of a wealthy sea captain. Tens of thousands of codfish bones lay outside the ship along the shore. Even the knife marks left on the bones from the gutting of the fish could be studied: they used the same methods that are employed today. The bones of a rat feeding on the fish also came from the excavations; the *San Juan's* timbers bore countless bite marks throughout the ship from the rats attracted by the pungent scent of whale oil.

The Red Bay wrecks are the oldest wrecks found in the Americas north of Florida. As such, they are a fascinating chronicle of sixteenth-century marine architecture, not of great warships, but of humble vessels, that did the day-to-day work of the commercial world, unsung, unheralded, year after year, with enormous loss of life over the centuries. Under one of

the ships Grenier even found the remains of a whaling boat, a *chalupa*, a 7m (23ft) long rowing boat that once carried up to six rowers and a steersman out to the hunt. They would harpoon the whale, then follow the drogue (the buoy at the end of the harpoon line) until the whale surfaced and could be speared to death. Towing the dead whale to shore could take hours, even days. It was a brutal, uncertain life, in which the men were paid in barrels of oil at the end of the season.

In the heyday of Labrador whaling, between 1560 and 1570, the trade was remarkably profitable, but it declined rapidly, partly because of indiscriminate killing. In less than half a century the Basques had killed more than 15,000 whales, decimating the population forever. When the whalers moved on, their foothold on the coast was forgotten until a persistent historian followed some dim clues deep into Spanish archives.

MARY ROSE

Basque whalers were already visiting Red Bay when another maritime tragedy unfolded – in front of England's King Henry VIII himself. July 19, 1545 was a fine summer's day, with only a light breeze blowing across the Solent Channel off Portsmouth. But the town was tense because Henry VIII faced a grave crisis – a French invasion fleet even larger than the Spanish Armada of four decades later threatened his fleet close offshore. Confronted as he was with a French invasion force of 235 ships and 30,000 men, Henry needed every ship he could find. He mustered 60, among them the jewel of his fleet – the *Mary Rose*.

Mary Rose had been in the king's service for 35 years. She had just emerged from the dockyard after a major refit that had made her a very formidable fighting ship. She bristled with heavy bronze cannon that could cripple the enemy with broadsides at long range. She had just been refitted with a new type of gun, mounted on a carriage, with barrels made by wrapping a single sheet of wrought iron into a cylinder. The massive barrels were reinforced with heat-shrunk hoops, and could throw heavy shot or cannon balls that burst on impact, causing carnage on a crowded deck. Iron linstocks decorated with dragons and crocodiles for holding slow matches were installed by each gun.

Mary Rose was a large warship for her day – about 36.5m (120ft) long, of about 700 tonnes burden, with lofty bow and stern castles. The dockyard strengthened the hull with massive timbers to accept the extra weight of the new cannons. But

Above *A magnificently preserved example of whaler's clothing, with knitted cap, a jacket or outer shirt, an inner shirt, knee-length breeches, socks or leg wrappings, and ankle-height leather shoes.*

unfortunately, they tried to cram too much aboard – not only additional guns, but more than 25 tonnes of extra weight in the form of archers crowding her decks, and no one had sailed the newly refitted ship in a breeze since her launching. Her instability manifested itself in battle, with fatal results.

Henry VIII and his court watched with the crowds as *Mary Rose* drifted out into the Solent. She was deeply laden with 415 sailors and 285 soldiers and archers. Her bottom gun ports were open, ready to engage the enemy. The ship was a brilliant sight, adorned with fine carving and gold leaf, with bright streamers and pennants at her masts and yards. She crept slowly out into open water, barely moving in the calm, and the king gazed at her in quiet satisfaction. A sudden gust ruffled the feathered hats of the court. *Mary Rose* heeled sud-

denly and veered to starboard. 'I have the sort of knaves I cannot rule,' cried out the Vice Admiral as the helmsmen fought vainly for control. The top-heavy warship tipped uncontrollably. Seawater poured into her open gun ports, flooding the lower deck in seconds. The horrified monarch watched helplessly as his pride and joy sank in less than a minute, taking all but 30 of her crew with her.

The *Mary Rose* was long remembered, but only some cannon were recovered from her before the position of the wreck was lost. Henry VIII himself bitterly mourned the loss of his flagship, but the French invasion was stemmed and the accident eventually forgotten. The ship lay in only 12.2m (40ft) of tide-swept water, her timbers periodically exposed by winter storms, but it took late twentieth-century

technology to find her.

Diver and journalist Alexander McKee was fascinated with the story of the *Mary Rose*. In the late 1960s, he teamed up with archaeologist Margaret Rule in a systematic search for the wreck, using historical records as a guide. Their quest lasted six years. Diving in the tidal waters of the Solent is quite unlike searching for wrecks in the clear tropical waters of Florida or the Caribbean. The only way McKee and Rule could hope to find *Mary Rose* was by using high technology – side-scan and sub-bottom radar that enabled them to detect subsurface features from the surface. When a promising image came on screen, divers would check it out.

McKee located what he suspected was *Mary Rose* in 1970 and recovered an iron cannon from the bottom. The divers were

Right *The only contemporary watercolour depicting the Mary Rose was painted in the margin of the Anthony Roll, an inventory of the king's ships published in 1546 by Sir Anthony Anthony, a civil servant. With flags and banners flying she must have been a magnificent sight. She carried 91 guns after her fateful refit in 1536 – their extra weight and that of the archers on her decks made her so unstable that a stiff breeze was enough to make her capsize and sink. When divers found the wreck in the 1970s,* **above,** *they had discovered a time capsule of Tudor seafaring life.*

lucky the following summer, because winter storms had exposed the massive ribs of the *Mary Rose* for the first time in some years. Only the blackened ribs of the ship were visible above the silt when McKee and Rule first dived on her. But 30,000 dives and four years later they had recovered more than 17,000 artifacts from the fine silt, a unique chronicle of Tudor life afloat.

The warship had sunk on her starboard side. The lower part of her hull had been sealed off by fine silt that buried the contents safe from destruction. Diving on the wreck was a nightmare. Visibility was minimal, the silt rose in murky clouds, and the tides and currents ran strongly across the wreck. But the divers found almost half the ship intact. The starboard side contained a rich treasure of finds, everything from weapons to personal possessions,

Above *A selection of personal effects found in the* Mary Rose *included those carried in decorative pouches worn by officers. Here, a pouch with a silk-embroidered front flap, complete with silver initials, was found to contain a boxwood comb, and a wooden seal. A pocket sundial, die, thimble ring, decorative clasp, tokens, and a wooden whistle were also among the many once-prized possessions that were found aboard the wreck.*

barber-surgeon's tools to a compass. These finds painted a vivid picture not only of the ship's last moments, but also of life aboard.

As well as powerful cannons, *Mary Rose* was armed with more than 200 archers. Her élite longbowmen could find their target with deadly accuracy from a distance of more than 270m (300yd), with deadly accuracy. They were the riflemen of Tudor times, capable of shooting off a dozen armour-piercing arrows a minute. The divers found 139 longbows and 2,500 arrows on the wreck. Many of the bows were so well preserved that they can be drawn today.

The archers' skeletons were jumbled on deck, close to their battle stations. One of the bowmen was a sturdy man in his mid-20s, who had been an archer for so long that his middle vertebrae had been twisted and deformed by the twisting motion of shooting a bow. His left forearm was enlarged and flattened by the strain of drawing the taut string. This right-handed archer was part of an élite corps of warriors who would shower an enemy ship with arrows from a distance, causing chaos on the crowded decks. Both this man and a younger archer had tried to scramble up a ladder over the side as the ship sank.

The *Mary Rose* saw action even in the few moments before she sank. We know this because the divers found skeletons lying on straw mattresses below decks. The ship had just left port, so they cannot have been people who were sick. Margaret Rule believes that they were wounded men who had been hustled down below out of sight so that the fighting men on deck could not witness their suffering.

Thousands of artifacts large and small enable us to reconstruct life aboard. The crew ate beef, mutton, pork and venison, fresh peas (some were even found in their pods), as well as bread and various fruit, among them plums and prunes, and hazelnuts. The officers dined off pewter dinnerware, quaffing ale from fine tankards. The crew used wooden plates and drinking vessels. The archaeologists found insect remains and the bones of the inevitable rats, even a pomander filled with spices used by an officer to ward off the smells aboard. Someone had also kept a small dog on the ship, perhaps to chase the rats away.

The seamen fished with hand lines that they carried into battle with them. The divers found the barber-surgeon's carved wooden chest, filled with the tools of his trade – even ointment. The surgeon was a dentist as well as a barber. The chest contained a bowl, pestle and mortar for medicines, surgical tools, cauterizing imple-

Right *The hull of the* Mary Rose *broke surface on October 11, 1982 after 437 years on the sea bed. All that remained of Henry VIII's magnificent warship hung suspended by cables beneath a 67 tonne underwater lifting frame.*

Below *A beautifully preserved leather book cover with embossed design probably once belonged to one of the officers that went down with the ship.*

Above *A superb bronze gun recovered from the wreck in 1979 rests on a replica of its original wooden gun carriage made by craftsmen at the Weald and Downland Museum in West Sussex. It was the sheer weight of guns like this one that sent the* Mary Rose *to her watery grave.*

ments, even a mallet for rendering victims senseless before surgery.

A seaman's chest yielded a magnificent gimballed steering compass, one of three found aboard. This is the oldest such instrument found in northern Europe. Some officers carried pocket sundials, presumably for telling the time. There were fragments of clothing including leather shoes, silver ornaments, two dozen gold coins, even sealed chests filled with spare cordage and ropes, stowed deep in the bilges. Some of the heavy blocks were in perfect condition, ready for use to this day.

Once the hull was excavated, the time had come to raise the *Mary Rose* herself. Divers suspended cables from a special cradle, working in conditions of almost zero visibility among the massive hull timbers. On October 11, 1982, as a huge fleet of yachts and small craft watched and cheered, Henry VIII's great carrack broke surface. The blackened hull fragments came to rest in a covered dry dock, sprayed 24 hours a day to prevent the waterlogged timbers from drying too fast and warping. *Mary Rose* was finally back in home port.

Few underwater archaeology projects are as spectacular as the raising of the *Mary Rose*. For the most part, the archaeologist working under the surface of lakes, rivers and oceans deals with humbler vessels. But these ships are just as important as great warships. They are a mine of information about the plain folk who manned them, and about their daily lives both afloat and ashore. The lives of ordinary people are what archaeology studies best of all.

Left *Now positioned in a controlled environment the hull of the Tudor warship towers to the height of a four-storey building. The hull is kept at a temperature of around 5°C (40°F) and at 95 percent humidity. The timbers are constantly sprayed with chilled water to prevent degradation and uncontrolled drying. When the cabin partitions, deck planks, and companion ways are back in position, long-term conservation can begin.*

PART THREE
UNSOLVED MYSTERIES

CHAPTER ONE
THE SYMBOLIC WORLD

CHAPTER TWO
MEGALITHIC MYSTERIES

THE SYMBOLIC WORLD

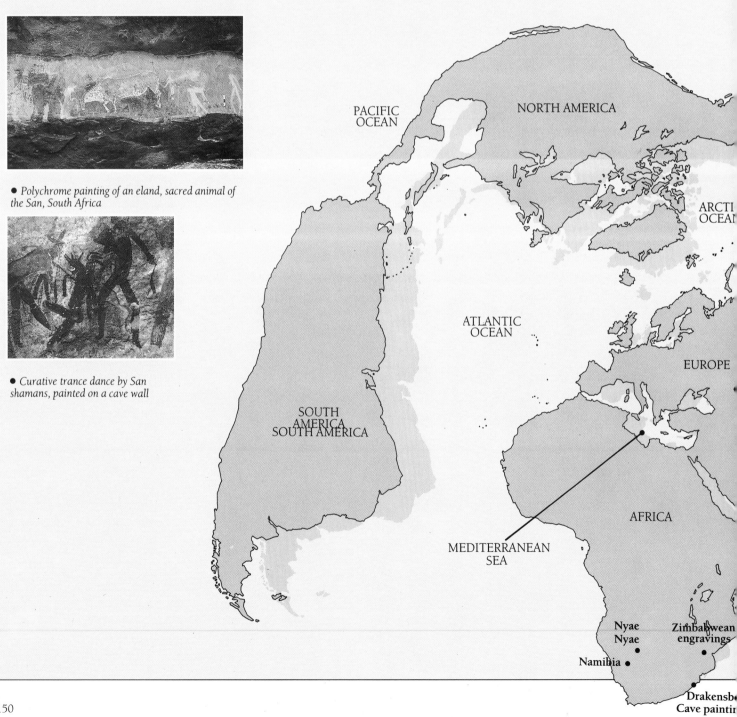

• Polychrome painting of an eland, sacred animal of the San, South Africa

• Curative trance dance by San shamans, painted on a cave wall

PACIFIC
OCEAN

NORTH AMERICA

ARCTIC
OCEAN

ATLANTIC
OCEAN

EUROPE

SOUTH
AMERICA
SOUTH AMERICA

MEDITERRANEAN
SEA

AFRICA

Nyae
Nyae

Zimbabwean
engravings

Namibia

Drakensb
Cave paintin

Many people still believe that archaeologists are like magicians. They associate them with lost civilizations and sunken continents – unexplained mysteries. They expect the archaeologist's spade to uncover Atlantis, to find long-forgotten temples in the high Andes. Though the stereotype persists, archaeology has changed. Archaeologists still work on complex mysteries, but these are often unspectacular problems that may take generations to solve – a far cry from the ancient-civilization-in-a-month syndrome of the 1880s. San rock art is such an example.

● *Superimposition of animals and figures on a San cave painting*

● *Modern !Kung San performing a trance dance*

● *San healer examining a wound*

ASIA

AUSTRALIA

INDIAN
OCEAN

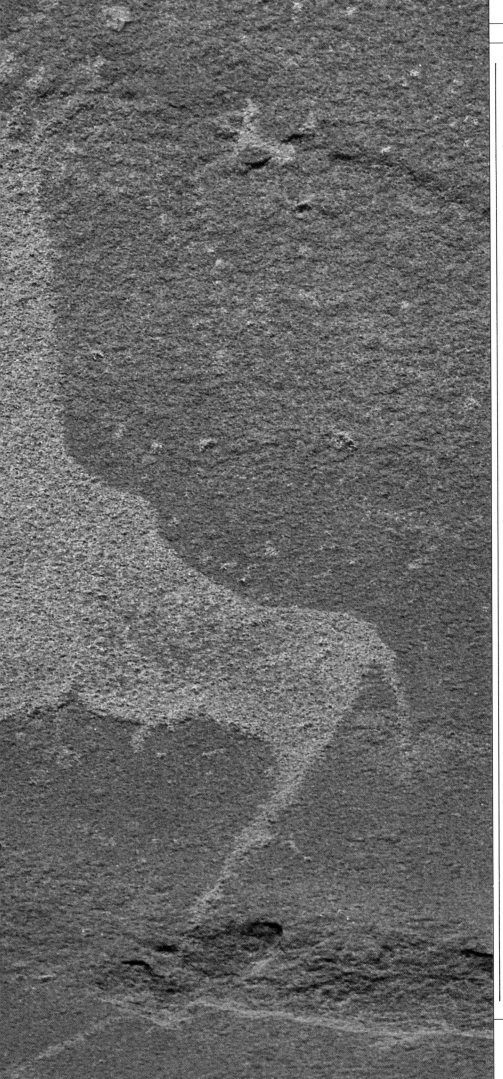

A beautiful rock engraving of two giraffe, from Twyfelfontein, Namibia, is just one of many such engravings left by the San as they were pushed north by Khoi Khoi and colonist farmers. Today we know that such images have a greater meaning than just a mere record of the animals they saw, but as few San remain today, discovering that meaning will be virtually impossible.

SAN ROCK ART

'The kloofs or chasms, washed by torrents of water . . . frequently leave a succession of caves, of which the Bosjesman chooses the highest . . . In one of these retreats were discovered their recent traces. The fires were scarcely extinguished, and the grass upon which they had slept was not yet withered. On the smooth sides of the cavern were drawings of several animals . . . Some of the drawings were known to be new; but many of them had been remembered from the first settlement of this part of the colony.'

Traveller John Barrow saw these magnificent rock paintings in the Cape Province of South Africa in the year 1797. He had heard rumours of cave paintings in the mountains, but had assumed that they were just caricatures, doodlings with no meaning at all. 'It was no disagreeable disappointment to find them very much the reverse,'

he wrote. The mystery of this prehistoric rock art has intrigued traveller and archaeologist alike ever since.

Barrow was an enlightened man by eighteenth-century standards, one of the few travellers of the day who found any redeeming features in the Bushmen (today, scholars call them the San). Skilled hunters and brilliant trackers, these diminutive Stone Age people would slip out of their mountain hiding places at night and steal cattle from under the noses of the Dutch colonists. The farmers cursed these wild nomadic people, who spoke an unintelligible clicking language. 'He has no religion, no laws, no government, no recognized authority, no patrimony, no fixed abode,' declared one missionary. He stated that Bushmen's souls were 'bound down and clogged by their animal nature'. In the 1830s, farmers hunted them on horseback on Sunday afternoons — for sport.

Today, only a few thousand San survive

— far to the north, in the arid Kalahari Desert of Botswana — and they are not painters. None of the San groups who painted caves and rock shelters survived the ravages of the nineteenth century. But they left an extraordinary chronicle behind them — thousands of painted rock surfaces and, in places, engravings — in the granite hills of Zimbabwe north of the Limpopo, in Namibia, and especially in South Africa in the Drakensberg Mountains and far to the south and east in the Cape. The paintings are delicate, sometimes even minuscule. Human figures are often only a few centimetres high. Reds, blacks, yellows, whites, the colours vibrate softly from the rock shelter walls in a complicated jumble of animals, humans and signs. There are even paintings of European caravels and British redcoats and their horses — the hunters pursuing the hunted, who calmly paused to paint their enemies. But San art in all its complexity remains a great archae-

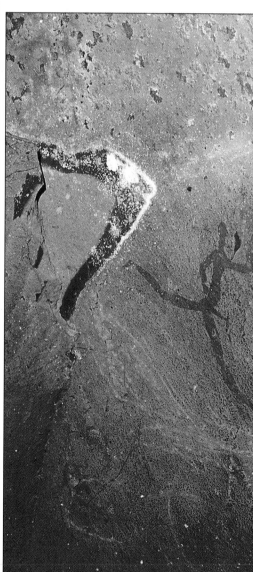

Above and right *San rock engravings from Twyfelfontein, Namibia, which depict gazelles, giraffes, zebras and antelopes, among other animals. Such engravings are sometimes found in areas where suitable rock outcrops provided 'canvases' for ancient artists.*

ological mystery. How old are the antelope and sticklike humans depicted in the paintings? Who painted them and, above all, why?

In 1930, anthropologist Mary How met a very old man named Mapote who, as a child, had painted with San in their caves. She persuaded him to paint for her. First Mapote chose a fairly porous piece of rock which would absorb his paint. Then he made some brushes by sticking small feathers into the ends of tiny reeds. Charcoal mixed with water served as black paint, and the white paint came from a powdered clay mixed with plant juice. To create red he mixed heated and pounded haematite with fresh ox blood. Now he was ready to begin. First he would paint an eland, he said, because the San of that part of the country 'were of the eland'. Beginning at the animal's chest, he moved the feather brush unerringly to complete two elands, then three human figures and a lion. Half a century later, Mapote's cryptic remark about elands was to become an important clue to the mystery of San art.

One of the first people to study the San was German linguist Wilhelm Bleek, in the 1870s. By chance, he learned that some /Xam San from semi-arid country in the Cape had been convicted of sheep stealing and brought to Cape Town to work on a new breakwater in Table Bay. Bleek persuaded the governor to let them live with him, so that he could study their language and customs. The San soon became Bleek's close friends, even continuing to live with the Bleeks after their sentences were over. In more than twelve thousand pages of verbatim text, Bleek's San tell of their way of life, their rituals, myths and beliefs.

The /Xam lived in small family groups of perhaps as many as 25 people, in a hunting and foraging society that was in a constant state of flux as people came and went. Occasionally tensions arose, sometimes as a result of social disputes, or because of food shortages. The /Xam medicine men concerned themselves with these tensions. Some were curers, healers with the ability to draw sickness out of a sufferer's body, often by causing nose bleeds. The blood would be smeared on the patient, to create a spell to keep evil away. Then there were medicine men of the game, and of the rain. The former were believed to control the movements of antelope herds, whereas the rain-makers were said to be able to trap a mythical, dangerous rain animal that they would lead over the land. Its blood and milk became rain. Bleek showed his informants some paintings in which they identified medicine men leading rain animals across their hunting territory.

Bleek also learned of the trance performances that the medicine men could use to control game or capture the rain animal. While the women clapped and sang the medicine songs, the men would dance.

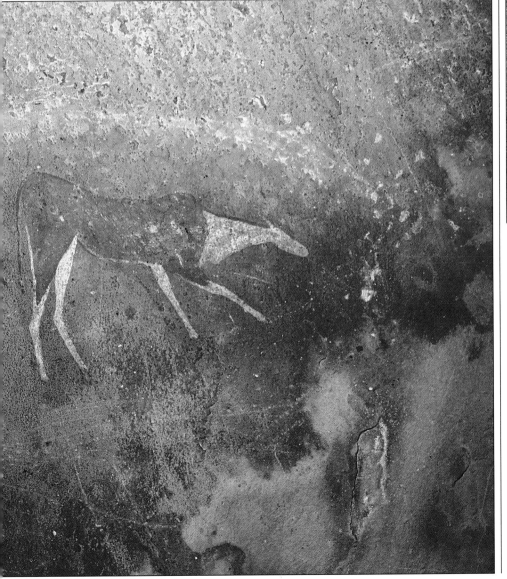

Left *A painting of an eland from Giant's Castle Reserve in the Drakensberg Mountains, Natal, South Africa. The San from this part of the country 'were of the eland' and may have regarded this animal, the most powerful of all the antelopes, as sacred, having great symbolic if not religious significance. In the rock paintings of the Drakensberg it is the animal which appears most often.* **Above** *This giraffe from a rockshelter in Zimbabwe is a good example of polychrome painting: the black may derive from charcoal, the white from clay, and the red from iron oxides in the earth, perhaps mixed with blood. Giraffes are a common animal in Zimbabwean rock paintings and it is possible that they had some religious meaning.*

Right *Recent research into the rock art of southern Africa indicates that it is essentially shamanistic. Human figures gather round a medicine man, or shaman, in a painting in Giant's Castle Reserve, Drakensberg Mountains, Natal.* **Below** *A line drawing of a trance scene in an Orange Free State rock shelter. Seated women clap the rhythm of 'medicine songs' as shamans dance, bending forward in a trancing posture. This posture is adopted when the dancers ask the gods for power. The surrounding lines may delineate the rock shelter or some forgotten shamanistic concept.*

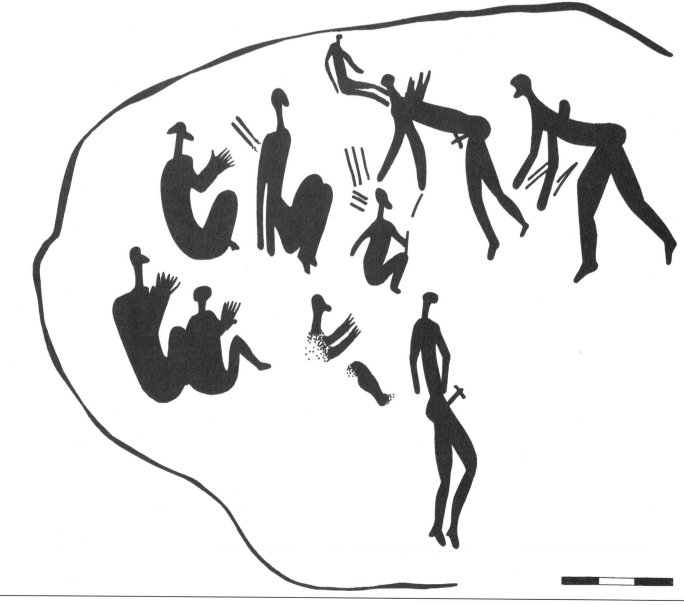

This activated a supernatural potency that made them tremble, sweat, experience a rising sensation, bleed from the nose and finally 'die'. In the trance, the /Xam medicine men's spirits were thought to leave their bodies to fight off evil influences, control game or capture the rain animal. Some of these men were painters.

COMPUTING ROCK ART

While Bleek was collecting San folklore, anthropologist George Stow was compiling 'a history of the manners and customs of the Bushmen, as depicted by themselves'. Ever since, archaeologists have assumed that the paintings are a pictorial record of Stone Age life going back far into pre-history, long before Europeans came. For generations they copied and photographed selected paintings that were the finest examples among hundreds of figures. Many of them assumed that the San were moved by a desire to produce beautiful paintings, to 'express themselves in paint'. In other words, San art was art for art's sake, and had nothing to do with their social life. Another school of thought argued that the artists were practising 'sympathetic hunting magic', encouraging the game to return – just as they may have done in distant Ice Age Europe. In fact, hunting is shown only rarely. Humans always outnumber animals. In one gorge, only 29 hunts were found among 3,909 paintings. What did the art mean? Only a few nineteenth-century San were ever asked to comment on paintings, and even these accounts were ignored.

During the 1960s and 1970s, scientists tried another approach. Instead of recording just selected paintings, they surveyed an entire area and studied every single image they could find. Experts such as Patricia Vinnicombe set down dozens of individual features from each painting, which they fed into a computer so that they could test hypotheses about the art against raw data. What were the most frequently depicted animals? How were such paintings distributed? How often were animals and humans associated? The computer data revealed that humans are more common subjects than animals, and that the antelope is the most frequently depicted animal. In Natal, to the east, the eland was the most common species among the antelope. So important was this large animal to the hunters that the artists painted them in vivid polychrome far more frequently than any other game. Surprisingly the painters almost never drew common game species like wildebeest.

Top *A shaman with a dancing rattle bleeds from the nose and collapses in a trance. To the left of him, a shaman, also with a bleeding nose and wearing a cap with ears, moves in to assist him. To the right a man dances with a flywhisk. The dances of some San groups were recorded before they died out and were found to be similar to these images.*

Above *A polychrome eland with accompanying human figures, in the Mountain Zebra National Park, South Africa. It is now known that the eland was painted in more than one colour in this region because it had great importance in San symbolism.*

Above *A complex scene from the Orange Free State, South Africa, depicts San dancers with an eland superimposed on the right of the frieze. The symbolism of this scene baffles modern experts, but it is now known that they were not superimposed at random but that each layer of the image was laid down according to certain conventions and linked the one below it to the one above it.* **Below** *Shaded polychrome eland are superimposed on therianthropes (human-like animals) clad in long karosses (skin cloaks).*

The computer data also revealed another interesting phenomenon. The artists would use the same rock 'canvas' again and again, superimposing paintings one on top of another in an intricate jumble of animals and human beings, rather than using the clean rock close by. Almost certainly, they were using the same places again and again as a deliberate way of linking paintings according to ancient conventions. When archaeologist Harald Pager analysed these superimpositions more closely in the late 1970s, he found that human figures were never painted on animals, but that animals would be painted on animals, and animals over humans. The artists preferred some animals such as the eland in superimposition, but avoided other combinations. Apparently they were painting according to rules, rules that were followed over quite large areas of the Drakensberg Mountains. The computer analyses disclosed some of the 'grammar' of San rock art, but not the meaning. But a century later it also led archaeologist David Lewis-Williams to Wilhelm Bleek's long-forgotten informants.

THE DEATH OF THE ELAND

Lewis-Williams remembered Mapote's strange comment in 1930, that the San were people 'of the eland'. The eland is the largest and fattest of all antelope, so bulky that an agile hunter can run it down. It is rich in meat and vital by-products that can sustain hunters for weeks. 'All other animals are like servants to the eland,' a San told Lewis-Williams. Small wonder the eland was important in an environment

where food supplies could be irregular. But Lewis-Williams soon found that the eland also figured large in nineteenth-century San myth and ritual. This, he guessed, was the reason the eland was so important in their rock art.

Bleek's informants had dictated several eland myths that associated the animal with honey, a substance with a strong, sweet smell similar to that which rises from a dead eland when it is skinned. Lewis-Williams soon discovered that this scent is considered to be redolent of power. Even today, San hunters in the Kalahari will dance next to the carcass of a freshly killed eland. In this dance, a medicine man, who

has special control of eland potency, enters a trance and cures everyone of ills by removing 'arrows of sickness' that may be directed against them.

Lewis-Williams examined thousands of paintings with this ritual in mind and found many depictions of elands associated with medicine men. Perhaps the southern San danced at eland carcasses, too. Lewis-Williams had seen dying elands trembling with wide-open nostrils, sweating profusely, melted fat gushing like blood from their nostrils. Did the San liken this phenomenon to 'death' in a medicine man's trance?

At Game Pass Shelter in the Drakens-

Below *A curing dance among the San from the Nyae Nyae area of Namibia. Dances like this provide clues to the dances on the rock paintings, which also depict medicine men in deep trances.*

Below *A curing dance among the San from the Nyae Nyae area of Namibia. Dances like this provide clues to the dances on the rock paintings, which also depict medicine men in deep trances.*

berg, Lewis-Williams found a painting of an eland staggering in its death throes with deeply sunken eyes. Dancers cavort around the animal, one adorned with cloven antelope hoofs crossed like those of the dying eland. White dots depict sweat drops falling from a dancer 'dying' in trance. Lewis-Williams believes that the dancers are acquiring the potency released by the death of the eland. The absorption of this potency is shown by the antelope heads, feet and hair on the dancers. The trance is so powerful that they have become like elands themselves. The same scene is repeated in dozens of other eland scenes, where the whole being of the medicine men, and the people, becomes merged with the most potent of all animals.

Therein lies the clue to this archaeological mystery. The painted and engraved animals of southern Africa were not just pleasing pictures, but complex metaphors that reflected symbolic values in the San world. But it was by no means every group that centred this metaphor on the eland, because other animals feature prominently in San art elsewhere. Each superimposition, each frieze, is a network of relationships that had profound meaning to the artists and medicine men.

We know from radiocarbon-dated excavations that Stone Age painters in southern Africa have been at work for at least 19,000 years. So their art may be as old as that of the Stone Age cave dwellers of southwestern France. But San symbolism survived into the late nineteenth century. When anthropologist George Stow showed some rock painting copies to an old San couple, the woman began to sing and dance. Her husband begged her to stop because the old songs made him sad. But she persisted and eventually the old man joined her. The aged couple were soon lost in the dance, exchanging looks of profound happiness, the present forgotten. Only now, more than a century later, are archaeologists trying to probe this forgotten world.

San from the Nyae Nyae area of Namibia form a dance circle for a curing dance. The young men form the trancing posture, bending forward with their arms outstretched as the women sing and clap. This very scene has been recorded in rock paintings many of which contain identical postures.

MEGALITHIC MYSTERIES

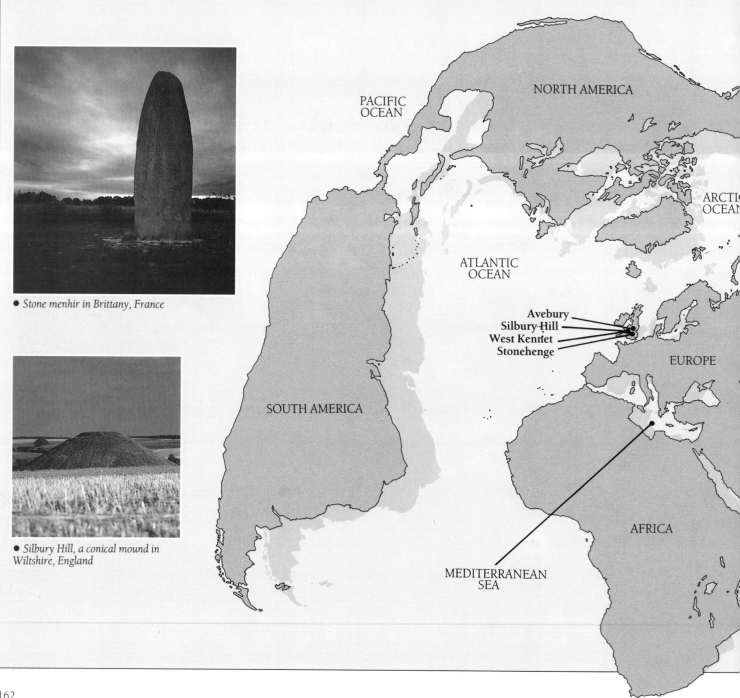

● Stone menhir in Brittany, France

● Silbury Hill, a conical mound in Wiltshire, England

PACIFIC OCEAN

NORTH AMERICA

ARCTIC OCEAN

ATLANTIC OCEAN

Avebury
Silbury Hill
West Kennet
Stonehenge

EUROPE

SOUTH AMERICA

AFRICA

MEDITERRANEAN SEA

Some of the greatest mysteries in archaeology surround the ancients' knowledge of the heavens, of the solar bodies that ordered their world. The stark rings of stones at Stonehenge and Avebury in southern Britain, and similar stone circles in France, evoke emotions of mystery and prehistoric power, of ancient knowledge brilliantly applied. They are a great archaeological puzzle.

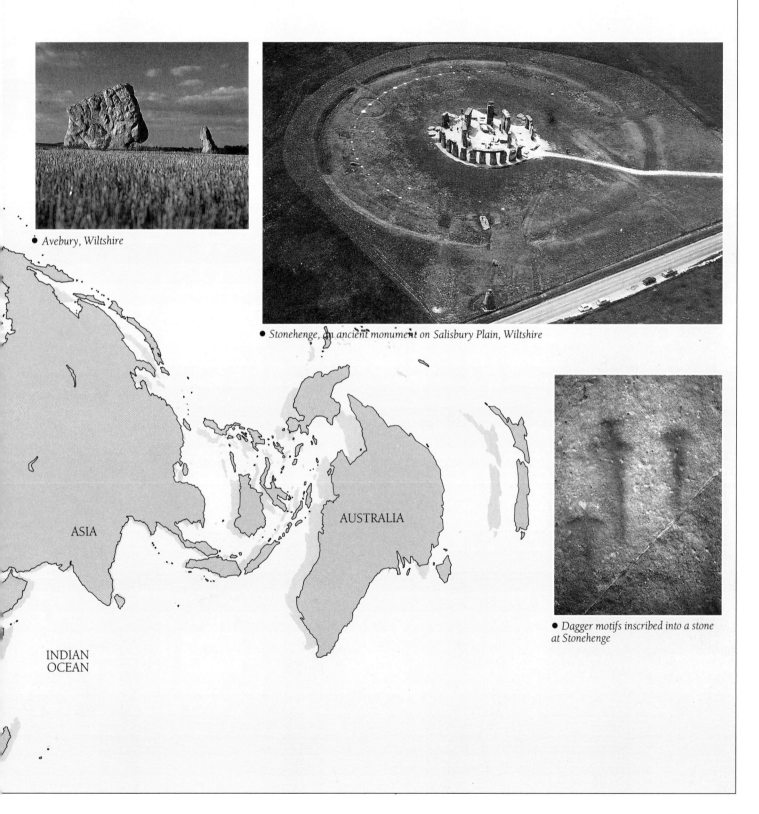

● *Avebury, Wiltshire*

● *Stonehenge, an ancient monument on Salisbury Plain, Wiltshire*

● *Dagger motifs inscribed into a stone at Stonehenge*

ASIA

AUSTRALIA

INDIAN
OCEAN

(preceding page) *Stonehenge, the most celebrated of all Bronze Age monuments, has been revered and studied for centuries. Despite the many theories about its astronomical significance recent researches do not support claims that Stonehenge was a sophisticated prehistoric astronomical computer.*

STONEHENGE

The gray stones have stood since time immemorial, impervious to wind and weather, majestic prehistoric circles in a fold of Salisbury Plain. Roman legions marvelled at the massive trilithons; Saxon farmers paused in their shadow. The same questions were on everyone's lips: who had erected Stonehenge and when? Monarchs and commoners, the learned and the curious contemplated Stonehenge. King Charles II even sent his architect Inigo Jones to make a plan of the stone circles. Some attributed Stonehenge to the 'Ancient Britons'. The celebrated antiquarian John Aubrey, too, knew all about them. They were, he wrote in the mid-seventeenth century, 'two or three degrees less savage, I suppose, than the Americans'.

By Americans Aubrey meant American Indians – about the only primitive peoples known to him who might have had a life somewhat akin to that enjoyed by his Ancient Britons, who lived long before Julius Caesar invaded Britain in 55BC. In reality, Aubrey was as puzzled as everyone else. It has taken generations of archaeological research to date this most mysterious and spectacular of archaeological sites. Even now the enigma remains – what was Stonehenge used for? Was it a simple shrine or a sophisticated astronomical observatory? Did its builders enjoy advanced mathematical knowledge and use abstruse calculations to orient the stones towards the heavenly bodies? Stonehenge is still one of archaeology's most tantalizing mysteries.

Thanks to several major excavations, we know today that Stonehenge is what archaeologists call a 'henge monument', an arrangement of stone circles bounded by a ditch and embankment, associated with burial mounds and other prehistoric sites near by. The site has been excavated many times, as archaeologists probe its complicated architectural history, which spans a period of more than 1,500 years, from as early as about 3000BC until about 1500BC. Its great 'trilithons', freestanding stones with massive lintels, are unique in the prehistoric world, so scientists have speculated for generations about the significance of Stonehenge.

Was Stonehenge a sophisticated astronomical observatory, a place where pre-

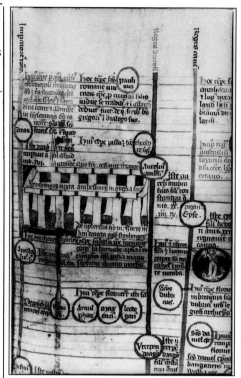

The earliest known illustration of Stonehenge, from a fourteenth-century manuscript, now in Corpus Christi College, Cambridge. The name of Aurelius Ambrosius appears above the image of Stonehenge. He was reputedly the father of Arthur, the builder of Stonehenge.

historic priests kept watch upon the heavens? As long ago as the eighteenth century, William Stukeley realized that Stonehenge was roughly aligned to the midsummer sunrise. He observed that the major features of the stone circle were arranged around a northeast-southwest axis. A long earthwork known as the 'Avenue' leads away from Stonehenge on its northeast side. This axis and the Avenue lie on an approximate line with the point on the horizon where the sun rises on midsummer morning. By the same token, the midwinter sunset is aligned with the other end of the axis. Even though our scientific predecessors were engrossed by prehistoric religion, because they lived in a far more religious age than ours, with this evidence it is hardly surprising that they believed that Stonehenge was associated with sun worship. From such beliefs, it is a short step to theorizing about Stonehenge's role as an astronomical observatory.

The crux of the Stonehenge mystery thus lies in proving or disproving alignments of stone circles and individual features of the monument. Everyone agrees on the midsummer-midwinter alignment. But every other attempt to demonstrate additional alignments founders on either archaeological, astronomical or mathematical grounds. The celebrated astronomer Fred Hoyle made extensive calculations and observations, and showed that *we* can indeed use Stonehenge for eclipse prediction, or to plot the movement of sun and moon. Thus, he argued, it would be astonishing if its prehistoric builders could not do the same. But this is a very different thing from *demonstrating* with a high statistical probability that Stonehenge was indeed used for these purposes thousands of years ago.

The astronomy of Stonehenge is a confusing morass of conflicting theories that are based on different astronomical bodies, even on elements of Stonehenge that are thousands of years apart in age. One researcher even used a rubbish dump dating

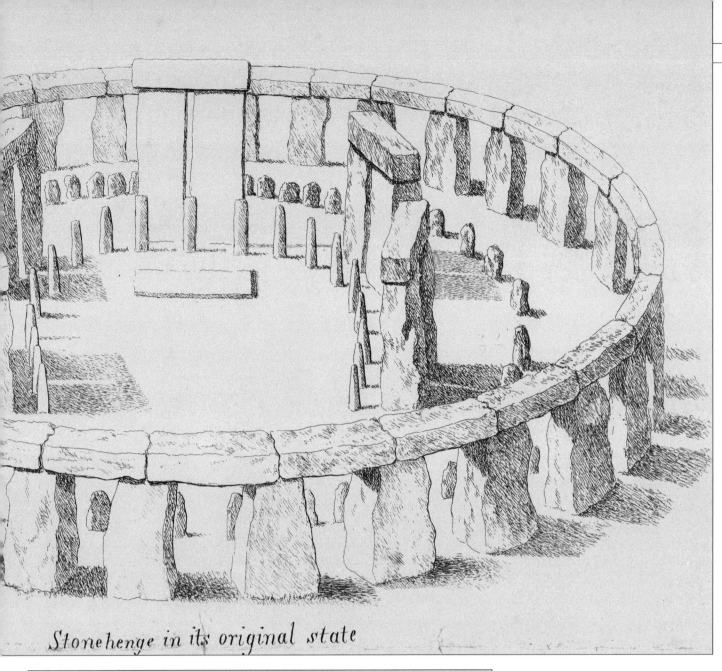

Stonehenge in its original state

Above *An ideal image of Stonehenge with all its trilithons and stones erected.*

Left *Located in a fold in the Salisbury Plain, the great trilithons of Stonehenge dominate the landscape.*

DEVELOPMENT OF STONEHENGE

*Stonehenge was in use for many centuries and evolved gradually from generation to generation. Archaeologists have now identified four broad phases in its development, **right**.*

Stonehenge 1 (c.2,800BC) consisted of a circular ditch and bank, 56 'Aubrey Holes' (named after John Aubrey, who found them in the seventeenth century) and four Station Stones. A small timber building may have stood at the centre.
Stonehenge II (c.2,100BC) boasted a double circle of Bluestones at the centre, imported from the Prescelly Mountains, Wales, but the circle was dismantled before completion. The entrance causeway was widened and the Altar Stone erected.
Stonehenge IIIa (c.2,000BC) saw a circle made of sarsen stones surrounding the centre and a horseshoe of five trilithons inside it. By that time the Altar Stone had been moved.
Stonehenge IIIb (of unknown date) saw the Altar Stone re-erected, also another Bluestone Circle and Horseshoe that were soon dismantled.
Below *Professor Fred Hoyle proposed in 1977 that the Aubrey Holes could have been a model of the sky, used for calculating the occurrence of eclipses. This diagram summarizes this theory.*

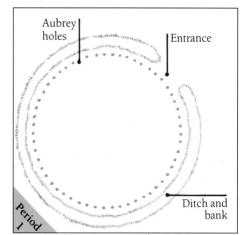

Period 1
Aubrey holes · Entrance · Ditch and bank

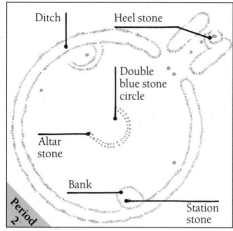

Period 2
Ditch · Heel stone · Double blue stone circle · Altar stone · Bank · Station stone

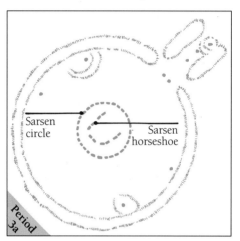

Period 3a
Sarsen circle · Sarsen horseshoe

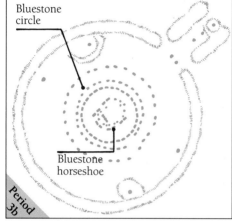

Period 3b
Bluestone circle · Bluestone horseshoe

Above *Stonehenge is one of the most frequently visisted archaeological sites in the world. It has been carefully restored and excavated in recent years, with archaeologists re-erecting stones that are known to have fallen in historical times. Here,*

Professors Richard Atkinson and Stuart Piggott discuss the final stages of re-erecting one of the stones. Atkinson stands on the left with his hand on the stone, and Piggott stands on the right, on the wooden plank, with his right arm on the stone.

from World War I to prove one of his alignments! But time and again, scientific archaeological observation has disproved these astronomical hypotheses.

Another promising 'alignment' came to light in 1966, when three pits were excavated on the site of the Stonehenge parking lot extension. The excavators believed that the pits were foundations for three massive wooden posts, quite different from those associated with Stonehenge itself. What then was their function? Astro-archaeologist Alexander Thom of Oxford University theorized that the posts were the supports for a timber platform that once carried temporary sighting markers. These markers were used to adjust a sight aligned with a spot a good 14.5km (9 miles) away! Another scholar argued that they were astronomical markers for solar and lunar events. All these calculations and theories collapsed when radiocarbon dates from the postholes gave readings between 9,180 and 8,140 years ago, fully 4,000 radiocarbon years before the Stonehenge features they were claimed to align with! The postholes may in fact have been nothing more than natural holes left by tree roots.

Period 3c

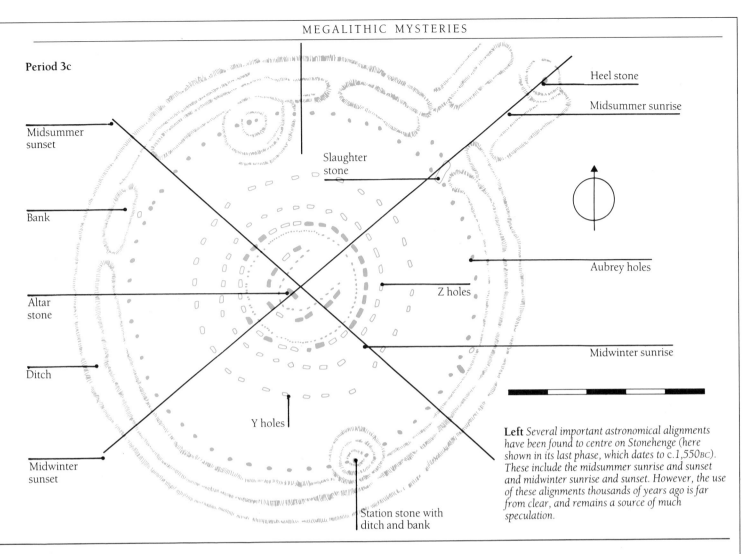

Midsummer sunset

Bank

Altar stone

Ditch

Midwinter sunset

Slaughter stone

Y holes

Station stone with ditch and bank

Heel stone

Midsummer sunrise

Aubrey holes

Z holes

Midwinter sunrise

Left *Several important astronomical alignments have been found to centre on Stonehenge (here shown in its last phase, which dates to c.1,550BC). These include the midsummer sunrise and sunset and midwinter sunrise and sunset. However, the use of these alignments thousands of years ago is far from clear, and remains a source of much speculation.*

CALCULATING PROBABILITIES

Theories about ancient observatories anywhere pit archaeology against statistical probability. The astronomer Gerald Hawkins caused a sensation in the late 1960s when he used an IBM computer to 'decode' Stonehenge's alignments. He used thousands of calculations to find astronomy in the stones.

The first Stonehenge was a circle of simple uncut stones and pits. Hawkins believes that the circle was set on very precise sight lines that were perpetuated in the much finer architecture of what archaeologists call Stonehenge III, the circle of trilithons erected centuries later. The computer spewed out thousands of probability calculations. There was, Hawkins claimed, a ten million to one chance that the two Stonehenges had the same alignments by accident.

British archaeologist Chris Chippindale points out that this sort of calculation is quite meaningless, because Hawkins has shown only that the stone configurations are astronomically valid and statistically improbable. What he has not done is to show that astronomical configurations of

that general type are improbable *as a whole*. What happened was that Stonehenge's stones and pits suggested a possibility to Hawkins. So he marshalled a spectrum of astronomical probabilities merely because Stonehenge suggested them. Unfortunately, the mystery remains because he cannot test his hypothesis against another Stonehenge. The site is unique. As Chippindale points out, all we can hope for is a theory that fits not only the observed features of Stonehenge, but the general archaeological evidence we have for this period of prehistory. This is the approach that much recent investigation has taken.

Many theories about Stonehenge can be dismissed out of hand, theories that claim, for example, that a circle of Stonehenge pits was used to make tidal predictions in the English Channel! For a start the holes were filled up soon after they were dug. And it seems unlikely that the Stonehenge people of 3000BC had the necessary knowledge of celestial mechanics possessed by the twentieth-century researcher! But fortunately, Stonehenge shares many architectural features with dozens of other stone circles, rows and shrines in Britain. Alexander Thom spent more than 30 years searching for such similarities, surveying and measur-

ing hundreds of these 'megalithic' monuments in Britain and France. After a while, he had acquired so much data that he could make statistical arguments based on dozens of sites.

In the 1960s, Thom claimed three major discoveries of megalithic science. First, he believed that the builders of stone circles and tombs had used exact units of length, including a megalithic 'yard'. These units were used to lay out precise geometric shapes on the ground – circles, ellipses, D shapes, even pointed egg shapes. Thom also claimed that the builders laid out precise astronomical alignments over many miles, alignments which coincided with solar and lunar events. In 1972, Sir David Kendall, a Cambridge statistician, calculated that the probability that the megalithic yard was a chance dimension was less than one per cent. This seemed to support at least part of Thom's claim for megalithic science.

But were the megalith builders such skilled artisans and astronomers? Many archaeologists believe that some units of length were used, but that they were far less accurate than Thom's calculations claim. For example, human paces are a convenient, reasonably accurate way of laying

Right William Stukeley's plan of Avebury shows the village in the middle of the great stone circle. Stukeley was an astute, accurate observer, who plotted the positions of individual stones, inner circles, and modern houses inside the monument.

Below Stonehenge's trilithons tower above the ancient temple. They once formed a circle, joined with lintels, some of which are still in place.

out circles and other shapes on the ground, even if the final geometry is less precise. Archaeologists of this persuasion argue, perhaps convincingly, that the irregular shapes of many circles and egg-shaped stone alignments may reflect people judging a circle by eye, then pacing it out.

AVEBURY

The greatest British stone circle is Avebury, east of Bristol. On January 7, 1648, a young country squire named John Aubrey came across Avebury while fox hunting. He was 'wonderfully surprised at the sight of those vast stones'. Soon he was comparing

Avebury to Stonehenge, to the latter's disadvantage, claiming that it 'does as much exceed in greatness the so renowned Stonehenge as a Cathedral doeth a parish church'. Avebury consists of two avenues of standing stones leading to a chalk bank broken by four entrances and causeways. Inside lies a great stone circle with the remains of two smaller concentric circles on either side of the centre. Generations of archaeologists have puzzled over the meaning of this remarkable monument.

Avebury stands on a low natural dome. Its ditch, which was dug in 2000BC, encloses 11.5ha (28.5 acres). The scale of the work was stupendous, especially if

undertaken by a tribal society. About 370,000m² (3,980,000ft²) of chalk were removed from the ditch and piled up on the surrounding bank. Before starting on the ditch, the builders measured out a circle with a diameter of 165.8m (544ft). According to Alexander Thom, they did so with a special rod about 2m (7ft) long, the length of a megalithic yard. This they laid out with precise care more than 300 times, with a slip in accuracy of no more than 2mm each time!

Aubrey Burl, a leading expert on stone circles, argues that far simpler methods were used to dig the ditch. Perhaps a long line set on a central peg was used to set out

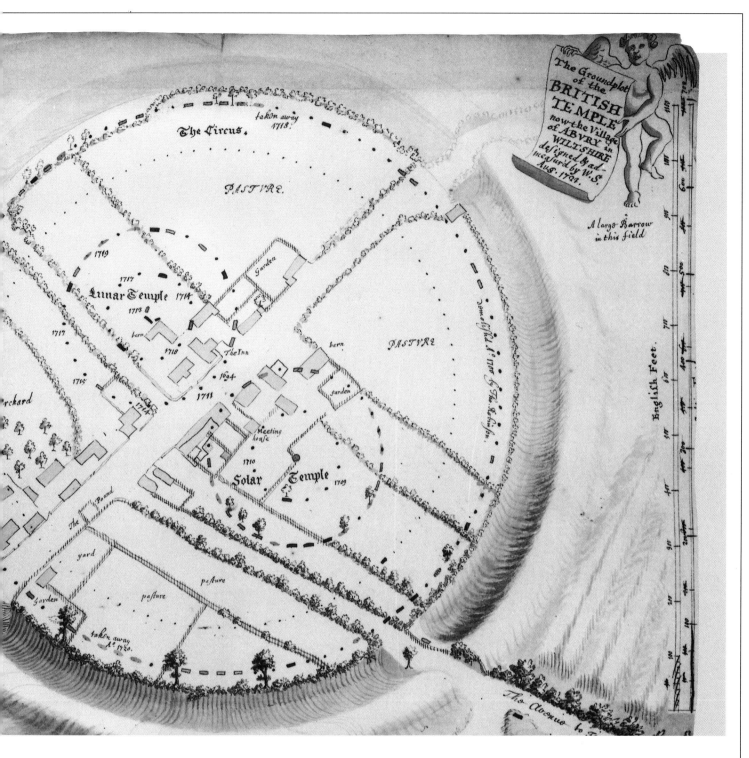

The Groundplot of the BRITISH TEMPLE now the Village of ABVRY in WILTSHIRE designed & admeasured by W.S. Aug. 1724.

A large Barrow in this field

English Feet.

a wavering circle that was interrupted by causeways set on NNW/SSE and WSW/ENE axes. A set of marker posts was set up to delineate the inner edge of the ditch; these have been identified from a single posthole found in 1965. This simple technique would have required no elaborate astronomy.

Then the construction work would have begun. Aubrey Burl reconstructs the scene: 'Then with antler-picks, ox shoulder blades, baskets, ropes of leather or animal hide, or even grass, the ditches were quarried, quadrant by quadrant, in sections, gangs of workers driving the antler tines into fissures, levering, pushing, until the chalk broke.' The rubble was levered out, manoeuvered into baskets, then carried up ladders and specially cut terraces. A circle of cut turf marked the core of the external bank. There the chalk was dumped, basketful by basketful. When each section of ditch was completed, the builders hacked away the balks between them until the circle was finished.

Another archaeologist, Richard Atkinson, used a formula based on the horizontal and vertical distance that the chalk had been moved, to calculate that it took 1,560,000 man-hours to build the ditch and bank alone, quite apart from the effort of erecting the great stones. Burl says that if 750 people worked at Avebury ten hours a day for two months a year after the harvest was in, they would have completed the task in four years.

If this was not enough, more than 190 stones weighing as much as 47 tonnes were towed laboriously from the nearby down to their final places in the stone circles close to the ditch edge. The men dug holes about 1m (3ft 3in) deep, sloping one side of each hole as a ramp for the stone. Each stone was slid down the ramp, then levered upright with levers and ropes. Timber props and clay supported the stone while it settled. Then it was jammed in place with packing stones which were rammed into

Below *Known as Adam and Eve, these two stones are the only remaining ones of the 200 or so stones that once formed the Beckhamton Avenue that led west from the Avebury Circle. They were the first two stones of the avenue.*

Right *Avebury village still nestles inside the great ditch and stone circle. Generations of villagers quarried the circles for building stone for these very houses, and not much of the stone circle remains.*

the pit. As many as 200 people were needed to move the largest uprights.

How many people lived around Avebury 4,000 years ago? Estimating prehistoric populations means entering a minefield of scientific uncertainty. In 1972, Richard Atkinson estimated that the entire population of England and Wales then was no more than 2,000 people, whereas a year later another archaeologist, Colin Renfrew, stated that there were at that time as many as 34,000 people in Wessex alone! More recent estimates are based on a much better understanding of the realities of prehistoric agriculture.

Aubrey Burl argues that a population of 1,500 people around Avebury would require 1ha (2.5 acres) of cultivated land per head, with as much lying fallow for later use when planted land was exhausted. Adding uncultivated marshes, hillsides, and forests, he comes up with a territory of 13,727ha (53 miles^2), and a population density of 28 people per 2.5km^2 (1 mile^2). Burl's figure is only an intelligent guess. For instance, if the people had been cattle herders rather than farmers, they would have needed much more land for their animals, between 155km^2 and 233km^2 (60 miles^2 and 90 miles^2). Burl believes that territories between 77km^2 and 233km^2 (30 miles^2 and 90 miles^2) supported a farming population of between 6,000 and 12,000 people some 4,000 years ago. This allows for sufficient people to build not only Avebury but other such enclosures in different territories, circles like Marden, about 11km (7 miles) south of Avebury and 16km (10 miles) north of Durrington Walls.

SILBURY HILL

The communal work that built Avebury continued for generations, transforming the prehistoric landscape, not only with long avenues, but with communal graves like the famous West Kennet long barrow and an astonishing artificial mountain – Silbury Hill – 1.6km (1 mile) south of Avebury.

Silbury is a conical mound about 39.6m (130ft) high, which was excavated by Richard Atkinson in the late 1960s by the simple expedient of tunneling into the core. He obtained a radiocarbon date from the centre that dates the great earthwork to the same period of Avebury, about 4,000 years ago. Atkinson estimated that it took 18 million man-hours to erect Silbury, a task that would have taken 500 workers more than half a century if they had worked for only a few weeks after the harvest was in.

West Kennet Long Barrow, **top right**, *is only 2.4km (1½ miles) south of Avebury, a communal sepulchre with large megalithic boulders protecting the forecourt. Inside the tomb lies a stone-lined passageway,* **right**.

The job would have taken 15 years with a full-time labour force.

Why would a society of prehistoric farmers undertake such large building projects that went on for generations? We can only guess at their motives, because all that remains are potsherds, stones, decaying earthworks, and scatters of food residues and human bones.

It seems certain that they were familiar with the movements of sun and moon, perhaps of some planets like Venus as well. It seems likely that they had some elementary knowledge of units of measurement that enabled them to build regular stone circles, even elaborate chamber tombs. The alignments of Stonehenge and Avebury, as well as of other stone circles, hint at some connection with the heavenly bodies, but no archaeologist-astronomer has yet shown conclusively that the sites were complex astronomical observatories.

The most likely theory is that places like Avebury and Stonehenge were locations where people congregated at certain seasons of the year, perhaps to trade, probably to conduct rituals that linked the world of the living to that of ancestors and of nature, the forces that supported bountiful crops. Aubrey Burl paints a colourful picture, of 'witch-doctors brandishing human bones, people dancing within the stones, the old and very young seated, swaying, hands and drums beaten rhythmically . . .'. He believes Avebury was a cult centre, a place where hundreds of prehistoric people came together to reaffirm their lives. Perhaps this is the closest we will ever get to the riddle of Avebury and Stonehenge.

Science can identify the sources of the stones, tell us how they were erected, and even perhaps, establish the geographical relationship between neighbouring monuments. But the voices of those who built them are gone forever, and no archaeologist however expert can ever hope to resurrect the chants and rituals they offered.

Left *Silbury Hill is a huge conical mound 39.6m (130ft) high, built about 4,000 years ago. Its significance is a complete mystery, despite excavations which tunnelled to its centre.*

PART FOUR
THE NEW FRONTIER

CHINA

CHINA

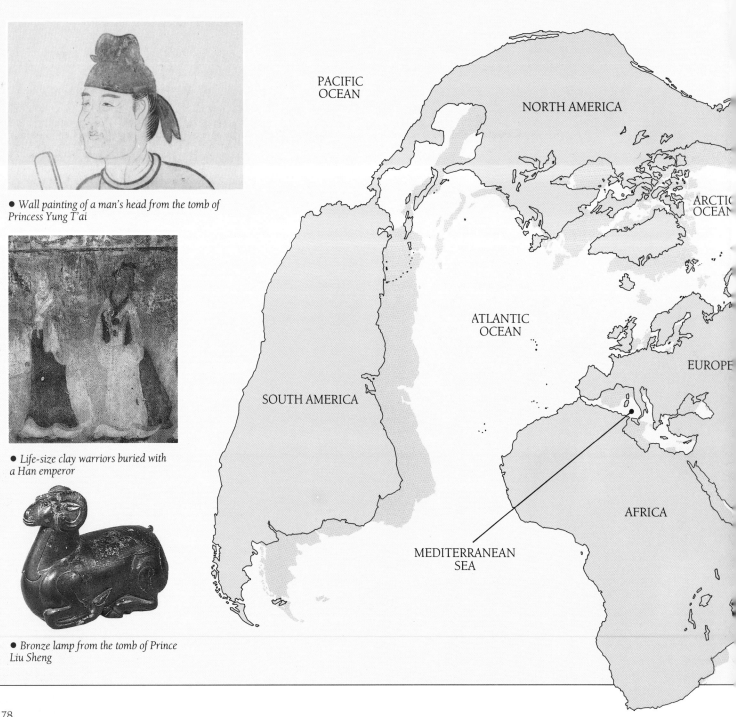

● *Wall painting of a man's head from the tomb of Princess Yung T'ai*

● *Life-size clay warriors buried with a Han emperor*

● *Bronze lamp from the tomb of Prince Liu Sheng*

PACIFIC
OCEAN

NORTH AMERICA

ARCTIC
OCEAN

ATLANTIC
OCEAN

EUROPE

SOUTH AMERICA

AFRICA

MEDITERRANEAN
SEA

By no means has every area of the world been explored by archaeologists, and discoveries remain to be made everywhere. In some cases archaeologists know the location of a site but for one reason or another have not been able to excavate it. If there is one area of the world where prodigious surprises await us, it is China, a land where modern archaeological exploration has hardly begun. The spectacular discoveries that have been made there recently are just a foretaste of what awaits archaeologists when they finally investigate the apparently undisturbed tombs of the mighty emperors of one of the world's oldest and richest civilizations. But it will be some time before they do because with amazing restraint and patience, Chinese archaeologists are refraining from excavating the royal sites until they have sufficient skill and expertise to do so properly.

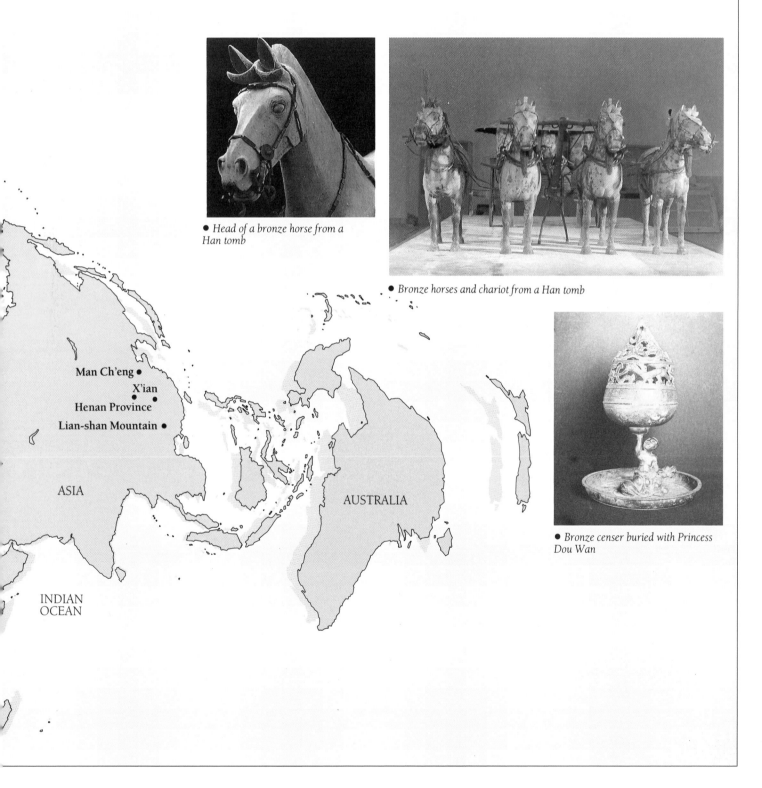

● *Head of a bronze horse from a Han tomb*

● *Bronze horses and chariot from a Han tomb*

● *Bronze censer buried with Princess Dou Wan*

Man Ch'eng ●

● X'ian

Henan Province ●

Lian-shan Mountain ●

ASIA

AUSTRALIA

INDIAN OCEAN

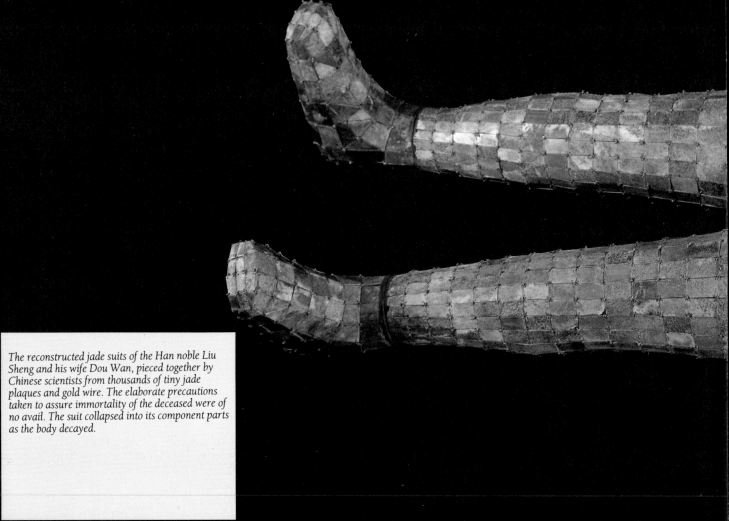

The reconstructed jade suits of the Han noble Liu Sheng and his wife Dou Wan, pieced together by Chinese scientists from thousands of tiny jade plaques and gold wire. The elaborate precautions taken to assure immortality of the deceased were of no avail. The suit collapsed into its component parts as the body decayed.

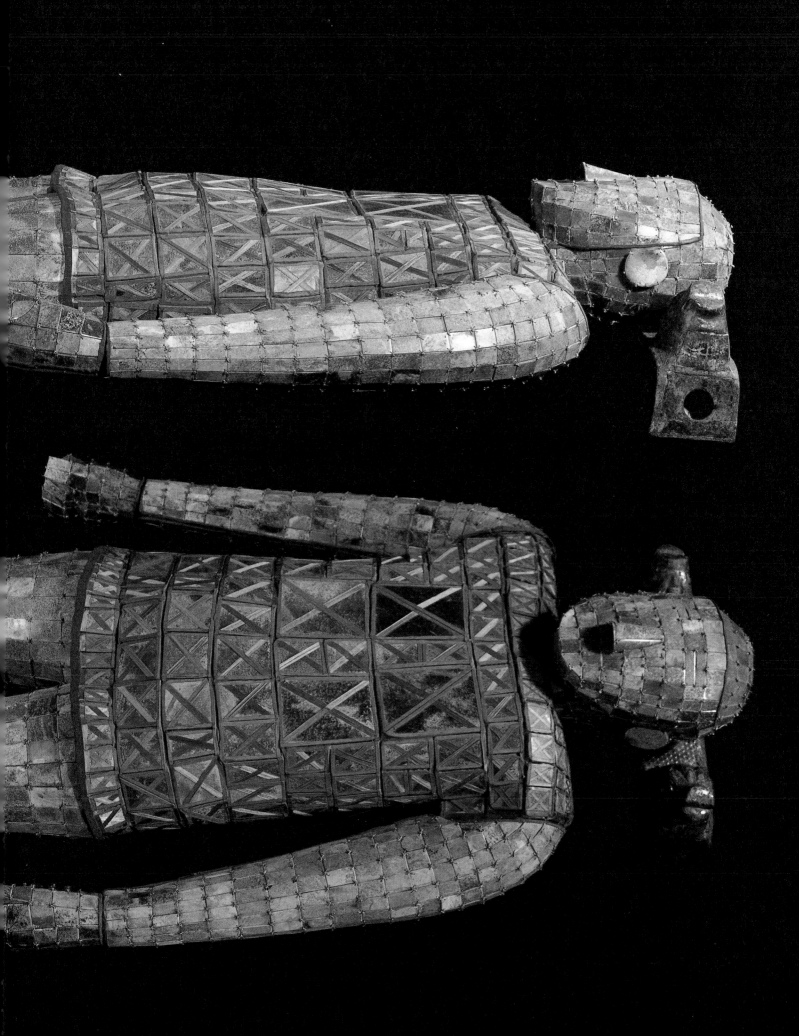

LIU SHENG AND DOU WAN

The Han Emperor Ching-ti took up residence in his tomb upon his death in 141 BC. He was buried in awesome splendour, under a great burial mound that was like a mountain. Thousands of convicts laboured on his lavish sepulchre. The entrance was sealed with stone blocks and molten iron. So far, archaeologists have not tried to excavate his mausoleum, but they have found some of the unfortunate men who constructed it, buried hastily with their neck and leg irons still in place. Some had been decapitated. Their skeletons are a tantalizing hint of the fantastic discoveries that await archaeologists in China.

The first Han leaders emerged in 206BC. Their dynasty was to rule China almost without interruption for 400 years. These brilliant and ruthless traders and administrators established the Great Silk Route that carried China's most famous product to the Roman Empire. Ching-ti ruled China during some of her most glorious years. Even today, the Chinese people call themselves 'the people of Han', in memory of those prosperous days.

At the apex of this great empire sat the emperor, the 'Son of Heaven'. He ruled over a despotic government administered by a vast bureaucracy of nobles and officials. His relatives maintained the imperial presence in ten principalities throughout his domains. They, in turn, ruled like emperors, accountable only to the Son of Heaven. Fortunately for archaeologists, the Han nobles and their lesser minions were preoccupied with the belief that they could take all their earthly possessions with them to the next world. They assumed they would transfer their pleasant earthly life into the next, with every amenity provided.

The teams of Chinese archaeologists who have dug into Han tombs have been accorded detailed insights into court life 2,000 years ago. They have unearthed acrobats modelled in clay performing before a noble family; miniatures of people, animals and farm houses; even models of carts and boats. The tombs provide an extraordinarily detailed record of how the ancient Chinese went about their business. No one has yet tried to excavate a Han royal burial, entombed as they are under vast artificial hills built with forced labour, and it is likely to be some time before the cautious Chinese embark on such an ambitious excavation project. They lack both the resources and the trained experts to tackle the task. In the meantime, they are learning their skills on other sites, some of which have proved startlingly spectacular.

In 153BC, the Han Emperor Wu-ti appointed his elder brother Liu Sheng to rule the populous Chung-shan principality near Beijing. Liu Sheng and his wife Dou Wan presided over the province for nearly 40 years until his death in 113BC. His wife survived him for about another decade. Both were depraved and corrupt nobles. Liu Sheng was 'fond of wine and women'. While thousands of their subjects starved as a result of terrible floods, Liu Sheng and his wife were laid to rest with lavish burial rites in deep, rock-cut chambers quarried into the barren hillsides near the town of Man-Ch'eng. There they lay undisturbed and forgotten, until June 1968, when a detachment of the People's Liberation Army made one of the most dramatic archaeological discoveries of all time.

The soldiers were on night patrol when they stumbled across a small hole that led deep underground. The company commander and his men made their way carefully into a narrow defile. They found themselves in a vast chamber, 'large enough to hold 100 men'. Their feeble flashlights caught the glint of gold, silver and jade; bronze and clay pots stood in long, orderly rows. The excited troops mounted guard over the tomb and summoned the authorities. Scientists from the Academy of Sciences in Beijing were on the scene within hours. Peering at the inscriptions on the funerary vessels, they soon identified the owner of the possessions as Prince Liu Sheng.

Meanwhile, the eager soldiers had scoured the neighbouring hillsides for more tombs. They came across huge piles of rocky chips on a nearby hill, poked around in the debris and unearthed the entrance to another cavern, this time a massive fortification of stone blocks sealed with molten iron. Was this another tomb? Under careful supervision, army demolition experts blasted open the entrance. It proved to be the burial ground of Liu Sheng's wife Dou Wan.

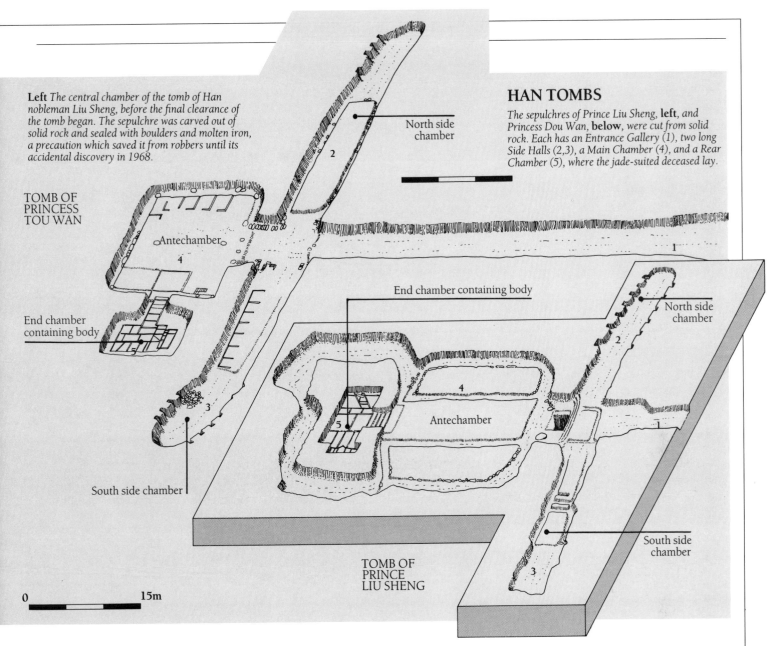

Left *The central chamber of the tomb of Han nobleman Liu Sheng, before the final clearance of the tomb began. The sepulchre was carved out of solid rock and sealed with boulders and molten iron, a precaution which saved it from robbers until its accidental discovery in 1968.*

TOMB OF
PRINCESS
TOU WAN

Antechamber

4

End chamber
containing body

5

South side chamber

3

0   15m

North side
chamber

2

HAN TOMBS

The sepulchres of Prince Liu Sheng, **left**, *and Princess Dou Wan,* **below**, *were cut from solid rock. Each has an Entrance Gallery (1), two long Side Halls (2,3), a Main Chamber (4), and a Rear Chamber (5), where the jade-suited deceased lay.*

End chamber containing body

North side
chamber

2

4

Antechamber

5

1

South side
chamber

3

TOMB OF
PRINCE
LIU SHENG

The contents of the tombs were so precious that the sites could be excavated only by carefully organized teamwork. The government formed an archaeological team of local and national experts, and called in the army to provide logistical support. The task was almost as complicated as that faced by British archaeologist Howard Carter when in 1922 he excavated Pharaoh Tutankhamen's tomb in Egypt's Valley of the Kings. Conservation and study of the contents of the two Chinese tombs continues to this day.

Liu Sheng's tomb was sealed with two brick walls. The cavity between them had been sealed with molten lava that must have been smelted on the site. The walls blocked an entrance passageway filled with earth and rocks that led to the tomb itself. The huge rock cavern beyond measured 52m (171ft) in length. Thousands of men had worked to excavate these chambers from the two hillsides, moving more than 64,000 tonnes of rock in the process.

The archaeologists penetrated the passageway and found themselves in an antechamber with two side passages. Liu Sheng's 6 carriages, 16 horses and 11 dogs lay in these defiles. A horse-drawn grindstone complete with horses and ample food and wine for a long journey lay nearby. The central chamber had originally been hung with finely embroidered curtains that had decayed over the centuries. It had wooden walls and a tiled roof. Hundreds of fine vessels and figurines lay in rows on the floor. A stone doorway at the far end of the chamber led to the burial chamber itself. In it, Liu Sheng's coffin lay on a platform at the north end, with a bathroom on the south side. A walkway extended around the stone-lined chamber. Dou Wan's sepulchre had the same design.

It took months to clear the two tombs. The archaeologists removed more than 2,800 funerary objects from them, including magnificent gold and bronze vessels, gold, silver and jade ornaments, fine clay

vessels, lacquered vases, even fine silks. Everything was of the finest possible quality, a quality that belonged to royalty and near-royalty alone.

Perhaps the most beautiful finds are a lamp and an incense burner. Dou Wan's body was watched over by a gilt-bronze lamp in the form of a young serving girl; the servant is kneeling, a lamp in her hands. The girl's head could be removed to fill the reservoir with oil, and the hollow right arm served as a chimney to divert the smoke away from the user. The lamp is inscribed with the title 'Lamp of the Palace of Eternal Trust'. Dou Wan's grandmother lived in a palace of that name; perhaps she gave the lamp to her granddaughter as a wedding present.

Liu Sheng took a magnificent incense burner with him to the next world. The bronze burner was fashioned into the shape of a precipitous mountain peak. Hunters cavort on its slopes, chasing wild animals over peaks which appear to float in clouds

Above *This rectangular clay tray from Dou Wan's tomb once held the figurines of four acrobats, eight musicians, two dancers, a conductor, and seven standing spectators. Today, one of the musicians is missing, but the performance goes on, just as it did in Han times (206BC to AD24). The tray is 67.5cm (26.5in) long.*

Left *Prince Liu Sheng's bronze incense burner was inlaid in gold. The upper part depicts mountain peaks interspersed with small figures of hunters and animals. The incense smoke would wreathe the 'mountain' in billowy clouds.*

Above *Two parcel-gilt bronze leopard figures inlaid with silver and garnets from Dou Wan's sepulchre. They are two of a set of four probably used to weigh down the corners of funerary palls Lesser peoples' palls were weighed down with summary jade carvings of pig-like animals.*

of silver and gold. When the incense was lit, the pungent smoke would swirl out through numerous holes in the burner and wreathe the mountain scene.

Some of the other bronze vessels were equally magnificent. They included two gilded wine containers modelled with intricate dragon and knob designs, which still glowed with lustrous colour after 2,000 years. There was another lamp too, in the form of a flying bird holding a round dish with three candles. The archaeologists were dazzled by the intricate patterns and the glitter of gold and silver inlay.

JADE CASKETS

The corpses of Liu Sheng and Dou Wan had been laid out in magnificent jade suits made up of thousands of small jade plaques. But, as the bodies decomposed and the wooden coffins rotted to dust, the jade suits collapsed and the gold or silk threads that tied the plaques broke. All that remained when the archaeologists discovered them was a tightly compacted jumble of jade and gold mixed with fragments of the wooden coffins. Even so, they managed to lift Liu Sheng's suit out in one piece, using an iron frame criss-crossed with fine wire and masked with plaster of Paris. The excavators approached Dou Wan's more fragmentary suit in a different way. They photographed each of the jade plaques, drawing and numbering them on a master plan, which helped them to reconstruct the suit.

The Han called the jade suits *yu-xia*, 'jade caskets'. A rigid etiquette surrounded these prestigious shrouds. Emperors and princes were buried in 'gold-threaded jade suits', and 'honorable ladies', such as imperial concubines, in jade linked with 'silver thread'. In the sixth century AD, Wu Jun wrote, 'upon burial the emperors of the Han were all laid out in jewelled jackets and jade suits. These suits resembled armour and were sewn together with gold thread'. Liu Sheng and Dou Wan's suits were the most complete ever found.

Liu Sheng's suit was in eight parts: helmet, mask, back and front upper garments, trousers, armlets, gloves and boots. Each component was tailor-made, fitted to the exact contours of the prince's body. The suit is 1.88m (6ft 2in) long, made up of 2,160 jade plaques and 1.1kg (2lb 7oz) of gold thread. Dou Wan's is 1.72m (5ft 6in) long, fabricated of 2,160 plaques and 700g (1lb 9oz) of gold thread.

Each piece of jade had been carefully colour-matched and numbered by the artisan, and each plaque polished on the outer surface, and shaped with tiny saws with

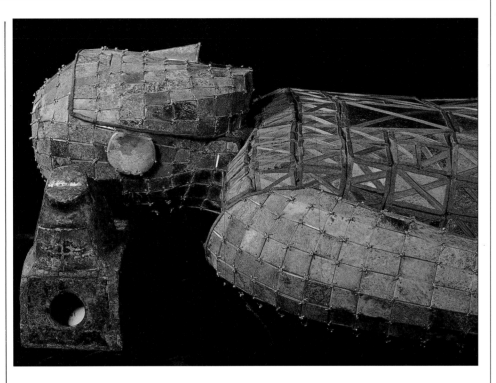

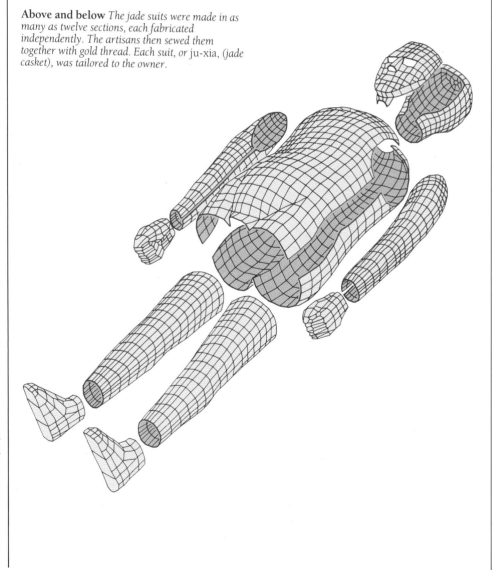

Above and below *The jade suits were made in as many as twelve sections, each fabricated independently. The artisans then sewed them together with gold thread. Each suit, or* ju-xia, *(jade casket), was tailored to the owner.*

delicate teeth. Then tiny holes were drilled along the edges. Fine gold thread was inserted into the holes and tied in intricate patterns with at least nine different knots, to join the plaques. Each part of the suit was edged with red cloth and set aside until the wearer died. These parts were sewn tightly to its neighbour so that no bit of the body was left exposed. The suited prince and princess were laid to rest in lacquered coffins, 'their heads reposing on bronze pillows inlaid with gold. The restorers estimated that each jade suit took a single craftsman more than ten years to complete.

Chinese archaeologists believe that the jade suits were an expression of the intimate association between the supposed spiritual qualities of jade and human afterlife, perhaps a key to eternity. It is possible, however, that the suits were of more importance as an instrument of political and social patronage, because the Han rulers used them as diplomatic gifts as well, bestowing them on foreign leaders. The suits were held in storage at the border city of Xuantu, near the modern city of Shenyang, until their owners died. With abundant supplies of nephrite jade near the eastern terminus of the Great Silk Route, the Han used the skill of their artisans to cement political relationships and to assure their own immortality. Not that the jade treatment was effective. All that remained of Liu Sheng – who had ruled and taxed 600,000 people – was a handful of teeth.

QIN SHI HUANG DI

Emperor Qin Shi Huang Di inherited the throne of the feudal kingdom of Qin in 246BC at the age of 13. The boy developed into a man of iron will, who subjected all of China by 221BC, calling himself Qin Shi Huang Di, First Emperor of Qin.

Huang Di started making plans for his death the moment he ascended his throne. Some 700,000 conscripts laboured on his great mausoleum for 36 years, while skilled artisans fabricated the elaborate grave furniture that would accompany the Emperor. The great historian Sima Qian, writing less than a century after the Emperor's death, described how an entire palace was built under a huge artificial burial mound. The subterranean palace contained a relief map of China modelled in bronze in which flowing mercury traced the courses of the Yangtze and Yellow Rivers. The palace ceiling was a huge depiction of the night sky, bright with the moon and stars. The Emperor also had slow-burning whale oil lamps lit in this palace.

The archaeologists took Sima Qian's

claim with a grain of salt until 1974, when some farmers who were digging a well east of Huang Di's great burial mound uncovered a vast subterranean pit that contained a pottery army of more than 6,000 life-size warriors. The men were drawn up in formation, each figure brightly painted with the correct insignia of rank, each with individual features. Two years later, two adjacent pits came to light, one with 1,400 warriors and horses, the other containing 68 figures, perhaps members of a command unit. Suddenly, Huang Di's claims looked a great deal more plausible.

Slowly, Chinese scholars are moving in on their ultimate target – the actual burial chambers inside the great mound. The opening of this tomb will be one of the great archaeological sensations of all time, but will come only when the Chinese feel that they have enough experience to excavate the mausoleum. Meantime, further confirmation of Sima Qian's description has come from soil analyses that reveal an unusually high level of mercury within the mound. So precise are these measurements that the archaeologists have been able to locate the exact position of Huang Di's palace inside the tumulus.

Further dramatic discoveries came in 1980, when excavations began on the west side of the weathered burial mound, which still stands 45m (147ft) above the surrounding countryside. Originally the tumulus was much larger, so the excavations 20m (65ft) west of the present earthwork may actually have been centred within the area of the burial ground itself. The excavators soon came across a large rectangular chamber built of wooden planks. Inside it, they discovered a pair of bronze carriages, complete with sculptures of drivers and teams of four horses each.

The wooden chamber had rotted away, crushing the chariots, leaving the archaeologists with an intricate restoration job. This conservation work is still going on, after which the dig will search for more trenches that may surround the burial mound – trenches that contain rich funerary goods.

A team of conservators worked for a full year to restore one of the two carriages. The carriage and its four horses is 3.3m (10ft 9in) long, and is of a type that was used by princes and others of high rank. The conveyance itself is 1.2m (4ft) long, a metre (3ft 3in) across and 43cm (17in) deep. The major parts were cast, and then fitted together by welding or riveting.

This was a comfortable vehicle; indeed an inscription on one of the reins reads 'comfortable carriage'. The occupant would have sat or reclined on a mattress in the back, separated from the seated driver by a partition. There are operable windows on three sides and a door fastened with a silver catch at the rear. An oval-shaped canopy, supported on 36 bronze strips, gave shade and privacy. The canopy was once covered with a layer of fine silk, and the insides and outsides of the carriage once gleamed with brightly painted cloud and geometric designs, as well as dragons and phoenixes.

The seated, mustachioed driver sits at the reins, a gentle smile playing on his lips giving him a benign air. He wears a bonnet and cap, a long blue robe and a sword at his belt. The Chinese believe that he may have been a civil official of the ninth grade. With

Above *The Emperor Qin Shi Huang Di's pottery regiment stands in marching order, displayed under cover at the site museum near the royal tomb. Each figure was modelled with individual features, each wore correct insignia of rank, and stood in its correct parade order. Chinese archaeologists excavated the terracotta regiment with infinite care,* **left**, *finding traces of the original paint adhering to the buried figures.* **Right** *A bronze driver and his steeds still hauled their carriage when unearthed close to Qin Shi Huang Di's tomb.*

astounding realism, the bronzesmith who cast him placed two sets of reins in his hands; four others lay on the dashboard, and a further two were attached to a ring at the forward end of the carriage.

The four horses – stocky, well-groomed steeds harnessed to a crossbar as a team – seem to be straining at their reins. They bare their teeth, holding their heads upright. Each stands 66cm (26in) high, and are about 115cm (45in) long. The bronzesmith cast the component parts, then cast or welded them into completed figures with joins so carefully finished that they are almost invisible. The effect is very lifelike. The two inner horses look ahead, the flanking ones slightly outwards, as if they are ready to respond to the slightest movement of the rein. They wear special copper wire tassles. The bridle and reins are intricate masterpieces of gold, silver and bronze wire.

Once the carriages were complete, the bronzesmiths coated them with a chromium preservative that fought corrosion for more than 2,000 years. Then, legend tells us, the smiths were executed and buried, so that the secrets of the Emperor's tomb died with them.

T'ANG TOMBS

T'ai Tsung the Great founded the dynasty named after him in AD627 and reigned over China until AD649. His capital at X'ian covered more than 80km² (31 miles²) and attracted merchants and travellers from as far away as Persia. A million people lived in the great city, another million outside its walls. Only Constantinople rivaled X'ian as a city at the time. The emperor's court lived in sumptuous splendour – its rich palaces were a renowned centre of poetry, music, and the arts.

In AD637 a lowly 12-year-old girl named Wu Chao joined the emperor's harem. Amid the luxury and intrigue of the court she rose to be a concubine of the second rank. The emperor died when she was 24, so she was banished to a nunnery, as custom dictated. But Wu Chao was both beautiful and a genius at getting her own way. In 655 she became the Empress of Emperor Kao Tsung, the son of her original master. Only five years later, the Emperor was paralysed. So the cunning Empress Wu gained absolute power until his death in 683. After deposing his sons, she became Empress in her own right and ruled with despotic severity until her death, at the age of 82. Paranoid to the degree of eccentricity, she eliminated everyone who threatened her position. When she heard that even her grandchildren had criticized her, she ordered them to commit suicide.

The T'ang emperors and Wu herself were buried in seemly splendour in the foothills near X'ian. Prominent crown princes, members of royal families and prominent officials were allowed to build their sepulchres nearby. Wu laid out the mausoleum for herself and her husband with characteristic lavishness. She selected a limestone mountain named Lian-shan 72km (45 miles) from X'ian and turned its surroundings into a funerary park. The mound that covered the underground royal tomb was once surrounded by 378 buildings. The sepulchre that held the body of the Emperor was re-opened in AD705 to receive Wu's remains, then the entrance was sealed with 30 massive stone blocks fused together with molten iron to make looting impossible.

A regal avenue leads to the mausoleum. It runs for 2.4km (1.5 miles) south to north, guarded by towers about 15m (49ft) high on small hills on either side of the avenue. Great sculpted figures of obelisks, winged horses, five pairs of horses with grooms, and ten pairs of warriors with heavy swords lined the avenue. So did 'scarlet birds' carved on stone slabs, birds that are said to have walked before the Emperor on public occasions, to peck out the eyes of anyone who dared to approach the ruler. Two huge seated lions marked the end of the majestic way, guardians of the royal tomb.

In front of the lions stand 60 male figures, each 1.5m (5ft) tall. They stand in four compact rows, 31 on the west and 29 on the east side of the avenue. The statues represent the foreign emissaries who attended the lavish funeral ceremonies and helped to pay the expenses. In gratitude, Wu ordered their statues to be placed in front of her mausoleum. Each is inscribed on the back with the name of the country represented. Only two figures survive: one is from Persia, the other perhaps from northern Afghanistan. Why were there so

Above *On the walls of her tomb, court ladies gather in attendance on the Princess Yung T'ai, their handmaidens carrying fans, dusters, and other possessions.*

many foreigners? The T'ang rulers believed that the presence of outsiders at their court was a sign of virtue, and at a royal funeral they would help in establishing credit for the deceased emperor in the afterlife.

The entrance to Wu's tomb was discovered in 1958, but Chinese archaeologists have so far not touched it. They have, however, excavated five burial chambers associated with the royal mausoleum. Three of them, which include the tombs of two crown princes named Chang Huai and Yi Teh, built in AD706, contain magnificent interior decoration that tells us much of T'ang life. One 12m (39ft) mural in Chang Huai's tomb depicts a polo game, a sport introduced to the court from Persia. The crown prince was obviously a keen player. In the mural some 20 players are raising their mallets, their horses galloping with hooves held high. One rider aims a backhand shot as his horse rears.

Another wall opposite depicts riders preparing for the hunt, as the crown prince sits on a white horse. A crowd of courtiers, guards, and animals surround him. Foreign dignitaries and courtiers stand a short distance away, perhaps guests who have brought a gift of horses from afar.

All the tombs are remarkable for their portraits of elegant ladies and hand-maidens. Crown Prince Chang Huai's sepulchre has a charming scene of women wandering through a garden admiring the flight of a hoopoe – a red-brown bird with a fan-shaped crest.

Princess Yung T'ai was only 17 when she was forced to commit suicide for criticizing her grandmother. A bride of one year, she was eventually buried in an imposing tomb near the royal mausoleum. Another regal avenue, lined with lions, warriors and ceremonial pillars leads to her tomb. The tomb is 87.5m (287ft) long and descends to the burial chamber 33m (108ft) below the burial mound. Four separate compartments in the corridor have wall niches that once contained numerous funerary goods. These included symbolic porcelain guardians – mounted male and female cavalry, each figure about 30cm (12in) high, and foot soldiers. Painted ceremonial guards stood at either side of the tomb doorway, together with the White Tiger of the West and the Dragon of the East, symbols of strength, bravery and imperial dignity. Guardsmen and their horses stand close by, their six halberds decked with bright pennons, held in tigers' muzzles.

The princess' name is carved on a black stone block in the front burial chamber. Groups of elegant court women are in attendance on the walls. Each group has a lady-in-waiting, while handmaidens carry fans, dusters, lacquer boxes and bundles, items that indicate precise roles in the harem hierarchy. These same brilliantly naturalistic figures are found in the burial chamber itself, where court ladies offer tasty morsels to pet birds on their wrists, or carry the tools of their trade. On the entrance doors, scholars hold scrolls, while

Above *The White Tiger of the West guards the tomb of Princess Yung T'ai. He was accompanied by painted ceremonial guards and the Dragon of the East, all of them symbols of imperial dignity.*

ladies hold a lacquered jewel box and a wine cup.

Princess Yung T'ai's tomb was looted by bold robbers, who tunneled 17m (56ft) below the ground to penetrate the sepulchre. One looter was trapped – the archaeologists found his skeleton surrounded by gold and silver coins. Despite the looting, more than 1,300 items were recovered, among them figurines of warriors, handmaidens and animals executed in superb tricolour glazes in brown, green and creamy beige. Jade ornaments, gold horse trappings and other precious fragments hint at the remarkable riches that once filled Yung T'ai's tomb.

THE LADY DAI

History was kinder to a Han noblewoman named the Lady Dai, the wife of a minor marquis, who lived between 193 and 141BC. She was buried on the summit of a low hill in Henan Province, her tomb a vertical, rectangular earthen pit approached by a sloping passageway. Thick jackets of dense white clay and more than 5,000kg (11,022lb) of charcoal lined the deep burial pit, which was dug more than 15m (50ft) into the hill. A six-walled wooden coffin lay in the centre of the pit, with the moisture-absorbent charcoal packed tightly against its sides. The charcoal kept out all oxygen as well as damp, preserving the Lady Dai and her possessions in pristine condition.

The wooden coffin, made from cypress, housed a series of nested coffins that fitted one inside the other perfectly. The outer and inner coffins were lacquered and decorated with beautifully coloured designs: multicoloured clouds chase each other across fair and stormy skies and humanlike monsters fight one another, play musical instruments or engage in the hunt. Fine satinstitch embroidery and hundreds of feathers glued delicately to the back-

ground fabric covered the inner coffin.

The innermost coffin contained Lady Dai. She had died when she was about 50 years old and was wrapped in more than 20 layers of cloth bound with silk ribbons. Two beautifully decorated quilts covered her ample frame. She lay on her back with her hands folded on her portly belly, and a ceremonial jade plaque filled her open mouth. Her skin was still soft. Pathologists at the Henan Medical College carried out a careful autopsy on the corpse. It was 1.54m (5ft) tall and weighed 39.3kg (86lb 9oz), although she probably weighed considerably more in life. Lady Dai had borne children in her youth; at the time of her death she had a bent posture and suffered from gallstones. She suffered from a serious heart condition that had killed her shortly after she ate a piece of watermelon. The pathologists described her as 'well nourished, with plenty of subcutaneous fat'.

Lady Dai's husband was prime minister

Below *Lady Dai's four outer coffins contained a jumble of priceless grave furniture.* **Right** *A restored, T-shaped painted silk banner with a male image in the centre, represented the occupant of the tomb. A somewhat similar banner came from Lady Dai's sepulchre.*

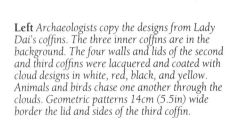

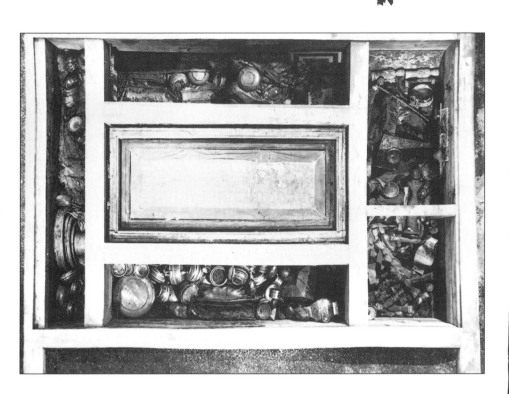

Left *Archaeologists copy the designs from Lady Dai's coffins. The three inner coffins are in the background. The four walls and lids of the second and third coffins were lacquered and coated with cloud designs in white, red, black, and yellow. Animals and birds chase one another through the clouds. Geometric patterns 14cm (5.5in) wide border the lid and sides of the third coffin.*

ficent funeral. Lady Dai went on her long journey to the afterlife with 312 bamboo slips that inventoried her possessions. Offerings of chicken, fish, and even eggs were packed in boxes. Lacquer boxes, chopsticks, jars, and 162 wooden figurines of servants, musicians, and attendants were packed in the tomb to ensure every comfort.

The archaeologists were astounded by Lady Dai's opulent wardrobe. Coats, stockings, gloves, shoes, and more than 40 boxes packed with rolls of silk accompanied her to eternity. The silks were both plain and brightly decorated, some adorned with animals, flowers, or delicate clouds, some of the finest gauze. This was the silk that reached the Roman Empire on the other side of the world, a material literally worth its weight in gold in Rome's markets.

The most remarkable silk object was a funeral banner draped over the inner coffin. It had been carried to the tomb in front of the carriage that bore the body to its burial. The deep red painted silk depicted an underworld populated by snakes and demons. A human-faced monster supports a platform where members of the lady's household make offerings. Lady Dai herself with stick and bent back stands on a second platform accompanied by five female attendants. A bird with a human face hovers over the scene. Perhaps the Lady Dai's soul is being welcomed back to her household for a short visit before it finally departs for ever. The sun and moon guard the final abode at the top of the banner, while two guardians await the noble lady at the gates. The primeval ancestor Tai-i sits at the very top of the banner, accompanied by five bird companions. He waits to receive the elements of Lady Dai's soul that will be carried by dragons.

Even though he was prime minister, Lady Dai's husband was a relatively minor official, who commanded the services of a mere 700 families. The income from his holdings may have been sufficient to ensure a rich burial both for himself and his portly wife, but the opulence of this obscure 50-year-old noblewoman's tomb must pale beside the astonishing riches that await excavation in China's royal tombs.

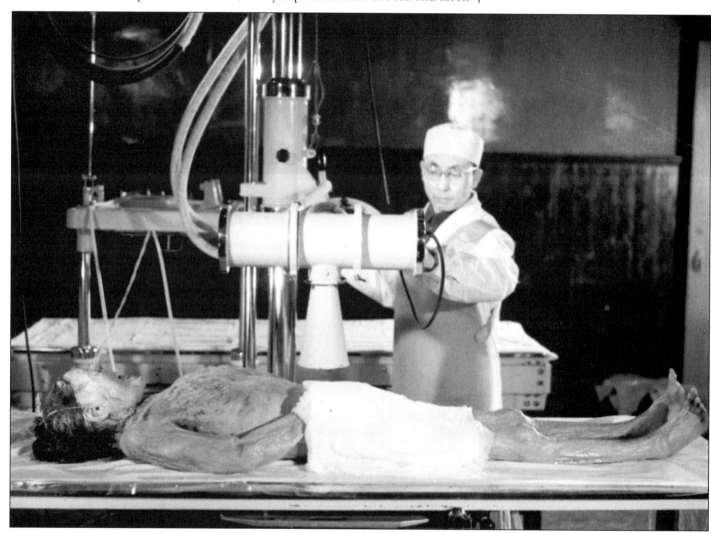

Above *Modern technology revealed Lady Dai's medical history in minute detail. Her body was astonishingly well preserved, the skin still elastic, joints mobile, hair still rooted. Even her hairpiece was still intact. Lady Dai was about 50 years old and overweight. She had borne children and had Group A blood. Her death was sudden, occurring just an hour or so after eating a melon – 138 melon seeds still remained in her esophagus, stomach, and intestines. The modern post-mortem revealed a severely occluded left coronary artery. Not that Lady Dai was healthy during her lifetime – X-rays revealed tuberculosis scars, a poorly set fracture in her right arm, and spinal problems which may have led to lumbago. Her internal organs contained gallstones and parasites.*

The wealth of Lady Dai's tomb astounded modern experts. Among her possessions they found a gauze silk gown of material as thin and light as modern nylon chiffon, 128cm (50.3in) long, which weighed only 49g (1.7oz). The lacquerware from the tomb was especially fine (far left and below). The Han artisans applied successive coats of lacquer over a thin base of carved wood or lacquered bamboo, until they had built up a hard, acid-resistant surface. Powdered minerals were added to the lacquer to give it vibrant colours. Their deft brush strokes added intricate flowers, grass patterns, and clouds to the surface. 180 lacquer pieces came from this one tomb alone. **Below** Five wooden musicians and dancers perform for their mistress in death. Three of the 30.4cm (12in) high figures sit before zithers, while their two companions play mouth organs.

CHART
EVENTS IN TIME

1,000,000 years ago   500,000 years ago   100,000 years ago   20,000BC

Africa
1.89 million years ago
Date of earliest known stone artifacts

Africa
1.6 million years ago
Emergence of *Homo erectus*

2,000,000 years ago

Africa
3.75-3 million years ago
Emergence of *Australopithecus afarensis*, in East Africa, of which 'Lucy' is an example.

Africa
1.75 million years ago
Emergence of *Homo habilis*

Global
120,000-12,000 years ago
LAST ICE AGE

Asia
460,000 years ago
Homo erectus had spread to China and Indonesia

Europe
300,000 years ago
Human settlements at Terra Amata in France and Torralba and Ambrona in Spain

1,000,000 years ago

500,000 years ago

Global
480,000-430,000 years ago
2ND ICE AGE

Africa 17,000BC
Evidence of cave painting in southern Africa

100,000 years ago   20,000BC   15,000BC

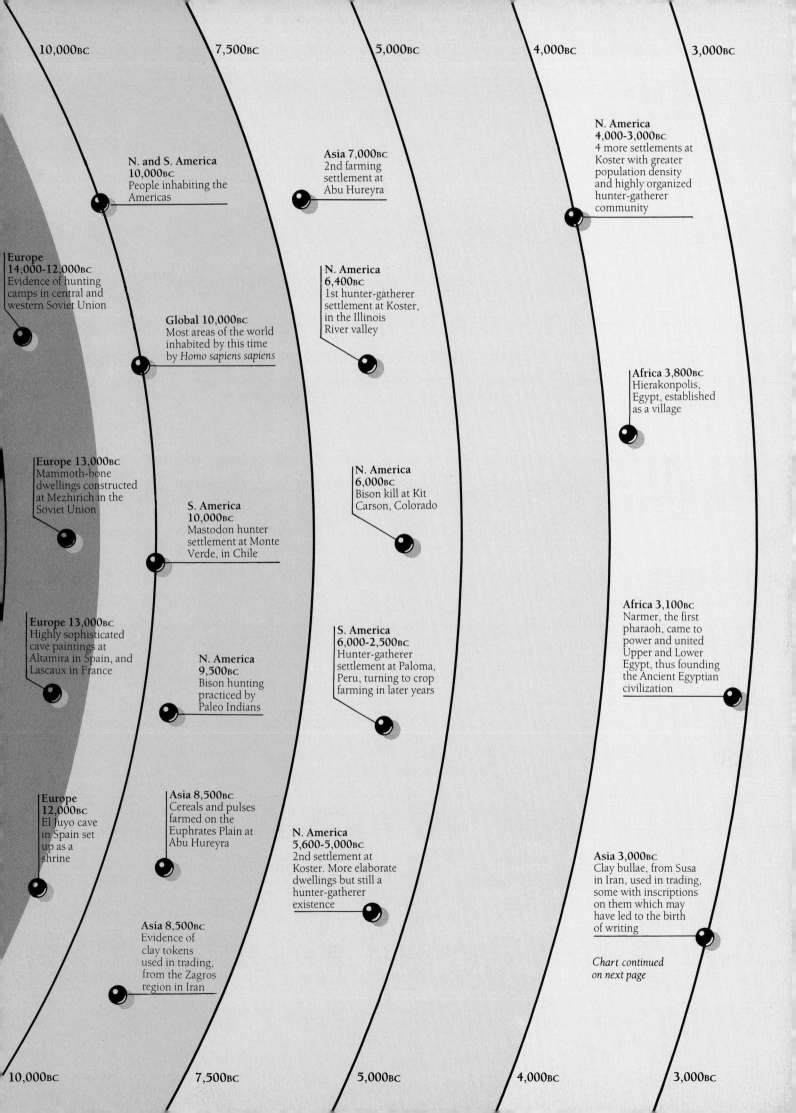

**N. and S. America
10,000BC**
People inhabiting the
Americas

Asia 7,000BC
2nd farming
settlement at
Abu Hureyra

**N. America
4,000-3,000BC**
4 more settlements at
Koster with greater
population density
and highly organized
hunter-gatherer
community

**Europe
14,000-12,000BC**
Evidence of hunting
camps in central and
western Soviet Union

Global 10,000BC
Most areas of the world
inhabited by this time
by *Homo sapiens sapiens*

**N. America
6,400BC**
1st hunter-gatherer
settlement at Koster,
in the Illinois
River valley

Africa 3,800BC
Hierakonpolis,
Egypt, established
as a village

Europe 13,000BC
Mammoth-bone
dwellings constructed
at Mezhirich in the
Soviet Union

**S. America
10,000BC**
Mastodon hunter
settlement at Monte
Verde, in Chile

**N. America
6,000BC**
Bison kill at Kit
Carson, Colorado

Europe 13,000BC
Highly sophisticated
cave paintings at
Altamira in Spain, and
Lascaux in France

**N. America
9,500BC**
Bison hunting
practiced by
Paleo Indians

**S. America
6,000-2,500BC**
Hunter-gatherer
settlement at Paloma,
Peru, turning to crop
farming in later years

Africa 3,100BC
Narmer, the first
pharaoh, came to
power and united
Upper and Lower
Egypt, thus founding
the Ancient Egyptian
civilization

**Europe
12,000BC**
El Juyo cave
in Spain set
up as a
shrine

Asia 8,500BC
Cereals and pulses
farmed on the
Euphrates Plain at
Abu Hureyra

**N. America
5,600-5,000BC**
2nd settlement at
Koster. More elaborate
dwellings but still a
hunter-gatherer
existence

Asia 3,000BC
Clay bullae, from Susa
in Iran, used in trading,
some with inscriptions
on them which may
have led to the birth
of writing

Asia 8,500BC
Evidence of
clay tokens
used in trading,
from the Zagros
region in Iran

*Chart continued
on next page*

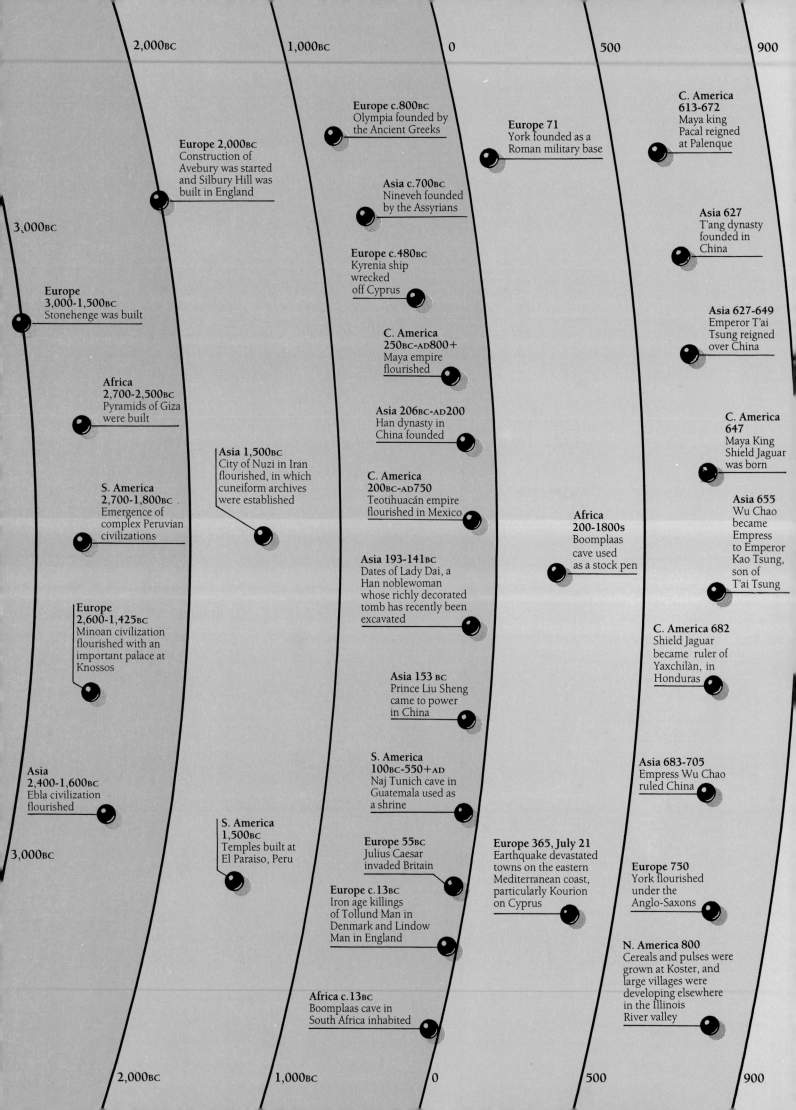

2,000BC   **1,000**BC   **0**   **500**   **900**

3,000BC

**C. America
613-672**
Maya king
Pacal reigned
at Palenque

Europe c.800BC
Olympia founded by
the Ancient Greeks

Europe 71
York founded as a
Roman military base

Europe 2,000BC
Construction of
Avebury was started
and Silbury Hill was
built in England

Asia c.700BC
Nineveh founded
by the Assyrians

Asia 627
T'ang dynasty
founded in
China

**Europe
3,000-1,500**BC
Stonehenge was built

Europe c.480BC
Kyrenia ship
wrecked
off Cyprus

Asia 627-649
Emperor T'ai
Tsung reigned
over China

**Africa
2,700-2,500**BC
Pyramids of Giza
were built

**C. America
250**BC-AD**800+**
Maya empire
flourished

Asia 1,500BC
City of Nuzi in Iran
flourished, in which
cuneiform archives
were established

**C. America
647**
Maya King
Shield Jaguar
was born

**S. America
2,700-1,800**BC
Emergence of
complex Peruvian
civilizations

Asia 206BC-AD**200**
Han dynasty in
China founded

**C. America
200**BC-AD**750**
Teotihuacán empire
flourished in Mexico

Asia 655
Wu Chao
became
Empress
to Emperor
Kao Tsung,
son of
T'ai Tsung

**Africa
200-1800s**
Boomplaas
cave used
as a stock pen

**Europe
2,600-1,425**BC
Minoan civilization
flourished with an
important palace at
Knossos

Asia 193-141BC
Dates of Lady Dai, a
Han noblewoman
whose richly decorated
tomb has recently been
excavated

C. America 682
Shield Jaguar
became ruler of
Yaxchilàn, in
Honduras

Asia 153 BC
Prince Liu Sheng
came to power
in China

**Asia
2,400-1,600**BC
Ebla civilization
flourished

Asia 683-705
Empress Wu Chao
ruled China

**S. America
100**BC-550+AD
Naj Tunich cave in
Guatemala used as
a shrine

3,000BC

**S. America
1,500**BC
Temples built at
El Paraiso, Peru

Europe 55BC
Julius Caesar
invaded Britain

Europe 365, July 21
Earthquake devastated
towns on the eastern
Mediterranean coast,
particularly Kourion
on Cyprus

Europe 750
York flourished
under the
Anglo-Saxons

Europe c.13BC
Iron age killings
of Tollund Man in
Denmark and Lindow
Man in England

N. America 800
Cereals and pulses were
grown at Koster, and
large villages were
developing elsewhere
in the Illinois
River valley

Africa c.13BC
Boomplaas cave in
South Africa inhabited

2,000BC   **1,000**BC   **0**   **500**   **900**

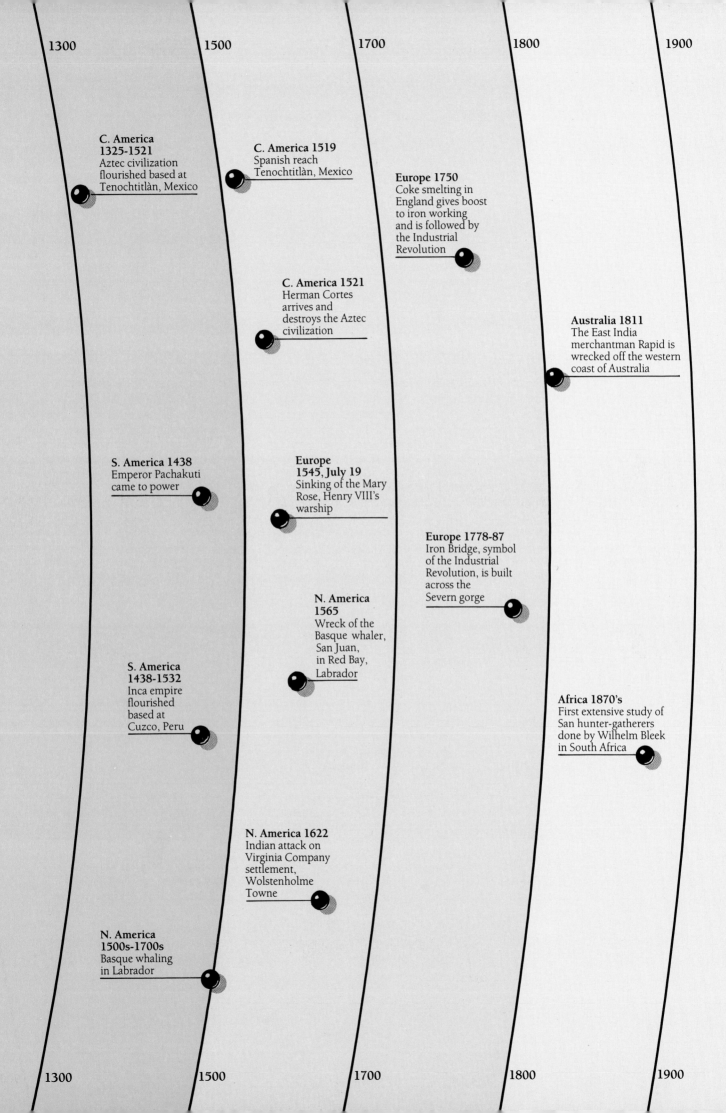

1300 1500 1700 1800 1900

**C. America
1325-1521**
Aztec civilization
flourished based at
Tenochtitlàn, Mexico

C. America 1519
Spanish reach
Tenochtitlàn, Mexico

Europe 1750
Coke smelting in
England gives boost
to iron working
and is followed by
the Industrial
Revolution

C. America 1521
Herman Cortes
arrives and
destroys the Aztec
civilization

Australia 1811
The East India
merchantman Rapid is
wrecked off the western
coast of Australia

S. America 1438
Emperor Pachakuti
came to power

**Europe
1545, July 19**
Sinking of the Mary
Rose, Henry VIII's
warship

Europe 1778-87
Iron Bridge, symbol
of the Industrial
Revolution, is built
across the
Severn gorge

**N. America
1565**
Wreck of the
Basque whaler,
San Juan,
in Red Bay,
Labrador

**S. America
1438-1532**
Inca empire
flourished
based at
Cuzco, Peru

Africa 1870's
First extensive study of
San hunter-gatherers
done by Wilhelm Bleek
in South Africa

N. America 1622
Indian attack on
Virginia Company
settlement,
Wolstenholme
Towne

**N. America
1500s-1700s**
Basque whaling
in Labrador

1300 1500 1700 1800 1900

GLOSSARY

Anglo-Saxons This term is used to describe peoples coming into Britain at the end of the Roman occupation in the early fifth century AD. The original Saxon homeland was to the south of Denmark, around the German rivers Elbe and Weser. The Angles came from southern Denmark. The Anglo-Saxon migration is taken to include the Jutes from northern Denmark and the Frisians from the coasts of northern Holland and northwest Germany. The Anglo-Saxon period ends with the Norman invasion and the death of Harold in 1066.

Amphora A strong and heavy pottery storage jar used for bulk transportation of liquids such as wine and oil in the Roman and Greek worlds. They are usually long and cylindrical with a narrow neck, two strong handles and with a strong pointed end. They could be held upright in a stand, pressed into the ground or leant one against the other. They could have been stacked together in ships, and groups of them are often recovered from underwater excavation of wrecks in the Mediterranean.

Amratian Period A pre-dynastic culture of Egypt, meaning before the time of written history. The Amratians were an early farming, or neolithic, community when copper was just beginning to be used to usher in the Copper and Bronze Ages. A distinctive black-topped red-ware was among the pottery used. The period is dated to the middle of the fourth millennium BC.

Assyrian Empire This began as the city-state of Assur on the River Tigris in northern Mesopotamia or modern Iraq; later capitals were Nimrud and Ninevah also on the Tigris. At the height of its power the empire stretched from Egypt to Anatolia and the Persian Gulf. The last major Assyrian king was Assurbanipal, 668-626BC, and the empire was finally overcome by King Nebuchadnezzar of Babylon in 605BC.

Aztecs The Aztecs were a phase of the Central American or Meso-american civilization. They established their capital at Tenochtitlán, modern Mexico City, in 1345. They maintained earlier practices of human sacrifice and military conquest. At the height of their power they dominated much of present-day Mexico. In 1521, the Aztecs succumbed to the Spaniard Fernando Cortez who had landed on the Mexican Gulf two years previously with just over 500 soldiers.

Baulk A baulk is a strip of earth left standing, during an archaeological excavation, between two adjacent rectangular trenches. The baulks display the stratigraphy of the site or the order of deposition of the archaeological strata; unless disturbed by the digging of pits or by burrowing animals the lowest deposit is the earliest. The term also describes the edge of a large area of excavation. The sides of the baulks, the sections, provide vital evidence for the interpretation of archaeological sites. In the final stages of an excavation the baulks between trenches may be excavated away to provide the complete plan of the site.

Biface Tools These are flint or stone tools which have been worked by man on both sides so as to form an effective chopping or cutting edge. The term was first used to describe hand axes of the Upper Paleolithic, the early part of the Old Stone Age in Europe.

Byzantine Empire The Roman empire was, by the end of the fourth century AD, under pressure from the tribes east and north of the Rhine-Danube border. The empire was thus split into two, the Western and Eastern Roman empires, so that the defences could be more effectively organized from Rome and Constantinople respectively. The Western empire disintegrated. Under the Emperor Heraclius, Greek became the predominant language of the Eastern empire and so historians use the term Byzantine Empire, named after the Greek form of Constantinople (modern Istanbul), from the end of the seventh century AD. The final, tumultuous days came in 1453 when the ever-shrinking remnant of empire was captured by the Turks.

Cuneiform The word means wedge-shaped and describes a form of writing, developed in Mesopotamia (Iraq), using a stylus or reed to make impressions in wet clay. It developed from a pictographic script, in which pictures represented words, into a set of schematic designs. It was the form of writing used by the Assyrian empire in the second millennium BC, the language being Akkadian. Letters in cuneiform were sealed into clay envelopes also inscribed.

Gerzean Period Like the Amratian period, this is another of the pre-dynastic periods of Egypt, from which it developed in the mid-fourth millennium BC. Copper was in wider use for axes and daggers. Patterns made on the pottery vessels included papyrus-made boats used on the Nile. Foreign contacts ushered in the period of writing in Egypt.

Han Dynasty The name of an ancient state and of several Chinese dynasties, it is generally restricted to the Western and Eastern Han empires of from 206BC to the early third century AD. Recent excavations of Han tombs have demonstrated the splendour of their burials. At the height of their power the Han empire extended far into central Asia.

Hectare This is a measure of area in the metric system, equal to 10,000 square metres; it is abbreviated to ha. One hectare is equivalent to 2.47 acres, where an acre is 4,840 square yards. More basically, an acre was the amount a plough team could plough in a day.

Henge A monument, probably of ritual use, consisting of a circular area surrounded by a ditch with the bank outside it. There are usually one or two entrances represented by gaps in the earthworks. Henges often have megalithic circles inside them, like Stonehenge and Avebury. These monuments are only known in Britain and were used in the Bronze Age, although they probably developed from simpler forms in the late neolithic period of the first farming communities.

Hominids A hominid is a member of the zoological family *hominidae*. This family

includes extinct and modern man as well as human-like remains of creatures still being found in Ethiopia and Kenya who practised a hunting, scavenging and foraging existence. An example is Lucy, found in 1974 in Ethiopia and dated to at least three million years ago.

Ice Age This term describes a period of sustained cold when ice covers much of the land surface. The last or Great Ice Age has been well researched and documented. In Europe four distinct phases, named after Alpine locations, are called Günz, Mindel, Riss and Würm. In North America these phases are called Nebraskan, Kansan, Illinoian and Wisconsin. They are followed by the post-glacial period covering about 10,000 years to the present day. The warmer periods between the glaciations are called interglacials. Neanderthal man lived in Europe during the Würm glaciation.

Incas The kingdom of the Incas was probably founded in the twelfth century in the mountains of southern Peru. During the fifteenth century the empire stretched from the borders of Colombia, through Peru and Bolivia, into Argentina. It was renowned for its system of administration, built on an extensive network of roads. The Incas were effectively conquered by the Spaniard Pizarro in 1532.

Mastodon This is an extinct mammal allied to the elephant.

Maya A civilized people occupying the Mexican peninsula of Yucatán, British Honduras and parts of Guatemala and Honduras. By about 200BC pyramids were being built in the lowlands of Guatemala. By the early tenth century AD great centres of the civilization had been abandoned. The Spaniards eventually overran the Yucatán in 1541.

Megalithic A megalithic monument is one built of large stones. Megalithic monuments include stone circles, alignments and chambered tombs. Examples are Stonehenge, Avebury and West Kennet Long Barrow, all in southern Britain.

Midden A midden is a pile of rubbish found on a settlement site. Specifically a kitchen midden is a pile of food debris such as sea shells left by food-gathering people who are used to eating in a spot where it is convenient to throw the debris.

Neanderthal Man An extinct form of man, named after a valley in Germany, where a skeleton was found in 1856. The head had prominent brow ridges with a receding forehead and weak chin; the brain was often larger than that of our own ancestors. There are interesting theories why the species with the larger brain died out. His position in any linear evolutionary sequence from the early hominids to modern man is still not clear. Remains have been found in Europe and the Near East and Neanderthal features were prominent during the last or Würm phase of the Ice Age. The development of Neanderthal man may have resulted from an adaptation to the cold.

Paleoanthropologist A person who studies the natural history of primitive man.

Photogrammetry A method of photographing areas from directly above or to the side in which a series of overlapping photos are taken. For mapping this is done from the air, for archaeological recording it can be done from a tripod. The method can also be used to record standing walls and the sides or sections of a trench. Markers can be set out in the form of a grid, on the ground or on a wall, so that scaled drawings can be produced from the photos even when the excavation is over.

Pollen Analysis The pollen grains of flowers, grasses and trees are very resistant to decay in some conditions and have characteristic shapes that can be identified under the microscope. Pollen analysis has been developed to monitor changes in man's environment. The technique has been used to study the climatic changes which have occurred in the post-glacial period since the end of the last Ice Age. The method can be used to some extent as a dating technique.

Potsherds Sherds or potsherds (or sometimes shards) are broken pieces of pottery. If properly fired, pottery is almost indestructible in the soil. On pottery-using sites they are usually the most abundant type of archaeological find. Since pottery types differ from culture to culture and change with time, much effort is given to establishing pottery sequences, so that groups of a few sherds – or sometimes a single distinctive sherd – can often be dated extremely closely.

Radiocarbon Dating, Radiocarbon Years Living matter is composed of two types of carbon. The greater part is Carbon-12, with an atomic weight of 12; this is the weight compared to the hydrogen atom.

There is also a small proportion of a radioactive Carbon-14. This latter component decays at a known rate with time when the wood, plant or bone dies. It is this changing proportion of Carbon-14 to Carbon-12 which can be measured in Radiocarbon laboratories around the world. The date established is always quoted with a plus-and-minus quantity called a standard deviation. This is a statistical figure such that there is a 2 to 1 chance that the date lies in the range of plus and minus one standard deviation, there is a 20 to 1 chance that it lies in the range of plus and minus two standard deviations, and there is almost certainty that it lies in the range of plus and minus three standard deviations. Thus a mean date should not be given on its own; a date range is always implied. As an example, if the determination is 1,000 ± 50AD, there is a 20 to 1 chance that the date lies in the range 900 to 1100AD. There are always errors and uncertainties in sophisticated scientific determinations and there remains, after corrections and calibrations, the possibility that the date in Radiocarbon Years may not be quite the same as the years as we understand them, however the relative dating between sites is thought reliable.

T'ang Dynasty T'ang is the name given to the imperial Chinese dynasty from AD618 to 906. After an earlier collapse of authority, the Duke of T'ang and his son achieved power and began one of the most famous ruling lines. They established power over much of central Asia. Recent excavations have demonstrated the wealth and splendour of this period of Chinese cultural history.

Upper Paleolithic The paleolithic period is of the Old Stone Age when tools were made principally of flint and stone. The Upper Paleolithic is the earliest phase of this, when biface tools were common.

Vikings These great Scandinavian sailors raided, traded and eventually settled in the lands within their reach: in parts of Britain in the ninth century and in northern France by permission of the French king in the early tenth century. These were the Norsemen or Normans. Further afield they reached Iceland, Greenland and Newfoundland, and travelled down the eastern European rivers to set foot in the Byzantine Empire.

BIBLIOGRAPHY

The following articles and books will provide additional information on the major sites and discoveries described in this book.

From a Treasure Hunt to a Science
Daniel, Glyn. *A Short History of Archaeology* Thames and Hudson, London (1981).

Edwards, I.E.S. *The Pyramids* Viking, New York (1973).

Fagan, Brian M. *The Adventure of Archaeology* National Geographic Society, Washington D.C. (1985)

Fagan, Brian M. *People of the Earth* Little, Brown, Boston. 5th ed (1986).

Hall, Richard. *The Viking Dig* The Bodley Head, London (1984).

Millon, Rene, and others. *Urbanization at Teotihuacan, Mexico* University of Texas Press, Austin (1974).

Noël Hume, Ivor. *Martin's Hundred* Alfred Knopf, New York (1982).

The First Humans
Cole, Sonia. *Leakey's Luck* Weidenfeld and Nicholson, London (1975).

Gamble, Clive. *The Palaeolithic Settlement of Europe* Cambridge University Press, Cambridge (1986).

Isaac, Glynn Ll. 'The Archaeology of Human Origins: Studies of the Lower Pleistocene in East Africa 1971-1981' *Advances in World Archaeology* 3:1-89 (1984).

Johanson, Don C. and Edey, Maitland. *Lucy: The Beginnings of Humankind* Simon and Schuster, New York (1981).

Leakey, M.D. 'Pliocene Footprints at Laetoli, Tanzania' *Antiquity* 52:133 (1978).

Leakey, Mary. *Disclosing the Past* Weidenfeld and Nicholson, London (1984).

Leakey, Richard, and Lewin, Roger. *Origins* Dutton, New York (1977).

Lewin, Roger. *Human Evolution* Blackwell Scientific Publications (1984).

Shipman, Pat. 'Scavenger Hunt' *Natural History* 93 (4):20-28 (1984).

Hunters and Foragers
Deacon, H.J. 'Excavations at Boomplaas Cave: a sequence through the Upper Pleistocene and Holocene in South Africa' *World Archaeology* 10:241-257 (1979).

Fagan, Brian, M. *The Great Journey* Thames and Hudson, New York (1987).

Parkington, John. 'Changing Views of the Later Stone Age of South Africa' *Advances in World Archaeology* 3:90-142 (1984).

Pfeiffer, John. *The Creative Explosion* Harper and Row, New York (1982).

Soffer, Olga. *The Upper Paleolithic of the Central Russian Plain* Academic Press, New York (1985).

Wheat, Joe Ben. *The Olsen-Chubbock Site* Society for American Archaeology, Washington D.C. (1972).

The First Farmers
Benfer, Robert A. 'The Challenges and Rewards of Sedentism' in Mark N. Cohen's and George Armelagos' (editors) *Paleopathology at the Origins of Agriculture* Academic Press, New York (1984).

Cohen, Mark. *The Food Crisis in Prehistory* Yale University Press, New Haven (1977).

Moore, Andrew M.T. 'The Development of Neolithic Societies in the Near East' *Advances in World Archaeology* 4:1-70 (1985).

Struever, Stuart and Holton, Felicia. *Koster* Doubleday Anchor Books, New York (1979).

Cities and Civilizations
Fagan, Brian M. *The Aztecs* W.H. Freeman, New York (1984).

Hoffman, Michael A. *Egypt Before the Pharoahs* Alfred Knopf, New York (1979).

James, Jamie. 'New Ways of Looking for the Past' *Discover,* September 1986: 64-75.

Moctezuma, Eduardo Matos. *The Aztec Great Temple and the City of Tenochtitlán* Thames and Hudson, London (1988).

Schmandt-Besserat, Denise. 'The Earliest Precursor of Writing' *Scientific American* 238(6): 50-59 (1978).

Decoding Maya Signs
Brady, James E. and Stone, Andrea. 'Naj Tunich: Entrance to the Maya Underworld' *Archaeology* 39(6): 18-25 (1986).

Coe, Michael. *The Maya* Thames and Hudson, London. 3rd ed (1984).

Hammond, Norman. *Ancient Maya Civilization* Rutgers University Press, New Brunswick, NJ (1982).

Freidel, David, A. and Schele, Linda. 'Symbol and Power: A History of the Lowland Maya Cosmogram' in Elizabeth Benson's and Gillette Griffin's (editors) *Maya Iconography* Princeton University Press, Princeton (1987).

Robicsek, Francis, and Hales, Donald. *The Maya Book of the Dead* University of Virginia Art Museum, Charlottesville, Va (1981).

Stuart, George. 'Maya Art Treasures Discovered in Cave' *National Geographic,* August 1985:220-235.

New Light on Old Worlds
Bermant, Chaim, and Weitzman, Michael. *Ebla: A Revelation in Archaeology* Times Books, New York (1979).

Conrad, Geoffrey W. and Demarest, Arthur A. *Religion and Empire: The Dynamics of Aztec and Inca Expansionism* Cambridge University Press, Cambridge (1984).

Hood, Sinclair. *The Minoans* Thames and Hudson, London (1973).

Matthiae, Paolo. 'Tell Mardikh: The Archives and Palace' *Archaeology* 30(4):244-253 (1977).

Stothert, Karen E. 'Unwrapping an Inca Mummy Bundle' *Archaeology* 32(4):8-17 (1979).

Warren, Peter. 'Knossos: New Excavations and Discoveries' *Archaeology* 37(4):48-57 (1984).

From Iron Age to Iron Bridge
Brothwell, D.R. *The Bog Man and the Archaeology of People* British Museum, London (1986).

Glob, Peter. *The Bog People* Faber and Faber, London (1969).

Longworth, Ian. *Prehistoric Britain* British Museum, London (1984).

Trinder, Barrie. 'Ironbridge: Industrial Archaeology in England' *Archaeology* 33(1):44-52 (1980).

Underwater Archaeology
Bass, George (editor). *A History of Seafaring Based on Underwater Archaeology* Thames and Hudson, London (1972).

Henderson, Graeme. 'Indiamen Traders of the Far East' *Archaeology* 33(6):18-25 (1980).

Katzev, Michael. 'Resurrecting the Oldest Known Greek Ship' *National Geographic* June 1970:841-857.

Katzev, Susan and Michael. 'Last Harbor of the Oldest Ship' *National Geographic* November 1974:618-625.

Rule, Margaret. *The Mary Rose* Conway Maritime Press, London (1982).

Tuck, James A. 'Discovery in Labrador: A 16th-century Port and its Sunken Fleet' *National Geographic* July 1985:41-71.

The Symbolic World
Bleek, W.H.I. and Lloyd, L.C. *Specimens of Bushman Folklore* Allen, London (1911).

Lee, Richard. *The !Kung San* Cambridge University Press, Cambridge (1979).

Lewis-Williams, David *Believing and Seeing: symbolic meanings in southern San rock art* Academic Press, New York (1981).

Vinnecombe, Patricia *People of the Eland* Natal University Press, Pietermarizburg (1976).

Megalithic Mysteries
Burl, Aubrey. *Prehistoric Avebury* Yale University Press, New Haven (1979).

Chippindale, Christopher. *Stonehenge Complete* Thames and Hudson, London (1983).

Heggie, Douglas C. *Megalithic Science* Thames and Hudson, London (1982).

Renfrew, Colin (editor). *The Megalithic Monuments of Western Europe* Thames and Hudson, London (1983).

China
Chang, Kwang-Chih. *The Archaeology of Ancient China* Yale University Press, New Haven (1977).

Cottrell, Arthur. *The First Emperor of China, the Greatest Archaeological Find of Our Time* Holt, Rinehart, and Winston, New York (1981).

Kao, Jeffrey and Zuosheng, Yang. 'On Jade Suits and Han Archaeology' *Archaeology* 36(6):30-37 (1983).

Swart, Paula, and Till, Barry D. 'Bronze Carriages from the Tomb of China's First Emperor' *Archaeology* 37(6):18-25 (1984).

Zhongshu, Wang. *Han Civilization* Yale University Press, New Haven (1982).

INDEX

CREDITS

p2 Werner Forman Archive. pp6-7 The Mansell Collection. pp8-9 York Archaeological Trust. pp10-11 (top) Photri. p11 (top) Ivor Noël Hume, National Geographic Society. p11 (bottom) Photri. pp12-13 Zefa. pp14-15 (top) Tony Stone Worldwide. p15 (centre) Science Photo Library. p15 (bottom) The British Museum. p16 Nick Saunders/Barbara Heller Library. pp16-17 Werner Forman Archive. pp18-19 The Bridgeman Art Library. p20 (top) G.S.F. Library. p20 (bottom) N.H.P.A. Photographic Agency. p21 (top right) I.P.I. Archive. p21 (bottom) Bruce Coleman Ltd. p21 (top left) Camerapix. pp22-23 John Reader. pp24-25 Cleveland Museum of Natural History. p26 (top) Bruce Coleman. p26 (centre) Picturepoint. p26 (bottom) Professor M.H. Day. p27 Camerpix. p28 (top) G.S.F. Library. p28 (centre) Camera Press. pp28-29 (bottom) G.S.F. Library p29 (top) Camera Press. p29 (centre) Bruce Coleman Ltd. p30 W. Bosler. pp30-31 John Reader. pp32-35 I.P.I. Archive. p36 (top) Picturepoint. p36 (bottom) Professor H.J. Deacon. p37 (top left) Picturepoint. p37 (top right) Frank Lane Picture Agency. p37 (bottom) H.J. Deacon. p38 Walter Rawlings. pp38-39 (top) The Buffalo Bill Historical Center. p39 (bottom) University of Colorado Museum. pp40-41 Picturepoint. p41 (centre) The Bridgeman Art Library. pp42-43 I.P.I. Archive. pp44-45 Professor Olga Soffer. p46 (top) Hutchison Library. p46 (centre) Professor T.D. Dillehay. pp46-47 (top) Professor T.D. Dillehay. p48 Professor T.D. Dillehay. pp 49-51 H.J. Deacon. pp52-53 (top left) Tell Abu Hureyra Excavation. p53 (top right and bottom) D.R. Baston. pp54-56, p57 (centre) Tell Abu Hureyra Excavation. p57 (top), pp58-59 Professor R.A. Benfer. pp60-67 D.R. Baston. p68 The British Museum. p69 Professor M.A. Hoffman. pp70-71 Hirmer Fotoarchiv. p71 (bottom), pp72-73, p74, p75 (bottom) Professor M.A. Hoffman. p75 (bottom) Doctor D. Schmandt-Bessrat. p76 (top) Doctor D. Schmandt-Bessrat. p76, p77 (centre) The British Museum. p77 Doctor D. Schmandt-Bessrat. pp78-79 Doctor David Soren. pp80-81 Walter H. Birkby/ National Geographic Society. p84 Ironbridge Gorge Museum Trust. p85 Werner Forman Archive. p86 (top) James Brady. p86 (centre and bottom) Werner Forman Archive. p87 (top left) James Brady. p87 (top right) Zefa. p87 (bottom) Werner Forman Archive. pp88-89 Peabody Museum, Harvard University/ Photograph by Hiller Burger. p90, p91 (top and bottom) Zefa. p91 (centre) Rijksmuseum voor Volkenkunde, Leiden. p92, p93 (centre left) University Museum, University of Pennsylvania. p93 (centre right), South American Pictures. p94 The British Museum. p95 (centre) Zefa. p95 (bottom left) Walter Rawlings. p95 (bottom centre) Werner Forman Archive. p95 (bottom right) South American Pictures. p96 Zefa. pp96-97 Peabody Museum Harvard University/Photograph by Hiller Burger. p98 (left) The Art Museum, Princeton University/Gift of Hans and Dorothy Widenmann Foundation. p98 (centre right) Werner Forman Archive. p99 Justin Kerr. p100 University Museum, University of Pennsylvania. p100, p101 (top), pp102-103 James Brady. p104 (top) P.M. Warren/The British School at Athens. p104 (centre) Aleppo Archaeological Museum/Hodder & Stoughton. p105 Karen Stothert. pp106-107 Paolo Mattiae/ Hodder & Stoughton. p106 (bottom right) Aleppo Archaeological Museum/Hodder & Stoughton. pp108-109 P.M. Warren/The British School at Athens. pp110-113 South American Pictures. pp114-115 Karen Stothert. p116 The British Museum. p117 (top left) The National Museum, Denmark. p117 (top right and bottom) Ironbridge Gorge Museum Trust. pp118-119 The National Museum, Denmark. p120 (left) Royal Danish Ministry for Foreign Affairs. p120 (bottom), p121 (bottom) The National Museum, Denmark. p121 (top) Silkeborg Museum. p121 (centre) Forhistorisk Museum, Moesgard. p121 (bottom left) The British Museum. p121 (bottom right) Department of Medical Illustration/University of Manchester. p122 (top and centre left) T. Holden. p122 (centre right), p123 The British Museum. p124 Ironbridge Gorge Museum Trust. pp124-125 Clive House, Shrewsbury Borough Museum Service. pp126-127 Science Museum. pp128-129 Ironbridge Gorge Museum Trust. p130 (top) Christie's. p130 (bottom), p131 (top left) Parks Canada. p131 (top right) Susan Womer Katzev. p131 (bottom) Frank Spooner Pictures. pp134-137 Patrick Baker/Western Australian Maritime Museum. p138 (centre left) Susan Womer Katzev. p138 (centre right) John Veltri. p139 (centre) Michael L. Katzev. p139 (bottom left and right), p140, p141 (centre) Susan Womer Katzev. p141 (top) Parks Canada. p141 (right), pp142-143 James A. Tuck/The Basque Project. p144 The Mary Rose Trust. pp144-145 By permission of the Master and Fellows, Magdalen College, Cambridge. p145 (top), pp146-147 The Mary Rose Trust. pp148-149 Robert Estall. p150, p151 (top left) Professor J.D. Lewis-Williams. p151 (top right) John K. Marshall. p151 (bottom) N.H.P.A. Photographic Agency. pp152-153 Gerald Cubitt. p154 (centre) Bruce Coleman. p154 (bottom), pp154-155 Gerald Cubitt. p155 (centre) J.D. Lewis-Williams. p156 (top) Gerald Cubitt. p156 (bottom), p157 (top) J.D. Lewis-Williams. p157 (bottom) Gerald Cubitt. p158 J.D. Lewis-Williams. pp159-161 John K. Marshall. p162, p163 (top left) Robert Estall. p163 (top right) Aerofilms. p163 (bottom), pp164-165 Robert Estall. p166 Corpus Christi College, Cambridge. pp166-167 The Mansell Collection. p167 (bottom) Robert Estall. p168 Topham. p170 Robert Estall. pp170-171 Bodleian Library, Oxford. pp172-173, p174, p175 (top), Robert Estall. p175 (bottom) Aerofilms. pp176-177 Zefa. p178, p179 (top left) Robert Harding. p179 (top right) China News Agency. p179 (centre and bottom), pp180-181 Robert Harding. p182, p184 (top and bottom left) China News Agency. p184 (bottom right) Robert Harding. p185 (top) Robert Harding. pp186-187 China News Agency. p186 (bottom) Frank Spooner Pictures. pp188-189, p190 Robert Harding. pp191-193 China News Agency.